THE

BILL OF RIGHTS

And What It Means Today

BY

EDWARD DUMBAULD

GREENWOOD PRESS, PUBLISHERS
WESTPORT, CONNECTICUT

Library of Congress Cataloging in Publication Data

Dumbauld, Edward, 1905-
   The Bill of rights and what it means today.

   Reprint of the 1st ed. published by University of
Oklahoma Press, Norman.
   Bibliography: p.
   Includes index.
   1. United States. Constitution. 1st-10th amend-
ments. I. Title.
KF4749.D8 1979   342'.73'085   78-12307
ISBN 0-313-21215-5

BY EDWARD DUMBAULD

Interim Measures of Protection in International Controversies
(The Hague, 1932)

Thomas Jefferson, American Tourist
(Norman, 1946)

The Declaration of Independence and What It Means Today
(Norman, 1950)

The Political Writings of Thomas Jefferson
(New York, 1955)

The Bill of Rights and What It Means Today
(Norman, 1957)

Reprinted in 1979 by Greenwood Press
A division of Congressional Information Service
88 Post Road West, Westport, Connecticut 06881

Library of Congress Catalog Card Number 78-12307

ISBN 0-313-21215-5

Printed in the United States of America

10 9 8 7 6 5 4 3

To the memory of
Robert Houghwout Jackson
who spoke with "the authentic voice of freedom."

PREFACE

AMAZINGLY little scholarly literature has been published
dealing with the Bill of Rights embodied in the first ten
amendments to the Constitution of the United States. Of course
commentators on the Constitution as a whole have made passing
mention of these amendments. Moreover several of them have
been the subject of monographs like Dean Erwin N. Griswold's
thoughtful little book on the Fifth Amendment.[1] Likewise Irving
Brant's biography of Madison, and Charles Warren's discussion
of the Judiciary Act of 1789 (a measure which competed with
the amendments to the Constitution for the attention of the First
Congress), have touched upon the topic incidentally. But the Bill
of Rights as a whole has not been treated by any writer until
recent months.

The distinction of being author of the first book devoted specifically to the Bill of Rights belongs, so far as my knowledge
goes, to Robert A. Rutland (a newspaperman, not a lawyer).
His volume, *The Birth of the Bill of Rights, 1776–1791*, came
into my hands after the historical part of the present study had
been completed. It is gratifying to record that nothing I had
written required modification in the light of his findings.

I have not limited my account of the Bill of Rights (as Rutland
does) to a narrative of the events leading up to its adoption, but
have also attempted a legal analysis of its scope. The material on
current judicial interpretation of the Bill of Rights gives the

---

[1] These are cited in the bibliography herein. The works of Stokes and Pfeffer
on church and state comment on the First Amendment. Lasson, Heller, and
Patterson have discussed the Fourth, Sixth, and Ninth Amendments.

reader a reasonably comprehensive view of the extent to which these constitutional rights for which our forefathers valiantly battled are given actual protection in the courts today. In the light both of history and of law, I have then ventured to offer in conclusion some thoughts on the value of the Bill of Rights. If these are found to contain hortatory and parenetic admonitions evincing kinship to the teachings of Thomas Jefferson, perhaps a sufficient explanation is to be found in his observation to Lafayette that "the waters must always be what are the fountains from which they flow."

Before beginning the present investigation into the sources and origin of the various specific provisions of the Bill of Rights, I was familiar with the fact that the English Bill of Rights had influenced Jefferson in drafting the Declaration of Independence and that the American Bill of Rights (the need for which Jefferson preached so strongly to Madison) was the vehicle whereby the political philosophy of the Declaration of Independence was incorporated into the Constitution. As Charles Warren puts it, the first ten amendments are the essential portion of the Constitution, the portion without which the Constitution itself would never have been accepted by the American people. Had it not been for the general understanding that amendments in the nature of a Bill of Rights would be adopted, it is altogether unlikely that the Constitution would have been ratified.

As I examined in detail the propositions for amendment that originated in the state ratifying conventions, I was pleased to learn that my native commonwealth of Pennsylvania had been the pioneer in proposing many of the provisions which were later embodied in the American Bill of Rights. This influence was partly indirect, many of the Pennsylvania proposals being later reiterated by Virginia. Undoubtedly, the Virginia Convention's demands were the major factor in shaping the amendments; for it is clear that without the persistent exertions of James Madison the Congress would not have adopted amendments, and that his zeal was stimulated by a desire to maintain his own political standing and reputation in Virginia. (It is of course possible that the Pennsylvania proposals themselves reflected the views of George Mason and Richard Henry Lee; for as Pittman states, it is not certain how early Mason's draft of the Virginia propositions was prepared.)

Study of the developments in drafting the Bill of Rights (what lawyers call "legislative history" of a measure in its course through Congress) is difficult because Senate sessions were secret during the period when these amendments to the Constitution were under consideration, and neither house then kept a verbatim record of proceedings similar to the present *Congressional Record*. The nearest equivalent is a publication known as the *Annals of Congress*, which is unreliable as well as incomplete. I have pointed out several errors in pertinent passages of the *Annals*. It is not safe to rely on this source alone, as many investigators do.

More dependable, but less informative, are the *Journals* of the House and Senate for the first session of the First Congress. These embody only action taken by vote of the respective bodies, and do not contain any account of the debates. Moreover, they are accessible in few libraries.[2] I used them at the library of the American Philosophical Society, at Philadelphia.

Documents in the National Archives are also helpful in showing how the propositions offered by Madison fared in Congress. Perhaps the most illuminating evidence regarding the successive stages in drafting the amendments is to be found in the printed documents preserved in the Rare Book Division of the Library of Congress and described in Vincent Eaton's valuable article. These include the Select Committee's report of July 28, 1789; the seventeen articles passed by the House on August 24, 1789; and the twelve articles passed by the Senate on September 9, 1789. All these are reproduced in my book.

The publication and study of these printed versions (together with the evidence of the *Journals*) should dispel much of the

[2] It is unfortunate that Patterson, in his *Ninth Amendment*, where he reprints the passages from the *Annals of Congress* dealing with the legislative history of the Bill of Rights, did not also reprint the pertinent passages from House and Senate *Journals*.

"mystery" regarding the legislative history of the amendments, which as late as 1951 perplexed so eminent an authority as Professor Zechariah Chafee.[3]

There has been no mystery, of course, about the final form of the amendments as ultimately adopted (in twelve articles) by Congress on September 25, 1789. These are enshrined in the National Archives for permanent public display; but it should be remembered that only the last ten of them received the requisite number of ratifications and became part of the Constitution on December 15, 1791, when Virginia ratified.

Likewise there appears to be no substantial uncertainty with respect to the original form of Madison's proposals as offered in Congress on June 8, 1789, although I have not found any text more authentic than that given in the *Annals of Congress* and reprinted in his published *Writings*. This, Eaton believes, came from the version published in the *New York Daily Advertiser* of June 12, 1789, and subsequently in other newspapers; apparently no official printing for the use of Congress is known.

It is my hope that this book will be useful, not only in contributing to the better understanding of an important aspect of the American heritage which has been too little understood by many of our citizens, but also in strengthening the sense of continuity and unity between past and present generations of patriots who have labored for the welfare of the nation.

A particularly striking instance of such solidarity with the past occurred at Philadelphia on August 24, 1955, in connection with the American Bar Association's commemoration of the bicentennial of the birth of Chief Justice John Marshall. At that ceremony in Independence Square, the Advance of the Colors was a thrilling and unforgettable spectacle. The pageantry of the occasion was heightened by the serene splendor of luminous sunlight and towering trees. To the music of drum and bugle, a procession of United States Marines moved towards Independence Hall bearing twenty-four battle flags of the Revolutionary War.

[3] Chafee, "Federal and State Powers Under the UN Covenant on Human Rights," *Wisconsin Law Review* (May, 1951), 449.

Next came the "Betsy Ross flag" of the original thirteen United States, borne and guarded by Marines attired in uniforms of that period; then the national colors, flanked by the insignia of the four armed services. The Chief Executive and the Chief Justice of the United States, whose speeches in tribute to the great Virginia jurist were to follow, witnessed the impressive scene in company with the venerable former senator from Pennsylvania, George Wharton Pepper, and other dignitaries of the legal profession. This was indeed a memorable experience.

Shortly before this ceremony, across the street in the Library of the American Philosophical Society, I had been examining the *Journals* of the First Congress.

Both experiences revived for me the memorable deeds of men who served their country well in an inspiring era of national greatness and patriotic achievement.

Edward Dumbauld

Uniontown, Pennsylvania
January 25, 1957

CONTENTS

ILLUSTRATIONS

THE BILL OF RIGHTS

And What It Means Today

I

ADOPTION OF
THE BILL OF RIGHTS

UNLIKE most of the state constitutions of the period,[1] the Constitution of the United States as drawn up in 1787 at Philadelphia contained no Bill of Rights. Typical of state pronouncements is the Virginia Declaration of Rights of June 12, 1776.[2] On August 16, 1776, Pennsylvania adopted substantially similar "provisions largely copied from the Declaration of Independence."[3] The people of Massachusetts approved in 1780 a constitution containing a notable Bill of Rights which was the handiwork of John Adams.[4] It was natural that these declarations of democratic theory should have been prevalent in American statecraft. Autochthonous autocracy was no more acceptable than the English variety. As Thomas Jefferson emphasized when the Virginia constitution of 1776 was being framed, the establish-

[1] The constitutions of New York, New Jersey, South Carolina, and Georgia contained no Bill of Rights. Connecticut and Rhode Island had no constitutions. Rhode Island continued under its colonial charter until 1842. Until Connecticut adopted a written constitution in 1818, its organic law was made up of usages. The other seven states had Bills of Rights. The state constitutions can conveniently be consulted in the collections of Poore and Thorpe.

[2] Edward Dumbauld, *The Declaration of Independence and What It Means Today*, 168–70. This pioneer Declaration of Rights was largely the work of George Mason. Julian P. Boyd, ed., *The Papers of Thomas Jefferson*, I, 329–86.

[3] Thomas Raeburn White, *Commentaries on the Constitution of Pennsylvania*, 32. The "Frame of Government," which, together with the Bill of Rights previously agreed to, comprised the constitution of the commonwealth, was adopted on September 28, 1776. *Conventions and Constitutions of Pennsylvania*, 51, 54, 61. For the text of the Bill of Rights see *ibid.*, 55–57. Neither the Virginia nor Pennsylvania constitutions of 1776 were submitted to popular ratification before going into effect. Charles Warren, *The Making of the Constitution*, 347.

[4] Harry A. Cushing, *History of the Transition from Provincial to Commonwealth Government in Massachusetts*, 235, 246–57.

3

ment of a satisfactory political system was the "whole object" of the Revolution, "for should a bad government be instituted for us in future, it had been as well to have accepted at first the bad one offered to us from beyond the water without the risk and expense of contest."[5]

Constitutional Convention Rejects Bill of Rights

At the Constitutional Convention efforts had been made to incorporate a Bill of Rights in the new plan of government. On September 12, 1787, shortly before the close of proceedings,[1] "It was moved and seconded to appoint a Committee to prepare a Bill of rights."[2] When this bare entry in the Journal of the Convention is supplemented by James Madison's notes, the fact comes to light that it was George Mason, author of the famed Virginia Declaration of Rights, who proposed this addition to the federal constitution.

The point came up during discussion of a proposal by Hugh Williamson, of North Carolina, that provision be made to guarantee jury trial in civil cases. Mason recognized the difficulty of drawing a line between equity cases and those in which juries were proper,[3] but felt that a statement of general principle "on

[5] To Thomas Nelson, Philadelphia, May 16, 1776. Edward Dumbauld, *The Political Writings of Thomas Jefferson*, 54. A decade later, after witnessing as envoy to Europe the evil effects of undemocratic government on the happiness of the people there, Jefferson was firmly convinced that in spite of the defects in state constitutions and in the Articles of Confederation, the political structure in America was better than any on earth. *Ibid.*, 70–71, 134.

[1] The Convention adjourned on September 17, 1787. James Wilson erroneously stated in the Pennsylvania ratifying convention on November 28, 1787, and December 4, 1787, that the proposal for a Bill of Rights at the Constitutional Convention never assumed the shape of a motion, and had not even been mentioned until three days before the end of the session. Max Farrand, *Records of the Federal Convention of 1787*, III, 143, 161; John B. McMaster and Frederick D. Stone, *Pennsylvania and the Federal Constitution 1787–1788*, 252–54, 313–14. Wilson denied that Virginia had a Bill of Rights, in spite of Smilie's statement that George Mason himself had advised him to the contrary.

[2] Farrand, *Records*, II, 582. The motion "passed in the negative" by a vote of ten states to zero.

[3] Historically, jury trial was never available in equity proceedings, where the Lord Chancellor, as keeper of the king's conscience, mitigated the strictness of

this and some other points" would suffice. "He wished the plan had been prefaced with a Bill of Rights, & would second a Motion if made for the purpose—It would give great quiet to the people; and with the aid of the State declarations, a bill might be prepared in a few hours." Elbridge Gerry of Massachusetts "concurred in the idea & moved for a Committee to prepare a Bill of Rights." Mason seconded the motion, but it was unceremoniously rejected, not receiving the favorable vote of a single state.[4]

Besides Mason's proposal for a comprehensive Bill of Rights, attempts had also been made at the Convention to secure recognition of certain specific rights. On August 20, 1787, there was referred to the Committee of Detail[5] a proposal offered by Charles Pinckney of South Carolina which covered liberty of the press, standing armies, supremacy of the civil over military power,

the common law. Blackstone, *Commentaries*, III, *426–41. But in many states there was no equity jurisdiction recognized in 1787. Jury trial was also excluded in admiralty cases. Extension of jurisdiction of the admiralty courts was one of the grievances complained of in the Declaration of Independence ("depriving us, in many cases, of the benefits of trial by jury"). Dumbauld, *The Declaration of Independence and What It Means Today*, 132–33. Jefferson introduced jury trial in equity and admiralty proceedings in Virginia after the Revolution, but the reform was short lived. *Papers of Thomas Jefferson*, I, 615, 648; II, 574, 594; IX, 71. Texas has jury trials in equity. Whitney R. Harris, "Jury Trial in Civil Cases," *Southwestern Law Journal*, Vol. VII, No. 1 (Winter, 1953), 5.

[4] Farrand, *Records*, II, 587–88, 628. Pique at this abrupt rejection may have influenced Mason in his refusal to sign the Constitution. Governor Edmund Randolph of Virginia and Gerry also refused. "Col. Mason left Philada. in an exceeding ill humor indeed. A number of little circumstances arising in part from the impatience which prevailed towards the close of the business, conspired to whet his acrimony. He returned to Virginia with a fixed disposition to prevent the adoption of the plan if possible. He considers the want of a Bill of Rights as a fatal objection." Madison to Jefferson, New York, October 24, 1787. *The Writings of James Madison*, V, 34. Mason's objections (Farrand, *Records*, II, 637–40) were published as a pamphlet and had considerable influence on the amendments later proposed by the states. Those of Virginia (see note 38, page 21) were based on a draft by Mason which was being circulated as early as June 9, 1788. R. Carter Pittman, "The Fifth Amendment: Yesterday, Today and Tomorrow," *American Bar Association Journal*, Vol. XLII, No. 6 (June, 1956), 512, 588.

[5] This was a committee of five, chosen on July 24, 1787, "for the purpose of reporting a Constitution" in accordance with the various decisions of the Convention. Farrand, *Records*, II, 85, 97.

and quartering of troops.[6] Nothing came of this suggestion. Again on September 14, 1787, Pinckney seconded a motion by Gerry to insert a declaration "that the liberty of the Press should be inviolably observed." This was defeated by a vote of seven states to four.[7]

In the course of a newspaper controversy in which Luther Martin, a delegate from Maryland, was engaged in 1788, he stated that he had prepared a Bill of Rights and would have offered it if there had been any likelihood of its acceptance by the Convention.[8]

The reasoning advanced by opponents of the inclusion of a Bill of Rights in the Constitution was that where no power had been granted there was no need of any protection against abuse of power. Indeed, a Bill of Rights against a government of

[6] Farrand, *Records*, II, 334, 341. Pinckney also made proposals regarding habeas corpus and religious tests. These bore fruit in Art. I, sec. 9, cl. 2 and Art. VI, cl. 3 of the Constitution. *Ibid.*, 438. Trial by jury in criminal cases was secured by Art. III, sec. 2, cl. 3. Bills of attainder and *ex post facto* laws were prohibited by Art. I, sec. 9, cl. 3 and Art. I, sec. 10, cl. 1. *Ibid.*, 375–76, 440.

[7] Farrand, *Records*, II, 617. Roger Sherman of Connecticut said the declaration was unnecessary, as the power of Congress does not extend to the press. Massachusetts, Maryland, Virginia, and South Carolina voted in favor of the declaration. *Ibid.*, 618. Sherman had the unique distinction of being a signer of "all three of the great American documents—the Declaration of Independence, the Articles of Confederation, and the Constitution." A shoemaker before becoming a lawyer, he was the eldest member of the convention after Benjamin Franklin, and was influential as sponsor of the "Connecticut compromise" regarding the representation of large and small States in the House and Senate. Warren, *The Making of the Constitution*, 55–56, 61, 207–208.

[8] Farrand, *Records*, III, 290: "I endeavoured to obtain a restraint on the powers of the general government as to standing armies, but it was rejected. It was my wish that the general government should not have the power of suspending . . . habeas corpus, . . . but I could not succeed. An honorable member from South Carolina most anxiously sought to have a clause inserted securing the liberty of the Press, and repeatedly brought this subject before the Convention, but could not attain it. . . . The more the system advanced the more was I impressed with the necessity of not merely attempting to secure a few rights, but of digesting and forming a complete bill of rights; . . . accordingly, I [prepared a draft of] such a bill of rights, and had it in readiness . . . I conversed with several members on the subject; they agreed with me on the propriety of the measure, but at the same time expressed their sentiments that it would be impossible to procure its adoption if attempted."

6

delegated powers was not only unnecessary, but might be dangerous. To formulate exceptions and prohibitions against exercise of
powers not granted might give color to claims that the powers
so restricted had been granted by implication.[9] The argument was
forcefully stated by Alexander Hamilton in the *Federalist* (No.
84): "For why declare that things shall not be done which there
is no power to do? Why, for instance, should it be said that the
liberty of the press shall not be restrained, when no power is
given by which restrictions may be imposed? . . . This may serve
as a specimen of the numerous handles which would be given
to the doctrine of constructive power, by the indulgence of an
injudicious zeal for bills of rights."[10]

James Wilson likewise relied on this contention when the
question came up in the Pennsylvania ratifying convention. His
explanation received extensive public circulation.[11] Charles Cotesworth Pinckney in South Carolina added a further reason why
the delegates in Philadelphia had eschewed a Bill of Rights: such
instruments usually begin by declaring that all men are born
free, and this would be awkward when much of the property of
South Carolinians consisted of men who were born slaves.[12]

Madison urged the usual grounds for omission of a Bill of
Rights in explaining his views to Jefferson: "My own opinion
has always been in favor of a bill of rights; provided it be so
framed as not to imply powers not meant to be included in the
enumeration. At the same time I have never thought the omission a material defect, nor been anxious to supply it even by
subsequent amendment, for any other reason than that it is

[9] See the argument of Sherman regarding freedom of the press, note 7,
page 6.

[10] *The Federalist*, 537. This reasoning overlooked the sweeping scope of the
"necessary and proper clause," as Madison recognized when he proposed amendments in Congress. Warren, *The Making of the Constitution*, 509; Madison's
Writings, V, 383.

[11] Farrand, *Records*, II, 143, 161.

[12] Farrand, *Records*, III, 256: "Such bills generally begin with declaring
that all men are by nature born free. Now, we should make that declaration
with a very bad grace, when a large part of our property consists in men who
are actually born slaves."

7

anxiously desired by others."[13] After giving reasons why he did not think a Bill of Rights important, Madison concluded that it nevertheless would serve two useful purposes: it would have an educative effect on public opinion;[14] and it would be of service on occasions when the government did wrong of its own motion (though Madison feared that in most cases of invasion of private rights the injury would result "not from acts of Government contrary to the sense of its constituents, but from acts in which the Government is the mere instrument" of a popular majority).[15]

Doubtless Jefferson himself was one of the "others" whose importunities influenced Madison to undertake the addition of amendments to the instrument drawn up at Philadelphia. As a fellow-Virginian, political mentor, and intimate friend, Jefferson's opinion carried great weight with Madison.[16] And Jefferson repeatedly and insistently demanded a Bill of Rights.[17] In his first letter to Madison commenting on the new Constitution, after enumerating the things in it that he approved, Jefferson continued: "I will now add what I do not like. First the omission of a bill of rights providing clearly & without the aid of sophisms for freedom of religion, freedom of the press, protection against standing armies, restriction against monopolies, the eternal and unremitting force of the habeas corpus laws, and trials by jury. . . . Let me add that a bill of rights is what the people are entitled

[13] Madison to Jefferson, New York, October 17, 1788. Madison's *Writings*, V, 269–75, at 271. With this important letter Madison enclosed a pamphlet giving "a collective view of the alterations which have been proposed."

[14] *Ibid.*, 273. Jefferson later wrote that even though "written constitutions may be violated in moments of passion or delusion, yet they furnish a text to which those who are watchful may again rally & recall the people; they fix too for the people the principles of their political creed." To Joseph Priestley, Washington, June 19, 1802. *The Works of Thomas Jefferson*, IX, 381–82.

[15] Madison's *Writings*, V, 272.

[16] On the lifelong association between the two Virginia statesmen, see Koch, *Jefferson and Madison*, 33–61.

[17] For Jefferson's views on the Constitution and his correspondence with Madison on the need for a Bill of Rights, see Dumbauld, "Thomas Jefferson and American Constitutional Law," *Journal of Public Law*, Vol. II, No. 2 (Fall, 1953), 381–83.

to against every government on earth, general or particular, & what no just government should refuse or rest on inferences."[18]

In later letters Jefferson developed in detail the contents which he thought the Bill of Rights should contain,[19] and delivered a *seriatim* rebuttal of the reasons Madison had advanced for omission of such safeguards.[20] In addition to the benefits which Madison had believed would be derived from a Bill of Rights,[21] Jefferson emphasized an additional "one which has great weight with me, the legal check which it puts into the hands of the judiciary. This is a body, which if rendered independent & kept strictly to their own department merits great confidence for their learning & integrity."[22]

In strongly championing a Bill of Rights, Jefferson was as usual a trustworthy barometer of public sentiment. The demand became overwhelming, and supporters of the new Constitution gracefully acceded to it.[23] Richard Henry Lee attempted in vain to add a Bill of Rights when the report of the Philadelphia Convention was under consideration by the Continental Congress before it was transmitted to the state legislatures for submission to ratifying

[18] To James Madison, Paris, December 20, 1787. Jefferson's *Works*, V, 371. The last sentence quoted is interlined in the manuscript, showing that it was a thought which struck Jefferson forcefully while he was writing. Library of Congress, Jefferson Papers. This letter was in reply to Madison's of October 24, 1787, transmitting a copy of the Constitution and commenting on it at length. Madison's *Writings*, V, 17.

[19] To Madison, Paris, July 31, 1788. Jefferson's *Works*, V, 426; to Madison, Paris, August 28, 1789. *Ibid.*, 492.

[20] To Madison, Paris, March 15, 1789. *Ibid.*, 461. Madison's arguments were set out in his letter of October 17, 1788, note 13, page 8.

[21] See page 8.

[22] To Madison, Paris, March 15, 1789. *Works*, V, 461. It is in this letter that Jefferson goes on to refute the reasons advanced by Madison to explain why a Bill of Rights was not thought important. See text at note 20, above. In Congress Madison urged the point about judicial enforcement when supporting his proposed amendments. Madison's *Writings*, V, 385.

[23] There was no real hostility on their part toward such a declaration, if others felt it desirable. Washington to Lafayette, Mt. Vernon, April 28, 1788. Farrand, *Records*, III, 298. See also Madison to Jefferson, note 13, page 8.

conventions.[24] But the ratifying conventions themselves made plain the trend of public opinion in favor of constitutional protection against arbitrary governmental action.

State Ratifying Conventions Recommend Amendments

Following Delaware's speedy and unanimous ratification on December 7, 1787, Pennsylvania was the second state to ratify.[1] There was strong opposition, however, in the Pennsylvania convention, and there had been unseemly violence employed in expediting ratification.[2] The dissenting minority in the convention on December 12, 1787, placed before that body fifteen propositions, and indicated their willingness to ratify if these proposed amendments to the Constitution were recommended.[3] The minority's propositions were rejected by a vote of 46 to 23, and were not even entered on the journal of the convention or in the shorthand reporter's account of the debates. On the same day the Constitution was ratified by the same majority, and the dissenters issued an address to their constituents[4] setting forth the propositions that they had offered in the convention.[5] On September 3, 1788, a

[24] Lee's proposed Bill of Rights dealt with rights of conscience, freedom of the press, trial by jury, standing armies, free and frequent elections, an independent judiciary, excessive bail, right of assembly, and unreasonable searches and seizures, *Letters of Richard Henry Lee*, II, 439, 442–44. He also urged a half dozen changes in the body of the Constitution.

[1] Subsequent ratifications were as follows: New Jersey, December 18, 1787; Georgia, January 2, 1788; Connecticut, January 9, 1788; Massachusetts, February 6, 1788; Maryland, April 26, 1788; South Carolina, May 23, 1788; New Hampshire, June 21, 1788; Virginia, June 25, 1788; New York, July 26, 1788. North Carolina rejected the Constitution on August 4, 1788, but ratified on November 21, 1789, after the new government had commenced to function. Rhode Island also ratified belatedly, on May 29, 1790.

[2] McMaster and Stone, *Pennsylvania and the Federal Constitution*, 65–71. On September 29, 1787, a member of the Pennsylvania assembly was forcibly brought into the house and kept there in order to make a quorum so that provision for the ratifying convention could be enacted before adjournment of the legislature.

[3] *Ibid.*, 421–23.

[4] *Ibid.*, 454–83. The minority's proposals appeared in the *Pennsylvania Packet and Daily Advertiser* for December 12, 1787, and were also printed as a broadsheet.

[5] *Ibid.*, 461–63.

gathering was held at Harrisburg (Albert Gallatin being one of the prominent participants) which petitioned the state legislature to ask Congress to adopt a dozen amendments. Considerable publicity was given to the Pennsylvania proposals by reason of the activities of the Harrisburg convention.[6]

The amendments desired by the Pennsylvania minority were thus among the earliest to be brought to public attention, and undoubtedly influenced the subsequent state ratifying conventions which proposed amendments. In Massachusetts, South Carolina, New Hampshire, Virginia, New York, and North Carolina, amendments were recommended by official action of the majority of the ratifying conventions.[7] Of these the Virginia proposals were the most influential, and they closely resemble the Pennsylvania minority's propositions.[8] Attention was also given

[6] *Ibid.*, 562–64; Henry Adams, *The Life of Albert Gallatin*, 77–79; Paul Leicester Ford, *The Origin, Purpose and Result of the Harrisburg Convention*, 10, 27–29, 34–39. According to Ford, delay caused by the severe winter prevented opponents of the Constitution from seriously jeopardizing its adoption. *Ibid.*, 14, 40.

[7] The Rhode Island convention also proposed twenty-one amendments when it ratified the Constitution on May 29, 1790, after the instrument had already gone into effect. See note 64, page 31. But since these were not formulated until over half a year after Congress had already adopted, on September 25, 1789, the articles which upon ratification by the states became the American Bill of Rights, it is obvious that Rhode Island's proposals have only an academic interest insofar as the genesis of the first ten amendments to the Constitution of the United States is concerned. In Maryland a committee was charged with the task of proposing amendments, but the convention took no official action with respect to them. See text at note 29, page 18. However, they were mentioned in Congress in 1789. *Annals of Congress*, I, 770.

[8] See text at note 38, page 21. Since Wilson went so far as to assert in the Pennsylvania convention that Virginia had no Bill of Rights, it is unlikely that the Pennsylvania propositions were copied from the Virginia Bill of Rights. More likely they were based on Mason's and Lee's objections, and on Pennsylvania's own Bill of Rights. The Virginia convention's proposals may have been drawn with knowledge of the Pennsylvania minority propositions. Originality is indicated by the suggestion in the Pennsylvania proposals of annual elections, a council to advise the president, and by the interest in killing game and fishing. Pennsylvania was also the first state to question the treaty power. Maryland, New York, and North Carolina later adverted to that topic. See text at note 12, page 13.

to the recommendations of the Pennsylvania minority by Madison and by Congress when considering the question of amendments in 1789.[9] In eight out of the ten amendments ultimately adopted the Pennsylvania minority was the first to propose an amendment on the subject matter treated therein.[10]

The Pennsylvania propositions were: (1) that "The rights of conscience shall be held inviolable; and neither the legislative, executive nor judicial powers of the United States shall have authority to alter, abrogate or infringe any part of the constitutions of the several States, which provide for the preservation of liberty in matters of religion"; (2) that in controversies about property and between man and man trial by jury shall remain as heretofore, in federal courts and in those of the several states; (3) that in all capital and criminal prosecutions a man has the right to demand the cause and nature of the accusation, as well in federal courts as those of the several states, and the right to be heard by himself or counsel, to be confronted with the accusers and witnesses, to call for evidence in his favor, and to a speedy trial by an impartial jury of the vicinage, nor shall he be compelled to give evidence against himself, nor shall he be deprived of liberty except by the law of the land or judgment of his peers; (4) that excessive bail and fines shall not be required nor cruel and unusual punishments imposed; (5) that warrants unsupported by evidence or to seize persons or property not particularly described shall not be granted; (6) that the people have a right to freedom of speech, of writing and publishing their sentiments, which shall not be restrained by any law of the United States; (7) that the people have a right to bear arms for the defense of themselves, their state, or the United States, and for killing game, and no law shall be enacted for disarming the people except for crimes committed or in a case of real danger of public injury from individuals, and standing armies shall not be kept up in time of peace, and the military shall be subordinate to the civil power; (8) that no law passed by the United States shall

[9] *Annals of Congress*, I, 770.
[10] See page 51 ff.

restrain liberty to fowl and hunt on one's own land or land not enclosed or to fish in any navigable waters or other waters not private property; (9) that no law of Congress shall restrain the legislatures of the states from imposing taxes, except imposts on goods imported or exported, and no taxes except imposts and duties on goods imported and exported or postage of letters shall be levied by Congress; (10) that the House of Representatives shall be increased in number, and elections shall remain free, and the states shall regulate elections without control by Congress, and the elections of representatives shall be annual; (11) that the power of organizing, arming and disciplining the militia shall remain with the states, and Congress shall not have authority to call or march the militia out of the state without the consent of the state, and then for such length of time only as the state shall agree; (12) that legislative, executive, and judicial powers shall be separated, and a constitutional council, who shall be responsible for the advice they give, be appointed to advise and assist the president;[11] (13) that no treaty opposed to the existing laws of the United States in Congress assembled shall be valid until such laws shall be repealed or made conformable to the treaty, nor shall treaties in contradiction to the Constitution of the United States or the constitutions of the several states be valid;[12] (14) that the federal judicial power be limited by eliminating "diversity of citizenship" jurisdiction,[13] and be limited in criminal cases to such only as are expressly enumerated in the Constitution,[14]

[11] The lack of a council was one of Mason's objections to the Constitution. See note 4, page 5.

[12] Participation of the House in exercise of the treaty power had been urged in the Constitutional Convention (Farrand, *Records*, II, 383, 392, 532, 538) and in Mason's objections (*ibid.*, II, 639). See text at note 61, page 31.

[13] Federal jurisdiction based on diversity of citizenship (in controversies "between citizens of different States") has been subject to much attack and little defense ever since it was conceived. Its only justification is the suspicion that state courts may be unfair to litigants from other states. It was one of the most widespread objections to ratification.

[14] The only power relating to crimes which is expressly granted by the Constitution is that given by Art. I, sec. 8, cl. 10 "to define and punish Piracies and Felonies committed on the high Seas, and Offences against the Law of Nations,"

and that Congress shall not have power to alter the descent and distribution and title of lands or goods or the regulation of contracts in the individual states; and (15) "that the sovereignty, freedom and independency of the several States shall be retained, and every power, jurisdiction and right which is not by this Constitution expressly delegated to the United States in Congress Assembled."[15]

Massachusetts was the first state which actually urged amendments at the time of ratifying the Constitution.[16] Jefferson had at first hoped that nine states would ratify the new frame of government, so that it would go into force and the benefit of its desirable features might be obtained, but that the remaining four states would reject it until a Bill of Rights was added. Later he came to favor the course Massachusetts had adopted, believing it better to accept first and to amend afterward; for "it will be easier to get the assent of nine States to correct what is wrong in the way pointed out by the Constitution itself, than to get

---

and by Art. I, sec. 8, cl. 6 "to provide for the Punishment of counterfeiting the Securities and current Coin of the United States."

The vast structure of present-day federal criminal law rests on the "necessary and proper" clause (Art. I, sec. 8, cl. 18). Yet an even more sweeping federal criminal jurisdiction over "common law crimes" was at first claimed by Federalists, and not until the cases of *United States* v. *Hudson*, 7 Cranch 32 (1812), and *United States* v. *Coolidge*, 1 Wheat. 415 (1816) was it determined that nothing could be a federal crime until it was so declared by Congress.

[15] Item (15) appears at the end of item (11) in the address of the minority to their constituents. McMaster and Stone, *Pennsylvania and the Federal Constitution*, 461–63. As to this proposal, see note 18, page 15.

[16] On January 30, 1788, John Hancock, president of the convention, made the proposition that amendments be urged at the time of ratification. This was formally moved by Samuel Adams, and on February 2, a committee was appointed, which two days later reported the resolution with some alterations. On February 6, 1788, the Constitution was ratified and the amendments recommended. Jonathan Elliot, *The Debates . . . on the Adoption of the Federal Constitution*, I, 129, 130, 132, 145–46, 151–52. For the amendments, see *ibid.*, 177–78; *Debates and Proceedings*, 82–85; *Documents Illustrative of the Formation of the Union of the American States*, 1018–19; and *Documentary History of the Constitution of the United States*, II, 94–95. Massachusetts was the sixth State to ratify.

thirteen to concur in a new convention and another plan of confederation."[17] This course was in fact followed.

The Massachusetts recommendations were nine in number: (1) that all powers not expressly delegated are reserved to the several states;[18] (2) that there be one representative to every 30,000 people until the membership of the House reaches 200;[19] (3) that Congress act with respect to elections only if a state fails to do so or makes regulations "subversive of the rights of the people to a free and equal representation in Congress";[20] (4) that

[17] Dumbauld, "Thomas Jefferson and American Constitutional Law," *Journal of Public Law*, Vol. II, No. 2 (Fall, 1953), 381–82. Madison had convinced Jefferson that calling a second constitutional convention, as New York had urged, would be dangerous. Fisher Ames argued in the Massachusetts convention that it would be easier to obtain desired changes by getting the assent of nine states after ratification of the Constitution than by getting thirteen states to accept the proposed provisions. Elliot, *Debates*, I, 160.

[18] The dissenting minority in the Pennsylvania convention had demanded an amendment equivalent to Article II of the Articles of Confederation, which provided: "Every State retains its sovereignty, freedom and independence, and every power, jurisdiction and right, which is not by this confederation expressly delegated to the United States, in Congress assembled." See text at note 15, page 14. The Massachusetts proposal, by reason of omission of the language at the beginning about the state's "sovereignty, freedom and independence" is essentially weaker, although it does, unlike the corresponding Virginia amendment and the Tenth Amendment to the Constitution as ratified, require that delegation be made "expressly." See text at note 32, page 42. Even under the Massachusetts language implied powers could not be excluded where resulting from interpretation of the scope of an express grant.

[19] The original Constitution in Art. I, sec. 2, par. 3, provided that "The number of Representatives *shall not exceed* one for every thirty thousand, but each State shall have at least one Representative"; and at the outset a membership of 65 was provided. Public opinion felt that the House which was to represent the people should be more numerous. George Washington's only speech at the Constitutional Convention was made in support of a last-minute change (after the document had already been engrossed for signature) increasing representation by substituting 30,000 for 40,000 in this paragraph. An amendment to increase representation was adopted by Congress in 1789 but was not ratified by the requisite number of states. See page 49.

[20] Art. I, sec. 4, par. 1 of the Constitution provides that "The times, places, and manner of holding elections for Senators and Representatives shall be prescribed in each State by the legislature thereof; but the Congress may at any time by law make or alter such regulations, except as to the places of choosing Senators." There was considerable popular apprehension that improper influence over elections might result from the exercise of this power by Congress;

Congress lay no direct taxes unless the impost and excise are insufficient, and then only if a requisition upon the states proves unsuccessful;[21] (5) that no monopolistic "company with exclusive advantages of commerce" be erected by Congress;[22] (6) that no person be tried for an infamous or capital crime until after indictment by a grand jury (except for cases arising in the armed forces); (7) that no federal court exercise "diversity of citizenship" jurisdiction in cases between citizens of different states unless the matter in dispute is of the value of $1500, and that the Supreme Court have jurisdiction in such cases only if the value is $3000;[23] (8) that every issue of fact in civil actions at common law shall be tried by jury upon request of any party; (9) that Congress shall at no time consent that any person holding an office of trust or profit under the United States shall accept a title of nobility, or any other title or office, from any king, prince, or foreign state.[24]

---

elections could be held at inconvenient and distant places. On the other hand, proponents of the Constitution felt that this authority in Congress was necessary, in order to ensure that the federal government would not collapse by reason of failure of the states to elect senators and representatives. Madison's *Writings*, V, 185. See page 43.

[21] One of the most notorious shortcomings of the government under the Articles of Confederation was the lack of power in Congress to impose taxes, and the failure of the states to respond to "requisitions" upon them for revenue. The "evil" of requisitions was regarded as "fatal" by Madison and given first place in his list of "Vices of the Political System of the United States" drawn up in April, 1787. Madison's *Writings*, II, 361. George Washington wrote to Jay: "Requisitions are a perfect nullity . . . Requisitions are actually little better than a jest and a byeword throughout the land." Warren, *The Making of the Constitution*, 18. In 1781 Congress asked the states for power to collect a five per cent duty on imports, but this plan fell through because of rejection by Rhode Island. Brant, *James Madison*, II, 211–12; *Papers of Thomas Jefferson*, X, 14, 16.

[22] This point, which had been one of Mason's objections (see note 4, page 5), is one that appealed to Jefferson. See page 8.

[23] See note 13, page 13.

[24] Samuel Adams was said to consider the 9th proposal important. Madison to Edmund Randolph, April 10, 1788. Madison's *Writings*, V, 118. Article VI of the Articles of Confederation contained an unqualified prohibition of acceptance of foreign titles; Art. I, sec. 9, cl. 8 of the Constitution prohibited such acceptance "without the Consent of the Congress." It is of interest to note that four of the nine Massachusetts proposals (Nos. 1, 2, 6, and 8) were included

Maryland, the seventh state to approve the Constitution, ratified on April 26, 1788. Advocates of the Constitution in that state's convention did not attempt to defend objectionable features in the instrument. They took the position that the convention was not empowered to propose amendments but had been appointed simply to "ratify the proposed Constitution, and that as speedily as possible."[25] Nevertheless after the Constitution had been ratified by a vote of 63 to 11, a resolution was adopted that a committee be appointed to consider and report such amendments as may be thought necessary to be recommended to the consideration of the people of the state if approved by the convention.[26] Thirteen amendments were agreed to by the committee,[27] while fifteen amendments were rejected by the majority of the committee.[28]

All the members of the committee who had voted for ratification declared that they would agree upon their honor to support the amendments which they had agreed to, both in their public and private characters, until they should become a part of the general government; but a great majority of them insisted on the express condition that none of the propositions which they had rejected, or any others, should be laid before the convention. The minority of the committee agreed to that arrangement except with regard to the first three of their fifteen propositions. These were again rejected by a vote of 8 to 5. On April 29, 1788, the convention resolved to consider no amendments except those proposed by the committee of thirteen. The committee being sent for by the convention, the majority then determined that they would make no report of any amendments whatever. A majority of the convention determined that the yeas and nays should not

in the amendments accepted by Congress in 1789. See Appendix 9, pages 220–22. Likewise six of the nine points proposed by Richard Henry Lee in the Continental Congress (see note 24, page 10) ultimately were adopted. Lee was dissatisfied because "The great points of free election, jury trial in criminal cases, and the unlimited rights of taxation and standing armies, remain as they were." Lee to Patrick Henry, September 14, 1789. *Letters of Richard Henry Lee*, II, 502.

[25] Elliot, *Debates* (2d ed., 1881), II, 548.

[26] *Ibid.*, 549.

[27] *Ibid.*, 550–52.

[28] *Ibid.*, 552–53.

be taken nor would they permit entry on the journal of the vote by which it was prohibited. The convention then adjourned.[29]

The amendments accepted by the Maryland committee were as follows: (1) that Congress shall exercise no power but what is expressly delegated by this Constitution; (2) that trial by jury in criminal cases shall be had according to the law of the state where the crime is committed, and no appeal involving questions of fact and no second trial after acquittal shall be allowed (except in the armed forces); (3) that in all actions on debts or contracts and controversies respecting property, trial of the facts shall be by jury if either party chooses; and that it be expressly declared that state courts have concurrent jurisdiction, and appeal from either federal or state courts shall be limited to matters of law and to controversies where a minimum amount is involved; (4) that inferior federal courts shall not have jurisdiction where less than a minimum amount is involved, and Congress may give the state courts jurisdiction in revenue cases, and in all cases of revenue appeal shall include questions of fact as well as of law; (5) that in trespasses done within the body of a county the party injured shall be entitled to trial by jury in that state; and that it be declared that state courts have concurrent jurisdiction with federal courts and there shall be no appeal from either except on matters of law; and no one shall be exempt from such jurisdiction and trial except ambassadors and ministers privileged by the law of nations; (6) that no federal jurisdiction shall arise from fictions or collusion; (7) that federal judges shall not hold any other office of profit under Congress; (8) that general warrants are oppressive and should not be granted; (9) that no soldier shall be compelled to serve for longer than four years except in time of war, and then only for the duration of the war; (10) that soldiers shall not be quartered in any house in time of peace without the consent of the owner; (11) that no mutiny bill shall be in force

29 *Ibid.*, 553–55. An account of the Maryland proceedings, including the two sets of proposed amendments, was furnished to Jefferson in John Brown Cutting's letter of July 11, 1788. Worthington C. Ford, *The Federal Constitution in Virginia*, 58–60.

longer than two years; (12) that "freedom of the press be inviolably preserved"; (13) that the militia shall not be subject to martial law, except in time of war, invasion, or rebellion.

The additional amendments desired by a minority of the Maryland committee were as follows: (1) that the militia, unless selected by lot or voluntarily enlisted, shall not be marched beyond the limits of an adjoining state without the consent of their legislature or executive; (2) that Congress shall have no power to interfere with elections unless a state neglects to provide for the same or is prevented by invasion or rebellion from doing so; (3) that direct taxes shall not be collected unless the state fails to pay the sum imposed; (4) that no standing army shall be maintained in time of peace without the consent of two-thirds of both branches of Congress; (5) that the president shall not command armed forces in person without consent of the Congress; (6) "that no treaty shall be effectual to repeal or abrogate the constitutions or bills of rights of the States, or any part of them"; (7) that no regulation of commerce or navigation act shall be passed without the consent of two-thirds of both branches of Congress; (8) that no member of Congress shall be eligible to any office of profit during his term; (9) that Congress shall have no power to lay a poll tax; (10) that no person with conscientious scruples shall be compelled personally to serve as a soldier; (11) that there be a responsible council to the president; (12) "that there be no national religion established by law; but that all persons be equally entitled to protection in their religious liberty"; (13) that all impositions and duties laid by Congress shall be credited to the state in which collected and be deducted out of such state's quota of the general expenses of government; (14) "that every man hath a right to petition the legislature for the redress of grievances, in a peaceable and orderly manner"; (15) that it be declared that all persons entrusted with legislative or executive powers in government are trustees and servants of the people and accountable as such, and that when the ends of government are perverted and the public liberty manifestly endangered, the people may of right reform the old or establish a new government;

19

and that the doctrine of nonresistance is absurd, slavish, and destructive of the happiness of mankind.

It will be noted that approximately half of the Maryland amendments had been previously proposed by the Pennsylvania minority or by the Massachusetts convention. It is also evident that most of the propositions put forward for the first time in Maryland appear in the recommendations of Virginia.[30]

The next ratifying convention to propose amendments was that of South Carolina. Of the four points which it advanced,[31] one was original:[32] to insert the word "other" before the word "religious" in Article VI, clause 3, of the Constitution which provides that certain officials "shall be bound by oath or affirmation to support this Constitution; but no religious test shall ever be required as a qualification to any office or public trust under the United States." This refinement of logic would have recognized the taking of the oath as a religious test rather than as a mere solemnity imposing an obligation under public law. No other state took notice of this meticulous reasoning, but unsuccessful attempts were made both in the House and in the Senate to have the suggestions of South Carolina incorporated in the American Bill of Rights during the debate on Madison's proposals.[33]

New Hampshire's list of desired changes copied those of Massachusetts,[34] and added three more: (1) that no standing armies

[30] The only original Maryland proposals that were not included in those of Virginia were amendments 4, 6, 7, and 11 of the committee, and 1, 5, and 13 of the minority of the committee, respectively.

[31] *Journal of the Convention,* 37–38; Tansill, *Documents,* 1023–24; *Documentary History,* II, 139–40. South Carolina ratified on May 23, 1788.

[32] South Carolina's first three points were equivalent to the Massachusetts 3rd, 1st, and 4th propositions, respectively.

[33] *Annals of Congress,* I, 709, 761–64, 778. See pages 44, 48.

[34] Bouton, *Miscellaneous Documents,* X, 20–21; Tansill, *Documents,* 1025–26; *Documentary History,* II, 142–43. New Hampshire ratified on June 21, 1788. The first nine of New Hampshire's proposals correspond to those of Massachusetts, except that the Seventh is even more restrictive of federal judicial power. Under the New Hampshire article all common law cases between citizens of different states would have to be begun in state courts, with no appeal to a federal court unless the value in controversy amounted to $3,000.

shall be maintained in time of peace without a three-fourths vote of each branch of the Congress, and that no troops shall be quartered in a private house in time of peace without the consent of the owner;[35] (2) that "Congress shall make no Laws touching Religion, or to infringe the rights of Conscience";[36] (3) that Congress shall never disarm any citizen except such as are or have been in actual rebellion.[37]

The amendments proposed by Virginia were probably the most significant, because Madison, "the father of the Constitution," was a native of that commonwealth and may have been more influenced by these proposals than by those from other states when he undertook in the first Congress under the new government the task of effecting the changes desired by public sentiment. The Virginia ratifying convention listed forty items: the first twenty were in the nature of a Bill of Rights largely identical with the Virginia Bill of Rights of 1776, and this general recital of political first principles was followed by twenty specific amendments to be inserted in the body of the Constitution itself.[38]

[35] The latter part of this article bore fruit in the Third Amendment to the Constitution of the United States. The Maryland committee had already advanced such a proposal.

[36] This provision was influential in debate in Congress resulting in the First Amendment to the Constitution. See text at note 20 page 39.

[37] The right to bear arms, going back to the English Bill of Rights, received recognition in the Second Amendment to the Constitution. See text at note 4, page 51. Counting this article, seven out of twelve of New Hampshire's proposals were ultimately accepted.

[38] For the Virginia proposals see *Debates and Other Proceedings of the Convention of Virginia*, III, 218–23; Elliot, *Debates*, II, 483–86; Tansill, *Documents*, 1028–34; *Documentary History*, II, 377–85. On June 25, 1788, the committee of the whole reported two resolutions, recommending ratification of the Constitution and that "whatsoever amendments may be deemed necessary" be recommended to Congress. Elliot, *Debates*, II, 473. A motion to substitute a resolution that a declaration of rights and other amendments should be referred to the other states for consideration "previous to ratification" was defeated by a vote of 88 to 80. *Ibid.*, 474. The resolution of ratification was then passed 89 to 79, and the second resolution regarding amendments also carried. *Ibid.*, 475–76. On June 27, 1788, George Wythe reported the amendments deemed necessary, which were adopted. *Ibid.*, 483, 487. Concerning these, Madison wrote to George Washington that he considered "several of them highly objectionable." Madison's *Writings*, V, 234. Undated drafts of the Convention's Bill of Rights (printed in

After proclaiming seven tenets of political philosophy set forth in the corresponding articles in the Virginia Bill of Rights, the convention in its eighth proposition, also taken from the same source, declared that in criminal cases the defendant was entitled to know the nature of the charge against him, to be confronted with accusers and witnesses, to call for evidence in his favor, to enjoy a fair and speedy trial by an impartial jury of his vicinage, without whose unanimous vote he can not be found guilty, "nor can he be compelled to give evidence against himself." The right to counsel was also specified, though this provision was not contained in the Virginia Bill of Rights. It undoubtedly was derived from similar provisions contained in the constitutions and early statutes of other states.[39]

The next item in the convention's Bill was a due process clause, reminiscent of Magna Charta, and now familiar in the form embodied in the Fifth and Fourteenth Amendments to the United States Constitution.[40]

The Tenth Article (and the Twelfth) are philosophical generalizations, also reminiscent of Magna Charta, to the effect that every freeman suffering a wrong should have a remedy without delay, denial, or venality in the administration of justice.

The Eleventh Article characterizes jury trial in civil cases as "sacred and inviolable." The Thirteenth directs that excessive bail ought not be required, nor excessive fines imposed, nor cruel and unusual punishments inflicted. The Fourteenth prohibits unreasonable searches and seizures, or general warrants. The Fifteenth permits peaceable assemblage and petition for redress of

Monaghan, *Heritage of Freedom*, 57–58) and of its amendments to the body of the Constitution, both in George Mason's handwriting, are preserved in the Library of Congress, together with other drafts (including suggestions by Richard Henry Lee). See also Rowland, *Life of George Mason*, II, 445–53.

[39] William M. Beaney, *The Right to Counsel in American Courts*, 16–20; *Powell* v. *Alabama*, 287 U.S. 45, 60–63 (1932). A Pennsylvania statute as early as 1701 recognized this right. England did not grant it (except in cases of treason) until 1836. The Pennsylvania minority's third proposal included this right. See page 12.

[40] This Ninth article is an expansion of the last clause of Article 8 of the Virginia Bill of Rights.

grievances. The Sixteenth guarantees freedom of speech and of the press. The Seventeenth declares the right of the people to bear arms, the subordination of the military to the civil power, the desirability of maintaining a well-regulated militia, and condemns a standing army in time of peace. The Eighteenth forbids quartering of soldiers in any house in time of peace without the consent of the owner. The Nineteenth provides that a conscientious objector should be "exempted upon payment of an equivalent to employ another to bear arms in his stead." The Twentieth protects freedom of religion.[41]

The important influence of the Virginia ratifying convention's proposed Bill of Rights is apparent when it is noted that (apart from the political generalities set forth in the first seven articles, and in the Tenth and Twelfth) every specific provision in the Virginia proposals later found a place in the federal constitution except the one allowing conscientious objectors to avoid bearing arms if they hired substitutes. Even that principle was included by Madison in the amendments which he proposed in Congress.[42]

With regard to the twenty particular modifications in the structure of the Constitution itself, the Virginia convention's proposals did not fare so well. Perhaps this was because in large part they were either too trivial or too controversial. Madison proposed in

[41] Of these articles, the Eleventh is the equivalent of Article 11 of the Virginia Bill of Rights; the Thirteenth of Article 9; the Fourteenth of Article 10 (with respect to general warrants); the Sixteenth of Article 12 (with respect to freedom of the press); the Seventeenth of Article 13 (except as to right of people to bear arms); and the Twentieth of Article 16. Article 14 of the Virginia Bill of Rights, relating to secession of Kentucky, and Article 15, recommending justice, moderation, temperance, frugality, virtue, and "frequent recurrence to fundamental principles" had no counterpart in the proposed federal Bill of Rights. The omission of Article 15 was criticized in the convention by Zachariah Johnson. Elliot, *Debates*, II, 470. He also pointed out that Article 1 had been revised so as to omit the affirmation that "all men are by nature equally free and independent."

[42] See Madison's seventh item, page 37. Possibly Madison's partiality toward the Virginia proposals may be due to the fact that in sponsoring amendments he was virtually fulfilling a campaign pledge; for his stand on this subject contributed to his election to Congress in Virginia. George Washington's inaugural address likewise recommended amendments. Douglas S. Freeman, *George Washington*, VI, 155, 188, 225, 248. See page 33.

Congress only such amendments as he considered acceptable to all parties and thoroughly unobjectionable. He believed that "it will be practicable . . . to satisfy the public mind . . . without endangering any part of the Constitution which is considered as essential to the existence of the Government by those who promoted its adoption."[43]

The Virginia proposals were: (1) that the states retain every power not delegated to the federal government; (2) that there be one representative per 30,000 population until the membership of the House reaches 200;[44] (3) that direct taxes and excises shall not be collected in a state raising its quota by local legislation;[45] (4) that members of House and Senate shall be ineligible to hold civil office during their term; (5) that the proceedings of the House and Senate be published yearly, except parts requiring secrecy;[46] (6) that receipts and expenditures of public money

[43] Madison's *Writings*, V, 375–76, 417–18. "The friends of the Constitution . . . wish the revisal to be carried no further than to supply additional guards for liberty, without abridging the sum of power transferred by the States to the general Government or altering previous to trial the particular structure of the latter." Madison to Jefferson, December 8, 1788. *Ibid.*, 311. See also text at notes 53, page 26; 3, page 34; 21, page 40; and 39, page 43. Madison's procedure in selection does not seem quite so capricious as Brant makes it appear. Brant, *James Madison*, III, 265. The Federalist party controlled both houses of Congress, and no amendment of Anti-Federalist tenor could have been successfully sponsored. For a list of members of the First Congress, First Session, see *Biographical Directory of the American Congress, 1774–1949* (Washington, 1950, 81 Cong., 2 sess., H. Doc. No. 607), 49–51. But Federalists like Madison did feel themselves bound in honor to accept those amendments without assurance of which ratification would have been impossible, especially since they regarded these changes as harmless. Madison to Richard Peters, August 18, 1789. Library of Congress, Madison Papers.

[44] It will be noted that these first two articles are the same as the first two Massachusetts proposals, and that they were included in the amendments proposed by Madison to Congress (as were the Fifteenth, Seventeenth, and Eighteenth, relating respectively to jury procedure, constitutional interpretation, and compensation of Congressmen and Senators). Madison's *Writings*, V, 380, 377, 378, 379. The first article is preserved in the Tenth Amendment to the Constitution; the Seventeenth, considerably modified, in the Ninth Amendment.

[45] Compare the fourth Massachusetts proposal, text at note 21, page 16.

[46] Article IX of the Articles of Confederation contained a similar provision requiring monthly publication.

24

be published; (7) that ratification of a commercial treaty shall require a two-thirds vote of the Senate, and a three-fourths vote of both houses shall be required for a treaty ceding or limiting territorial rights or claims, or fishing in American seas or navigating American rivers; (8) that navigation laws and laws regulating commerce shall require a two-thirds vote of both houses; (9) that a standing army in time of peace shall require a two-thirds vote of both houses;[47] (10) that no soldier shall be enlisted for longer than four years or the duration of a war; (11) that militia shall be subject to state regulation except when in federal service; (12) that the power of Congress over federal districts shall be limited to police regulation; (13) that no one shall be president more than eight out of any sixteen years;[48] (14) that the judicial power be restricted so that no lower federal courts shall be established except for admiralty matters, and so as to eliminate diversity jurisdiction and appellate jurisdiction in questions of fact at common law, and so as to exclude controversies originating before ratification of the Constitution (except territorial disputes between states, disputes involving lands claimed under grants of different states, and suits for debts due to the United States);[49] (15) that the defendant in criminal cases may challenge or except to the jury; (16) that Congress shall not interfere with elections unless a state fails to act; (17) that language prohibiting action by Con-

[47] In the Virginia convention Madison opposed this proposition, lest "the national security . . . be frustrated" by a fraction of the people. Madison's *Writings*, V, 232. See note 38, page 21.

[48] This proposal, limiting perpetual re-eligibility of the president, dealt with an issue which Jefferson thought important.

[49] Cf. the seventh Massachusetts proposal. Charles Warren observes that 16 out of the 79 amendments proposed by state conventions related to the Judiciary article of the Constitution. Warren, "New Light on the History of the Federal Judiciary Act of 1789," *Harvard Law Review*, Vol. XXXVII, No. 1 (November, 1923), 55–56. The principal relief sought was jury trial in civil cases, appellate power limited to questions of law, no federal courts of first instance, no diversity jurisdiction. See *ibid.*, 81, 84. Many lawmakers were of the opinion that matters relating to the functioning of the judiciary could be adequately regulated in the statute then pending in Congress rather than by constitutional amendment. *Ibid.*, 114. For Madison's comment on fears regarding the judiciary article, see his *Writings*, V, 387.

gress shall not be interpreted as an implied grant of power but as an exception or as a precaution; (18) that laws (after the first one) relating to compensation of congressmen and senators shall become effective only after an intervening Congressional election;[50] (19) that some tribunal other than the Senate be provided for trying impeachments of senators; (20) that salaries of judges may be changed only by general revision at seven-year intervals.

Important matters, but of a controversial nature, were involved in the Virginia proposals relating to commercial treaties and navigation laws.[51] Southern fears of being sacrificed for the benefit of New England shipping and mercantile interests were extremely prevalent. Jay's negotiations with Spain regarding the Mississippi had been a source of constant alarm to the frontiersmen of Virginia and other states of that region.[52] These conflicts had led to the requirement subjecting the treaty power to a two-thirds vote of the Senate. Madison did not wish to reopen issues that had been decided in the Constitutional Convention. Amendments which merely expressed dissatisfaction with agreements that had been reached, which merely voiced the political opposition of those who were antagonistic to the new form of government, were systematically ignored by Madison in formulating the amendments which he offered in the first Congress.[53]

The New York ratifying convention was probably the most hostile to the new Constitution of any of the state conventions which did ratify the instrument. (North Carolina refused to

[50] An amendment to this effect was adopted by Congress in 1789 but was not ratified by the requisite number of states. See page 49.

[51] Seventh and eighth Virginia proposals.

[52] Warren, *The Making of the Constitution*, 24, 654–58, 748; Dumbauld, *Political Writings of Thomas Jefferson*, xvii–xviii.

[53] Among the amendments proposed by the states which would have reopened controversies settled in the Constitutional Convention may be noted the following: two-thirds vote for navigation laws (Warren, *The Making of the Constitution*, 461, 501, 578–84, and see note 52, above; no direct taxation until failure of requisition (*ibid.*, 221, 497), and see note 21, page 16; no inferior federal courts except for admiralty jurisdiction (*ibid.*, 537–39; no standing army in time of peace (*ibid.*, 483).

ratify, and did not become a party to the Constitution until after its entry into force. Rhode Island also came into the Union after the new government had commenced operation.) Sentiment in New York was adverse to the Constitution because the power to regulate commerce given to the federal government would prevent that state from enjoying the profits theretofore derived from taxes collected by New York on articles passing through the state to and from inland consumers or producers in New Jersey or Connecticut. George Clinton, a prominent Anti-Federalist (later vice-president of the United States in Jefferson's second administration) was president of the New York ratifying convention. It ratified the Constitution by a majority of only three votes[54] (in Virginia and New Hampshire there had been a majority of ten, though in Rhode Island there was only a majority of two).

The New York act of ratification was an involved and lengthy document, commencing with a detailed Bill of Rights, declaring that the rights enumerated therein were inviolable, but expressing the opinion that the explanations thus set forth were consistent with the provisions of the Constitution, and expressing also the confident expectation that the amendments proposed by the New York convention would speedily become a part of the Constitution. It was therefore ratified "in full confidence nevertheless" that until the amendments desired became effective Congress would not call the militia out of the state for more than six weeks without the consent of the legislature, or interfere with elections, or impose an excise on any article produced, grown, or manufactured in the United States except ardent spirits, or impose direct taxes unless excises and imposts were insufficient and then not until

[54] Elliot, *Debates*, I, 358. New York ratified on July 26, 1788. On the previous day the New York convention had resolved that a circular letter be sent to all the states recommending that a general convention be convened to consider amendments. Madison and other friends of the new government were alarmed by the suggestion of a second convention, and advocated that appropriate amendments should be sought pursuant to the procedure provided in Article V of the Constitution itself. Madison to G. L. Turberville, November 2, 1788, Madison's *Writings*, V, 298–300; to Jefferson, December 8, 1788. *Ibid.*, 311–12. See also note 17, page 15.

requisitions proved unavailing. The thirty-two specific amendments proposed were then set forth.[55]

These proposals covered the following subjects: (1) that there be one representative in Congress for each 30,000 people until the membership of the House reaches 200; (2) that no excise be laid upon articles (except ardent spirits) grown, produced, or manufactured in the United States; (3) that no direct taxes be imposed unless impost and excise are insufficient and then not until after requisitions have proved fruitless; (4) that Congress not interfere with elections of representatives or senators unless the states fail to take action; (5) that no person shall be president, vice-president, or serve in either house of Congress who is not a freeholder and is not a native-born citizen or one naturalized before July 4, 1776 or a person who held a commission during the Revolutionary War and later became a citizen; (6) that no monopoly or company with exclusive advantages of commerce be created by Congress; (7) that no standing army shall be maintained in time of peace except by a two-thirds vote of each house; (8) that no money shall be borrowed on the credit of the United States except by a two-thirds vote of each house; (9) that war shall not be declared except by a two-thirds vote of each house; (10) that habeas corpus shall not be suspended longer than six months or 20 days after the next meeting of Congress; (11) that Congress in legislation for the federal district shall not exempt such district from taxes imposed in the state in which the district is located, nor confer privilege from arrest for crimes committed or debts contracted outside the district; (12) that Congress shall not make laws to prevent state laws from extending to places purchased for the use of the United States except as to persons in the service of the United States, nor as to them with respect to crimes committed outside of such places; (13) that laws relating to compensation of representatives and senators shall not become effective until after an election has intervened; (14) that the journals of Congress (except parts requiring secrecy) shall

[55] Tansill, *Documents*, 1039–44; *Documentary History*, II, 196–203. See also Elliot, *Debates*, I, 351–56.

be published at least once a year, and that the doors of both houses shall be open except when secrecy is required, and that the yeas and nays shall be recorded at the request of two members; (15) that no capitation tax shall ever be laid by Congress; (16) that no person shall be senator more than six out of twelve years, and that the states may recall a senator at any time; (17) that no senator or representative shall hold office under the United States; (18) that the authority of the executive of the states to appoint senators to fill vacancies shall be given to the legislatures of the states; (19) that the bankruptcy power of Congress shall be limited to merchants and traders and that the states shall have authority to enact insolvent laws for other descriptions of debtors; (20) that the president shall not serve more than two terms in office; (21) that the executive shall not grant pardons for treason without the consent of Congress, but may grant reprieves until the matter is laid before Congress; (22) that the president shall not command an army in the field in person "without the previous desire" of Congress; (23) that letters patent, commissions, pardons, writs, and process shall run in the name of the people of the United States; (24) that no inferior federal courts shall be established except to exercise appellate and admiralty jurisdiction; (25) that a tribunal for the trial of impeachments be provided for, composed of the Senate, the Supreme Court, and the senior judge from the highest court of every state; (26) that persons aggrieved by Supreme Court decisions in cases of original jurisdiction shall be entitled to have the president issue commissions to seven or more men learned in the law to correct errors and do justice to the parties; (27) that no judge of the Supreme Court shall hold any other office under the United States or any state; (28) that the judicial power shall not extend to controversies concerning lands except between states or under the grants of different states; (29) that the militia of any state shall not be compelled to serve outside the state longer than six months without the consent of the legislature; (30) that the words "without the consent of the Congress" shall be deleted in Article I, section 9, clause 7 [8], of the Constitution;[56] (31) that senators, repre-

[56] See note 24, page 16.

29

sentatives, and all executive and judicial officers of the United States shall be bound by oath "not to infringe or violate the Constitutions or Rights of the respective States"; (32) that the legislatures may provide that electors of election districts shall choose a citizen who has been an inhabitant for one year before the election for one of the representatives of such state in Congress.

The New York amendments, though the most numerous, were perhaps the least influential of those proposed by any of the state conventions. One amusing idea advanced was that parties aggrieved by Supreme Court decisions should have the right to apply to the president in order that he might issue commissions to seven men "learned in the law" who would correct errors and do justice to the parties.[57]

Of the amendments suggested by New York which had not been already proposed by other states, none were ultimately embodied in the American Bill of Rights.

The same is true of the amendments favored by the North Carolina convention at Hillsboro which on August 2, 1788, refused to ratify the Constitution, holding that "a declaration of rights, . . . together with amendments to the most ambiguous and exceptionable parts of the said constitution of government, ought to be laid before Congress, and the convention of states that shall or may be called for the purpose of amending the said Constitution, for their consideration, previous to the ratification of the Constitution aforesaid on the part of the state of North Carolina."[58]

North Carolina's proposals were essentially the same as Virginia's.[59] The Declaration of Rights, containing twenty articles,

[57] This idea was advanced in recent years (apparently independently) by one Everett C. McKeage of San Francisco in *American Bar Association Journal*, Vol. XLI, No. 2 (February, 1955), 106.

[58] Elliot, *Debates*, III, 210, 219. A motion to substitute a resolution of ratification and recommendation of six subsequent amendments was defeated by a vote of 184 to 84. *Ibid.*, 209, 216–19. North Carolina later ratified the Constitution on November 21, 1789.

[59] For the North Carolina recommendations, see *Proceedings and Debates*, 271–75; Elliot, *Debates*, III, 210–15; Tansill, *Documents*, 1043–51; *Documentary History*, II, 266–75.

was identical with that emanating from the Virginia convention. Of the twenty-six additional proposed amendments, twenty were the same as Virginia's, and one was copied from Massachusetts.[60] The five new items added by the Hillsboro convention were: (1) that Congress shall not declare any state to be in rebellion except by a vote of two-thirds "of all the members present in both houses" (Twelfth Article); (2) "that no treaties which shall be directly opposed to the existing laws of the United States in Congress assembled, shall be valid, until such laws shall be repealed, or made conformable to such treaty; nor shall any treaty be valid which is contradictory to the constitution of the United States" (Twenty-third Article)[61]; (3) that Article I, section 9, paragraph 5 [6] of the Constitution be amended so as to read: "Nor shall vessels bound to a particular state be obliged to enter or pay duties in any other;[62] nor when bound from any one of the States, be obliged to clear in another" (Twenty-fourth Article); (4) that Congress shall not interfere with redemption of paper money already emitted by any state, or in liquidating and discharging the public securities of any state (Twenty-fifth Article); (5) that Congress shall not introduce foreign troops into the United States without the consent of two-thirds of the members present of both houses (Twenty-sixth Article).[63]

When Rhode Island belatedly ratified the Constitution, a form of ratification like that of New York was followed. The amendments proposed by Rhode Island, however, were only twenty-one in number.[64] Since these were not promulgated until long after

[60] The first eleven articles bear the same numbers as Virginia's. The Thirteenth through the Twenty-first are Virginia's Twelfth through Twentieth, respectively. The Twenty-second is the Fifth in the Massachusetts list of amendments.

[61] The Pennsylvania minority had already proposed a more comprehensive amendment on this topic; so had the Maryland minority in its Sixth proposition. See pages 13, 19.

[62] That provision in the Constitution reads: "nor shall vessels bound to or from one State be obliged to enter, clear, or pay duties in another."

[63] This Twenty-sixth Article is reminiscent of a grievance complained of in the Declaration of Independence. Dumbauld, *The Declaration of Independence and What It Means Today*, 143.

[64] Tansill, *Documents*, 1056–59; *Documentary History*, II, 316–19. Rhode Island ratified on May 29, 1790. Five new points were put forward by Rhode

Congress had adopted and referred to the states for ratification the twelve articles ten of which, upon receiving the requisite ratifications, became the American Bill of Rights, it is obvious that Rhode Island's proposals had no influence upon the first ten amendments to the Constitution of the United States.[65]

If the proposals of Rhode Island are excluded as having had no effect upon the formulation of the Bill of Rights, but those of Pennsylvania and Maryland are included (although they were not adopted by official action of the conventions held in those states), the number of amendments proposed by the states reaches 186. This figure becomes 210 if the 24 items in the preliminary recitals of the New York act of ratification, which do not purport to be amendments, are counted (as is done in the following summaries). With duplications eliminated, 80 substantive propositions emerge.[66] All eight states, it will be noted, sought an amend-

---

Island: (1) that after 1793 consent of eleven states be required for adopting amendments to the Constitution; (2) that no person be compelled to do military duty otherwise than by voluntary enlistment except in cases of general invasion; (3) that no direct taxes be laid without the consent of three-fourths of the states; (4) that importation of slaves be prevented as soon as possible, since such traffic "is disgraceful to the cause of liberty and humanity"; (5) that Congress should have power to establish "a uniform rule of inhabitancy, or settlement of the poor of the different States throughout the United States." (Amendments Nos. 4, 6, 9, 17 and 19).

[65] Congress completed its action on the Bill of Rights on September 25, 1789.

[66] This figure becomes 83 if the three original proposals in the New York preliminary recitals (the eighteenth, nineteenth, and twenty-first) are counted. (These provide that states may apportion their representatives among districts, that *ex post facto* laws include only those concerning crimes, and that federal jurisdiction of cases in which a state is a party does not extend to criminal prosecution or authorize a suit against a state.) More minute subdivision according to subject matter (as set forth in the table in Appendix 1, page 160) yields a total of 87 items. The number commonly given is 124. This is based on Ames, *The Proposed Amendments to the Constitution*, 19, 307–10. Ames includes Rhode Island's 21 proposals, but omits the 40 items in the nature of a Bill of Rights proposed by Virginia and North Carolina. If these are counted as well as the amendments put forward by those states to be incorporated in the body of the Constitution, the total for all states comes to 164 (or 188, if the 24 New York preliminary items are included). A total of 231 is reached if the 43 Pennsylvania and Maryland proposals are added. Thorpe, *The Constitutional History of the United States*, II, 199, speaks of 200 or more amendments.

ment prohibiting Congress from interfering with the time and place of holding elections. There was also unanimity in demanding restrictions upon federal power to tax, and a declaration that powers not delegated to the federal government were reserved to the states. Seven states spoke in favor of jury trial in civil cases. Six states called for an increase in the number of members of Congress, for protection of religious freedom, and for prohibition of standing armies in time of peace. Five states demanded prohibition of quartering troops, and of unreasonable searches and seizures. An equal number favored state control of militia, the right to bear arms, trial by a jury of the vicinage, and freedom of speech and of the press. Four states desired recognition of the right to due process of law, speedy and public trial, assembly and petition; curtailment of federal judicial power; and a ban on monopolies, on excessive bail, on unconstitutional treaties, and on the holding of other federal offices by members of Congress.

More than half of the proposals just mentioned which were supported by a substantial consensus of state opinion were ultimately embodied in the Bill of Rights. Of twenty-two amendments which were supported by four or more states, fourteen were incorporated by Madison in his recommendations to Congress. The others were rejected as inconsistent with decisions already made by the Constitutional Convention at Philadelphia.

Madison's Proposed Amendments in the First Congress

When the Constitution had gone into effect and the first Congress convened, Madison took the lead in proposing amendments. Not only were the supporters of the Constitution honor bound by the circumstances under which ratification had taken place to accord such satisfaction to their opponents, but Madison himself was practically obliged to do so in fulfillment of his campaign promises. A material factor in procuring his election to Congress was his announcement that he favored amendments.[1]

[1] Madison to George Eve, January 2, 1789, Madison's *Writings*, V, 319–21. A similar letter to T. M. Randolph was published in the *Virginia Independent Chronicle* of January 28, 1789, shortly before election day (February 2). See also Edward Carrington to Madison, February 16, 1789. Library of Congress, Madison Papers.

Madison hoped to allay the fears of those who were dissatisfied with the new form of government by proving that "those who had been friendly to the adoption of this Constitution . . . were as sincerely devoted to liberty and a Republican Government, as those who charged them with wishing the adoption of this Constitution in order to lay the foundation of an aristocracy or despotism." He particularly desired to conciliate North Carolina and Rhode Island, so as to hasten their re-entry into the Union.[2] At the same time he opposed any modifications injurious to the "structure & stamina" of the government, or offensive to those "who approve the Constitution in its present form."[3] He eschewed controversial topics, realizing that the necessary legislative majorities to effect a constitutional amendment could not be mustered in behalf of any such proposals.[4] In sponsoring amendments, Madison received little help from his colleagues. The Federalists did not wish amendments at all; the Anti-Federalists desired more than Madison offered, and knew that adoption of his amendments would kill the prospect of any radical changes in the future.[5]

[2] Madison's *Writings*, V, 374–75; Hugh Williamson to Madison, July 2, 1789. Library of Congress, Madison Papers.

[3] Madison to James Madison, Sr., June 15, 1789; to Tench Coxe, June 24, 1789. On June 13, 1789, Madison wrote to Jefferson, sending the amendments which he had proposed in the House "as most likely to pass" and which would "if passed be satisfactory to a majority of those who have approved the Constitution. I am persuaded they will be so to a majority of that description in Virginia." Replying on August 28, 1789, Jefferson indicated his approval of the amendments, but said that he would have been for going further. Madison's proposals were regarded by Federalists as "an anodyne to the discontented" and "a soporific draught to the restless." Edmund Randolph to Madison, June 30, 1789. Library of Congress, Madison Papers.

[4] Madison to Edmund Pendleton, June 21, 1789. "Two or three contentious additions would even now prostrate the whole project," Madison wrote to Pendleton on August 21, 1789. Library of Congress, Madison Papers. See also Madison's *Writings*, V, 409, 417–18.

[5] Hardin Burnley to Madison, November 5, 1789. Library of Congress, Madison Papers.

[6] Materials utilized in tracing the development of the Bill of Rights in its course through Congress include the following: *Journal of the House of Representatives* (original in the National Archives; printed by Francis Childs and John Swaine, New York, 1789; reprinted by Gales & Seaton, Washington, 1826); *Journal of the First Session of the Senate* (original in National Archives;

In the House of Representatives on May 4, 1789, Madison gave notice that he intended to bring up the matter of amendments,[6] and on June 8 he moved that the House go into committee of the whole in order to consider this subject.[7]

Meeting with considerable opposition, he pressed for action. In an address to the House he set forth at length the proposed amendments which he desired to insert in the Constitution, and moved that they be referred to a select committee, since his request for their consideration in committee of the whole had not been well received. Elbridge Gerry of Massachusetts, though professing a desire for early consideration of amendments, thought it would be disrespectful to the states which had proposed amendments if a select committee were to take up instead the recom-

printed by Thomas Greenleaf, New York, 1789; reprinted by Gales & Seaton, Washington, 1820). References, unless otherwise stated, are to the 1789 printed Journals, available in the library of the American Philosophical Society. These will be cited "J. H. Rep." and "J. Sen." respectively. National Archives Record Group No. 46, Sen 1A–C2, includes: (1) a printed text for use of the Senate of the 17 articles adopted by the House, on which Senate amendments are noted in ink (this is item 50 in *The Formation of the Union: An Exhibit*, National Archives Publication No. 53–15, Washington, 1952); (2) a list in the handwriting of Oliver Ellsworth of 26 unnumbered amendments by the Senate (these correspond with the numbered amendments referred to in J. H. Rep. 146, 152); (3) a partially torn text of the 12 articles adopted by the Senate, printed at New York by Thomas Greenleaf, with pencilled "ag" opposite those agreed to by the conference committee, and marks in ink indicating that Articles I, III, and VIII were amended in conference; (4) report of the conference committee, in the handwriting of Oliver Ellsworth. In the Rare Book Room of the Library of Congress are printed texts of the Select Committee's report of July 28, 1789, of the seventeen articles passed by the House on August 24, 1789, and of the twelve articles passed by the Senate on September 9, 1789. (These are all printed by Thomas Greenleaf; in the Archives copy of the House version the printer's name has been cut out and in Article VIII the spelling "offense" appears instead of "offence.") To follow the debate in the committee of the whole and in the House the only source available is the less reliable *Annals of Congress*, which was compiled from newspapers and Thomas Lloyd's *Congressional Register*. Regarding its inadequacies, see *A National Program for the Publication of Historical Documents*, 93–94. A good account of the genesis of the Bill of Rights, though based largely on the *Annals*, is given in Thorpe, *The Constitutional History of the United States*, II, 199–263. A concise summary of the pertinent data in the *Journals* of the House and Senate appears in *History of Congress*, 152–73.

[7] *Annals of Congress*, I, 248, 424.

35

mendations of an individual member.[8] Other speakers also opposed the motion. Finally Madison then moved his propositions by way of resolutions to be adopted by the House. Thereupon a motion to consider them in committee of the whole was agreed to, and the House adjourned.[9] On July 21, the committee of the whole was discharged, and Madison's proposals were referred to a select committee, composed of one member from each state and empowered to take up the subject of amendments generally.[10]

Madison's proposed amendments were a distillate of the proposals emanating from the state conventions.[11] In nine formal amendments he embodied nineteen substantive items:[12] (1) that there be prefixed to the Constitution a declaration that all power is derived from the people, for whose benefit government is instituted, and who have a right to reform or change it whenever it is found inadequate to its purposes; (2) that there be one representative for every thirty thousand population; (3) that no law varying the compensation of senators and representatives become operative before the next ensuing Congressional election; (4)

[8] *Ibid.*, 444–46.

[9] *Ibid.*, 449–50; J. H. Rep. 57.

[10] J. H. Rep. 79–80; *Annals*, I, 660–65. The committee was composed of John Vining of Delaware, James Madison of Virginia, Abraham Baldwin of Georgia, Roger Sherman of Connecticut, Aedanus Burke of South Carolina, Nicholas Gilman of New Hampshire, George Clymer of Pennsylvania, Egbert Benson of New York, Benjamin Goodhue of Massachusetts, Elias Boudinot of New Jersey, and George Gale of Maryland.

[11] Madison's *Writings*, V, 376–80; *Annals of Congress*, 433–36; *Congressional Register*, I, 426–29. A useful list of precedents for Madison's proposals is given in Thorpe, *The Constitutional History of the United States*, II, 199–211. In formulating his proposals Madison doubtless used the convenient little pamphlet printed by Augustine Davis at Richmond in 1788, containing the amendments recommended by New York, Massachusetts, New Hampshire, Maryland, South Carolina, Virginia, and North Carolina. This was probably the pamphlet enclosed by Madison to Jefferson on October 17, 1788. Madison's *Writings*, V, 271. A copy is preserved in the Library of Congress in Madison Papers, Vol. 76, p. 35. See note 13, page 8.

[12] The number of substantive items is 32 rather than 19 if each distinct right is counted separately; for example item 9 has four subsidiary parts. Of the 33 items offered by Madison, two were apparently original, and one was a formal renumbering of Article VII. The remaining 30 were drawn from state proposals. See table in Appendix 1, page 160.

that "the civil rights of none shall be abridged on account of religious belief or worship, nor shall any national religion be established, nor shall the full and equal rights of conscience be in any manner, or on any pretext, infringed"; (5) that freedom of the press shall be inviolable, and the people shall not be deprived of their right to speak, write, or publish their sentiments; (6) that the right of peaceful assemblage and petition for redress of grievances shall not be restrained; (7) that the right to bear arms shall not be infringed, but no conscientious objector shall be compelled to render military service in person; (8) that no soldiers shall in time of peace be quartered in any house without the consent of the owner, nor at any time except in a manner warranted by law; (9) that no person shall be subject to double jeopardy (except in case of impeachment) nor shall be compelled to be a witness against himself, nor be deprived of life, liberty, or property without due process of law, nor be obliged to relinquish property for public use without just compensation; (10) that excessive bail shall not be required, nor excessive fines imposed, nor cruel and unusual punishments inflicted; (11) that unreasonable searches by means of general warrants shall be forbidden; (12) that in criminal prosecutions the accused shall enjoy the right to a speedy and public trial, to be informed of the nature and cause of the accusation, to be confronted with his accuser and the witnesses against him, to have compulsory process for obtaining witnesses in his favor, and to have the assistance of counsel for his defence; (13) that exceptions shall not be construed so as to enlarge delegated powers but as limitations or precautions; (14) that no state shall violate the equal rights of conscience, or the freedom of the press, or trial by jury in criminal cases; (15) that no appeal to the Supreme Court shall be allowed where the amount in controversy is less than a minimum value, nor shall any fact triable by jury be otherwise re-examinable than in accordance with common law principles; (16) that criminal trials (except impeachment and in the armed services) shall be by an impartial jury of freeholders of the vicinage, with unanimity required for conviction, the right of challenge, and other accustomed requisites; and presentment by a grand jury shall be essential in all crimes punishable with loss of life or member, provided that in case of enemy occupation or insurrection the law may authorize trial in some other county of the same state; and that in case of crimes not committed within any county, the trial may be in such county as the laws shall have prescribed; (17) that in civil suits at common law trial by jury should remain inviolate; (18) that neither the legislative, executive, nor judicial departments shall ever exercise the powers vested in another department; (19) that the powers not delegated by the Constitution nor prohibited by it to the states are reserved to the states respectively.[13]

Although it was to satisfy the scruples of others rather than his own that Madison took the initiative in proposing amendments, he diligently set himself to the task of pushing them through the legislative treadmill in spite of the inertia and opposition of his colleagues.[14]

Fisher Ames of Massachusetts, on whose motion the select committee was appointed, said of the measure: "I hope much debate will be avoided by this mode and that the Amendments will be more rational and less *ad populum* than Madison's. It is necessary to conciliate, and I would have Amendments. But they ought not be trash, such as would dishonor the Constitution, without pleasing its enemies." On the day before the committee reported, Ames derisively wrote: "We shall make a dozen or two rights and privileges for our posterity."[15]

[13] All the above items, except the first, were to be inserted at appropriate places in the body of the Constitution. Thus items (4) through (13) were to be added to Art. I, sec. 9, which enumerates restrictions on the powers of Congress; item (14) was to be placed in Art. I, sec. 10, which imposes restrictions on the States; items (15) through (17) were to be inserted in Art. III, which deals with the Judicial Power; items (18) and (19) were to become Art. VII, and Art. VII was to be renumbered as Art. VIII. Not until later in the course of debate did Madison yield to the insistence of Roger Sherman of Connecticut that the amendments be appended to the Constitution instead of being inserted in it. Brant, *James Madison*, III, 275; Madison's *Writings*, V, 416, 418–19; *Annals of Congress*, I, 778. See pages 39 and 44.

[14] *Annals of Congress*, I, 426–27, 704; Brant, *James Madison*, III, 267–68. See pages 7–8.

The select committee to which Madison's proposals for amendments had been referred brought in a report on July 28, which was taken up in committee of the whole on August 13, after further efforts to delay action were fought off by Madison's persistent pressure.[16] Sherman then moved that the amendments be added at the end of the Constitution. He strongly opposed attempting to "interweave our propositions into it." Other congressmen supported Sherman's suggestion, one upon the ground that to insert amendments in the body of the text would be to concede imperfection in a document signed by George Washington and would attribute to that patriot language not included in the instrument at the time his signature was affixed. Sherman's motion was defeated for the time being, however, and the House proceeded to consideration of the amendments.[17]

Provisions for increased representation in Congress and for postponement of salary increases until after an election intervenes were adopted.[18] Debate was evoked by the proposal to add to the prohibitions directed against Congress in Article I, section 9, of the Constitution a provision that "No religion shall be established by law, nor shall the equal rights of conscience be infringed."[19] Madison took part in the discussion, offering to clarify the provision by inserting the word "national" before "religion." Gerry disliked that term, and Madison withdrew his suggestion. Samuel Livermore of New Hampshire proposed the language contained in that state's amendments: "Congress shall make no laws touching religion, or infringing the rights of conscience." This version was adopted by a vote of 31 to 20.[20] Next passing

[15] Warren, "New Light on the History of the Federal Judiciary Act of 1789," *Harvard Law Review*, Vol. XXXVII, No. 1 (November, 1923), 117–18.

[16] J. H. Rep. 85, 88, 100; *Annals*, I, 707. Debate in committee of the whole took place August 13, 14, 17, 18. J. H. Rep. 100–103. For the report of the select committee see pp. 210–12.

[17] *Annals of Congress*, I, 704–707, 710, 717. Cf. *ibid.*, 766. See note 13, page 38, and note 43, page 44.

[18] *Ibid.*, 719, 728.

[19] *Ibid.*, 729.

[20] *Ibid.*, 731. See note 36, page 21. This clause was considerably changed in the Senate and in conference.

to freedom of speech and of the press and of assemblage, the House rejected a motion to strike out "assemble and." A motion by Thomas Tudor Tucker of South Carolina to insert "to instruct their representatives" was also defeated after Madison urged the rejection of doubtful amendments. The clause was adopted as reported.[21] Gerry charged Madison with the fondness of an author for his own work, and an unwillingness to see it disfigured by others. Gerry commented also on a remark by Michael Jenifer Stone of Maryland that the proposal about instructing representatives would make the government a democracy. That is what Gerry had thought it was, but perhaps the designation of aristocracy would fit it better. Gerry also remarked that the warm weather was causing heated debate.[22]

Proceeding on August 17 to the clause relating to the right to bear arms, a motion to strike out the exemption to conscientious objectors was defeated for the time being. The clause was adopted as reported. Likewise lost was a motion to prohibit a standing army without a two-thirds vote of both Houses. This motion was offered by Aedanus Burke of South Carolina, author of the pamphlet which had aroused public opinion against the Cincinnati. After rejection of several amendments, the clause on quartering soldiers was adopted as reported by the select committee.[23]

Important prohibitions against double jeopardy, self-incrimination, deprivation of life, liberty, or property without due process of law, and taking of property for public use without just compensation were adopted after two proposed changes were lost.[24] Prohibition of excessive bail or fines and cruel and unusual punishments was quickly accepted. In the clause relating to unreasonable searches and seizures, the committee of the whole adopted an amendment by Gerry, correcting an inadvertent omission.[25] His attempt to substitute "impair" for "disparage" in the

[21] *Ibid.*, 733, 738, 747.

[22] *Ibid.*, 740, 742, 748.

[23] *Ibid.*, 751–52.

[24] *Ibid.*, 753–54. A motion by John Laurence of New York to add "in criminal cases" to the prohibition against self-incrimination was carried.

[25] *Ibid.*, 754. Two other amendments were defeated. One of these was the

40

clause relating to constitutional construction, however, received no second.[26]

Madison's original proposition to protect the rights of conscience, free speech, free press, and jury trial against *state* action was then approved, as restated in affirmative language by Livermore: "The equal rights of conscience, the freedom of speech or of the press, and the right of trial by jury in criminal cases, shall not be infringed by any State." Madison thought this provision important, since some states did not have bills of rights.[27]

An amendment by Theodore Sedgwick of Massachusetts to increase to $3,000 from $1,000 the minimum for federal appellate jurisdiction was defeated. Livermore's motion to add the right to trial in the state where the offense occurred prevailed.[28]

An August 18, 1789, Gerry moved in the House to refer to the committee of the whole all the amendments proposed by the states which had not been included in the report of the select committee. This was defeated by a vote of 34 to 16.[29] Consideration of the select committee's report in committee of the whole was resumed, and the articles dealing with procedural rights in connection with trial of criminal cases, and with the right to jury trial in civil cases at common law, were quickly adopted,[30] as was the article on separation of powers.[31] When the provision relating to reserved powers was taken up, Tucker moved to prefix to it the words "All power being derived from the people" and also to insert the word "expressly" before "delegated." Madison spoke

proposal by Egbert Benson of New York to say "and no warrant shall issue" rather than "by warrants issuing." Though there is no record of any further action by the House on this point, Benson apparently succeeded in inserting the phraseology which he preferred during his service as a member of the committee of three appointed to prepare a proper "arrangement" of the amendments accepted by the House. See note 43, page 44. Lasson, *The History and Development of the Fourth Amendment*, 101.

[26] *Annals*, I, 754. See Madison's 13th item, page 37.

[27] *Ibid.*, 755. This proposal was later eliminated by the Senate.

[28] *Ibid.*, 756. This may be an error in the *Annals*.

[29] *Ibid.*, 757; J. H. Rep. 102.

[30] *Annals*, I, 759–60. Burke's proposal to change "vicinage" to "district or county" was defeated.

[31] *Ibid.*, 760.

in opposition to the latter proposal, pointing out that the same change had been considered and abandoned in the Virginia ratifying convention. The amendments were defeated.[32] After Boudinot reported on behalf of the committee of the whole on August 18, Tucker moved to refer to the committee of the whole seventeen additional proposed amendments to the Constitution. These were all defeated.[33]

On the following day, the House began consideration of the report of the committee of the whole.[34] On August 21, seventeen

[32] *Ibid.*, 761. The same proposal to insert "expressly" was again defeated when made in the House by Gerry (J. H. Rep. 108; *Annals*, I, 767) and in the Senate (J. Sen. 122). According to the *Annals of Congress*, Daniel Carroll of Maryland proposed to add "or to the people" after "reserved to the States," and the amendment was accepted. However, the printed document in the National Archives (see note 6, page 35) as well as the versions in J. H. Rep. 107 and J. Sen. 106 show that these words were not in the proposed articles as adopted by the House but were added by the Senate. J. Sen. 122–23. This is doubtless an error in the *Annals*, although it is not too clear what changes the House may have made in the report of the committee of the whole. J. H. Rep. 107–108. According to *Annals*, I, 768, on motion of Sherman the House on August 21 adopted the language which the Senate clearly inserted on September 7, shown as Senate amendments No. 25 and No. 26 in the Senate amendments dated September 9, 1789, in the National Archives (see note 6, page 35).

[33] J. H. Rep. 103–104; *Annals*, I, 761–63. These were: (1) no person to serve as representative more than six out of any eight years; (2) after 1795, election of senators to be annual, with no person serving more than five out of any six years; (3) Congress to have no power over elections; (4) each state to be judge, according to its own laws, of elections of senators and representatives; (5) power to expel members to be eliminated; (6) no senator or representative to be appointed to civil office during his term; (7) no direct tax except upon failure of requisition; (8) no inferior federal tribunals except courts of admiralty; (9) Congress to have no power to prevent state laws from applying to federal district when persons outside such district are aggrieved; (10) power of Congress to permit holding of foreign titles to be eliminated, saving the rights of present holders during their lifetime; (11) state duties on exports or imports to be uniform in operation on foreign nations and citizens of the several states, as well as consistent with treaties; (12) no president to serve more than eight out of any twelve years; (13) president to "have power to direct (agreeably to law) the operations" of army and navy, instead of being commander-in-chief; (14) president to have power to suspend for twelve months an unfit officer, Congress to have power to provide for removal; (15) same as (8); (16) "diversity jurisdiction" to be eliminated; (17) "other" to be inserted before "religious test" in Art. VI.

42

articles were adopted.[35] The proposed recital to be added to the Preamble of the Constitution declaring that all power is derived from the people failed to receive the necessary two-thirds vote.[36] During debate several amendments in wording were made,[37] and numerous proposals rejected.[38] Lengthy argument marked Burke's proposal to add a provision, desired by many states, forbidding interference by Congress with state regulations of elections. Ames replied that it was important for Congress to have such authority. Madison stated that he would not have objected to the offering in committee of the whole of Burke's proposal, but repeated his insistence that the amendments found acceptable should not be delayed by the consideration of doubtful proposals. "But I cannot agree to delay amendments now agreed upon, by entering into the consideration of propositions not likely to obtain the consent of either two-thirds of the House or three-fourths of the State legislatures." He further explained that he "was willing to make every amendment that was required by the States, which would not tend to destroy the principles and the efficacy of the Constitution; he conceived that the proposed amendment would have that tendency, he was therefore opposed to it." The proposal was defeated by a vote of 28 to 23.[39]

Another radical restriction on federal power which many states had called for was offered by Tucker on August 22. This was the proposal to prohibit direct taxes unless duties, imposts, and excises were insufficient and a requisition on the states had proved unproductive. It was defeated by a vote of 39 to 9 after extensive

[34] Debate in the House took place August 19, 20, 21, and 22. J. H. Rep. 106–12.

[35] J. H. Rep. 107–109.

[36] *Annals*, I, 707, 766.

[37] According to *Annals*, I, 766, on motion of Fisher Ames the fourth article (relating to freedom of religion) was amended to read "Congress shall make no law establishing religion, or to prevent the free exercise thereof, or to infringe the rights of conscience." A motion to add "in person" to the conscientious objector clause was accepted. *Ibid.*, 767. See also *ibid.*, 767, 773.

[38] J. H. Rep. 109–16; *Annals*, I, 767, 768–73, 777, 778, 783.

[39] J. H. Rep. 109; *Annals*, I, 768–70. This was No. 3 of the Massachusetts amendments.

debate.[40] Tucker then proposed to abolish lower federal courts except admiralty courts, and to offer the South Carolina amendment inserting "other" before the words "religious test." Both measures were rejected.[41] Gerry then offered two of the Massachusetts amendments: to prohibit monopolies and acceptance of foreign titles. Both were defeated.[42]

Madison finally was obliged to yield to Sherman's insistence that the articles of amendment be added as a supplement to the Constitution, instead of being inserted in it. A committee composed of Benson, Sherman, and Sedgwick was appointed "to prepare and report a proper arrangement of, and introduction to the articles . . . agreed to by the House."[43] The committee reported on August 24, 1789, and the House approved the seventeen articles of amendment and transmitted them to the Senate.[44]

Changes in the Senate and in Conference

The Senate, after defeating a motion to postpone the subject until the next session of Congress, began consideration of the articles on September 2.[1] Minor changes were made in the articles

[40] J. H. Rep. 110; *Annals*, I, 773, 777. This was No. 4 of the Massachusetts amendments.

[41] J. H. Rep. 111; *Annuals*, I, 778. See page 20.

[42] J. H. Rep. 111; *Annals*, I, 778. See page 16.

[43] J. H. Rep. 112; *Annals*, I, 778. See notes 13, page 38 and 17, page 39.

[44] J. H. Rep. 112–13; *Annals*, I, 779. Comparison of J. H. Rep. 107–109 with J. Sen. 104–106 shows the changes in arrangement made by the committee. Article 7 had been 9, 8 had been 7, 9 had been 13, 10 had been 14, 11 had been 12, 12 had been 15, 13 had been 8, 14 had been 11, 15 had been 10. The first six and last two articles retained their former position.

[1] J. Sen. 106; *Annals*, I, 74. For the text of the articles as proposed by the House, see J. Sen. 104–106. The Senate debated this subject September 2, 3, 4, 7, 8, and 9. *Ibid.*, 114–31. Of the amendments proposed by the House, Senator Maclay of Pennsylvania, a staunch Democrat, noted: "They were treated contemptuously by Izard, Langdon, and Mr. Morris. Izard moved that they should be postponed till next session. Langdon seconded, and Mr. Morris got up and spoke angrily but not well. They, however, lost their motion, and Monday was assigned for taking them up. I could not help observing the six-year class [of senators] hung together on this business, or the most of them." Edgar S. Maclay, *Journal of William Maclay*, 134. During debates in the Senate on the Bill of Rights, Maclay was ill; but the questions that visitors discussed with him related

relating to the number of representatives and to the salaries of members of Congress.[2] The article on freedom of religion gave rise to considerable uncertainty in drafting. At first a proposal to delete "religion or prohibiting the free exercise thereof" and substitute "one religious sect or society in preference to others" was defeated, but then on reconsideration accepted. A motion to eliminate the entire article was lost. The same fate met two other proposed versions: "Congress shall not make any law, infringing the rights of conscience, or establishing any Religious Sect or Society"; and "Congress shall make no law establishing any particular denomination of religion in preference to another, or prohibiting the free exercise thereof, nor shall the rights of conscience be infringed." The Senate likewise rejected a motion to adopt the article in its original form as it came from the House; but finally accepted it in that form with the omission of the words "nor shall the rights of conscience be infringed."[3] Later (on September 9) another wording was adopted when the provisions on freedom of religion were combined with those on freedom of speech, press, and assemblage: "Congress shall make no law establishing articles of faith or a mode of worship, or prohibiting the free exercise of religion, or abridging the freedom of speech, or the press, or the right of the people peaceably to assemble, and petition the Government for the redress of grievances."[4] This language may have been intended by Richard Henry Lee and New England proponents of establishment to permit the federal government to give financial support to churches.[5]

to salaries for federal officials and location of the seat of government. Nothing more was mentioned in his journal about the Bill of Rights. *Ibid.*, 144–50, 166.

[2] J. Sen. 115, 116. Regarding Senate amendments generally, see the documents in National Archives described in note 6, page 35.

[3] J. Sen. 116–17; *Annals*, I, 74.

[4] J. Sen. 129. Article IV in the House version thus became part of the Senate's Article III and subsequent articles were correspondingly renumbered. Articles X, XI, XIV, and XVI of the House version were eliminated by the Senate, so that in renumbering XII became IX, XV became XI, and XVII became XII. Articles VI, VII, IX, XIII, XV were approved by the Senate without change.

[5] Brant, *James Madison*, III, 269–71. The Senate language was later modified in conference. See page 49.

After rejecting an amendment condemning standing armies and requiring "strict subordination" of military to civil power, the Senate adopted the article relating to the right to bear arms.[6] Articles dealing with quartering of soldiers and with search and seizure passed without change. The Senate rewrote two articles, combining the provisions relating to indictment by a grand jury with those relating to double jeopardy, self-incrimination, due process, and eminent domain.[7] Provisions dealing with jury trial in civil cases were likewise combined.[8] No change was made in the articles specifying certain rights of the accused to a fair trial[9] and prohibiting excessive bail or fines, as well as the infliction of cruel and unusual punishments.[10]

The Senate rejected Madison's proposal imposing limitations on the states.[11] A statement affirming the principle of separation

[6] The Senate version read: "A well regulated militia, being the best security of a free State, the right of the people to keep and bear arms shall not be infringed." J. Sen. 119. Comparison with the House version (*ibid.*, 104) shows that the Senate omitted the words "composed of the body of the people" after "militia," and also deleted the provision exempting conscientious objectors from personal service. Later this language was improved by substituting "necessary to the" for "the best." J. Sen. 129.

[7] Article VIII was approved with the substitution of "be twice put in jeopardy of life or limb by any public prosecution" for "except in case of impeachment to more than one trial or punishment." Besides double jeopardy, this article covered self-incrimination, due process, and just compensation. Article X was stripped by the Senate of all the provisions relating to trial by a jury of the vicinage, and cut down to "No person shall be held to answer for a capital or otherwise infamous crime, unless on a presentment or indictment by a grand jury." On September 9 these articles were combined and renumbered as VII (now the Fifth Amendment). J. Sen. 119, 130.

[8] The Senate struck from the House version of Article XI the provision prohibiting appeals to the Supreme Court involving less than $1,000, and also rejected a substitute proposal which would have eliminated "diversity of citizenship" cases below a minimum value. The Senate imposed a $20 limitation when accepting the guarantee of jury trial in suits at common law contained in Article XII. These provisions were later (September 9, 1789) combined and renumbered as Article IX (now Amendment VII). J. Sen. 119, 121, 130.

[9] Article IX (covering speedy public trial, nature and cause of the accusation, confrontation, right to process to obtain witnesses, right to counsel) was renumbered as VIII by the Senate. J. Sen. 119, 130. This is now Amendment VI.

[10] J. Sen. 121, 131. This was Article XIII (renumbered by the Senate as X). It is now Amendment VIII.

of powers also failed of approval.[12] On the other hand, the declarations regarding non-disparagement of powers not enumerated and reservation of powers not delegated were accepted, the former without change, and the latter as amended by adding the words "to the United States" after "delegated," and the words "or to the people" after "reserved to the States respectively."[13]

On September 8, the Senate amended the language of the introductory resolution submitting the proposed amendments to the states, and also voted down numerous proposals offered by advocates of more extensive amendments.[14] These embodied the recommendations of the Virginia convention which had not been accepted by Madison. They were doubtless offered by the Virginia senators in compliance with the instructions of that state's convention. On September 7, during debate on the article dealing with non-disparagement of powers not enumerated (Article XV),

11 J. Sen. 121; *Annals*, I, 76. See text at note 27, page 41. This was Article XIV. Madison's proposals to require the states to observe the basic rights specified in Article XIV tested the sincerity of those who professed to favor liberty and republicanism. See text at note 2, page 34. The fact that Jefferson approved all of Madison's proposals, as far as they went (see note 3, page 34), shows that he, like Madison, was more interested in human rights than in States' rights. The Pennsylvania proposals likewise applied to State action.

12 J. Sen. 122. This was Article XVI.

13 J. Sen. 122, 123. These were Articles XV and XVII (renumbered by the Senate as XI and XII), now Amendments IX and X. The perennial proposal to insert "expressly" before "delegated" was also rejected again. See page 42.

14 J. Sen. 123, 124–27. The twenty-one proposals rejected by the Senate included all but three of the Virginia propositions which Madison had not accepted. See text at note 42, page 23 and note 44, page 24. Items 1–5, and 10 and 12 of the Virginia convention bill were offered in the Senate. Apparently items 6 and 7 (relating to freedom of elections and executive suspension of laws) were not thought to be of sufficient practical importance. Madison had accepted items 8, 9, 11, 13–20. Of the Virginia convention's amendments to the body of the Constitution, items 4–14, 16, 19 and 20 were offered in the Senate. Item 3 (on taxation) had been defeated on the preceding day (as had item 16 on elections). Madison had accepted items 1, 2, 15, 17, and 18. For proposals rejected in the House, see text at notes 33, page 42, and 38–42, pages 43–44. As Jefferson said regarding adoption of the Declaration of Independence by Congress, "the sentiments of men are known not only by what they receive, but what they reject also." Jefferson's *Works*, I, 33–34.

the Senate had also rejected other demands, some of which had been proposed by Massachusetts and South Carolina: that taxation be permitted only upon failure of requisitions; that "other" be added between the words "no" and "religious test" in Article VI, clause 3; that Congress may interfere with elections only in case of neglect by a state or in case regulations are made which are "subversive of the rights of the people" to a free and equal representation in Congress; that no monopoly be created; that Congress shall not consent to acceptance of foreign titles or offices; and that no person indebted to the United States shall sit in either house of Congress.[15]

On September 9, 1789, the Senate adopted its resolution of concurrence in the House resolution as amended, and notified the House accordingly.[16] On the following day the House received the Senate's message that it had agreed to the House's resolution of September 2 with several amendments.[17] On September 19, the subject was taken up. On September 21, the House agreed to some of the Senate's amendments and disagreed with others. A conference was desired; Madison, Sherman, and Vining being the managers on the part of the House.[18] On September 23, Madison made his report to the House.[19] The report of the conference committee was considered and accepted on September 24 by the House.[20] On Friday, September 25, 1789, the Senate concurred.[21] Therefore this date is celebrated as the anniversary of the Bill of Rights.

Under the terms of the conference report, the House accepted all the Senate amendments, provided that further changes should be made in three articles. In Article I, "more" was to be substi-

[15] J. Sen. 121–22.

[16] J. Sen. 131; *Annals*, I, 77.

[17] J. H. Rep. 134; *Annals*, I, 889.

[18] J. H. Rep. 145–46; *Annals*, I, 905.

[19] J. H. Rep. 151. On September 24, Ellsworth reported to the Senate. J. Sen. 145.

[20] J. H. Rep. 152–53; *Annals*, I, 913. The message from the House was received by the Senate on the same day. J. Sen. 148.

[21] J. Sen. 150–51; *Annals*, I, 88. The message from the Senate was received by the House on the same day. J. H. Rep. 156.

tuted for "less" in the original House provision regarding the number of representatives in Congress. Article III regarding freedom of religion was finally worded as follows: "Congress shall make no law respecting an establishment of religion, or prohibiting the free exercise thereof, or abridging the freedom of speech, or of the press; or the right of the people peaceably to assemble, and to petition the government for a redress of grievances." In Article VIII, there was inserted in the clause guaranteeing a speedy and public trial the words "by an impartial jury of the State and district wherein the crime shall have been committed, which district shall have been previously ascertained by law."[22]

Twelve articles were sent to the states for ratification,[23] but only ten of these twelve received the requisite ratification by three-fourths of the states. (Articles I and II were not ratified. Hence the numbers of the amendments in the Constitution are lower by two than in the Senate numbering.) Quite fittingly, it fell to Secretary of State Thomas Jefferson to notify the governors of the several states of the ratification of the Bill of Rights.[24] Massachu-

[22] On the date of his conference report, Madison wrote to Edmund Pendleton: "It will be impossible I find to prevail on the Senate to concur in the limitation on the *value* of appeals to the Supreme Court, which they say is unnecessary, and might be embarrassing in questions of national or Constitutional importance in their principle, tho' of small pecuniary amount. They are equally inflexible in opposing a definition of the *locality* of Juries. The vicinage they contend is either too vague or too strict a term, too vague if depending on limits to be fixed by the pleasure of the law, too strict if limited to the County. It was proposed to insert after the word Juries, 'with the accustomed requisites,' leaving the definition to be construed according to the judgment of professional men. Even this could not be obtained. The truth is that in most of the States the practice is different, and hence the irreconcileable difference of ideas on the subject. In some States, jurors are drawn from the whole body of the community indiscriminately; in others, from large districts comprehending a number of Counties; and in a few only from a single County. The Senate suppose also that the provision for vicinage in the Judiciary bill, will sufficiently quiet the fears which called for an amendment on this point. On a few other points in the plan the Senate refuse to join the House of Reps." Madison's *Writings*, V, 424. See also *ibid.*, 420–21.

[23] *Documentary History*, II, 321–24; Frank Monaghan, *Heritage of Freedom*, 54–56.

[24] His letters conveying official notice of this important event and transmitting a printed text of the articles of amendment and of the ratifications were dated

setts, Connecticut, and Georgia belatedly ratified in 1939 the first ten amendments to the Constitution.[25] They had been in full force and effect since December 15, 1791, when the ratification of Virginia completed the process of incorporating them into "the supreme law of the land."

The American Bill of Rights

In the light of the foregoing discussion of the stages which preceded the formulation and ratification of the first ten amendments to the Constitution, it will now be profitable to turn to the wording of the American Bill of Rights as finally embodied in the nation's fundamental law, and to summarize the genesis and significance of each of these amendments.

ARTICLE I

Congress shall make no law respecting an establishment of religion, or prohibiting the free exercise thereof; or abridging the freedom of speech, or of the press, or the right of the people peaceably to assemble, and to petition the Government for a redress of grievances.

Insofar as it relates to freedom of religion, this article is derived from Madison's fourth item, as modified during its consideration by the House and Senate and in conference. It goes back to the Virginia convention bill's twentieth article, based upon Article 16 of the Virginia Bill of Rights of 1776. The Pennsylvania minority was the first to propose an amendment on this subject.

Insofar as freedom of the press is concerned, Madison's fifth item, the Virginia convention bill's sixteenth article, and Article 12 of the Virginia Bill of Rights furnish the lineage of the pro-

March 1, 1792. National Archives, records of the Department of State, American Letters, Vol. IV, pp. 355–56. Apparently two copies of the pamphlet with blue paper wrappers (in the Rare Book Room of the Library of Congress), believed by Eaton to have been printed by Francis Childs and John Swaine at Philadelphia, were enclosed to each recipient.

[25] Denys P. Myers, *Massachusetts and the First Ten Amendments to the Constitution*, 8; Myers, *The Process of Constitutional Amendment*, 11–14, 15, 17.

visions set forth. Here again the Pennsylvania minority was the first to speak out. Charles Warren asserts that the right to freedom of *speech* (as distinguished from freedom of the press) "was *created* by the First Amendment to the Federal Constitution" and "was not found in the Bill of Rights . . . of any American State in 1788."[1] However, the Pennsylvania Bill of Rights contained a provision "that the people have a right to *freedom of speech*, and of writing and publishing their sentiments; therefore the freedom of the press ought not to be restrained."[2] The Pennsylvania minority, as well as the Virginia convention bill (in their sixth and sixteenth propositions, respectively), urged an amendment to the federal constitution on this subject.

With respect to peaceable assemblage and petition for redress of grievances, the Amendment is based upon Madison's sixth item, the Virginia convention bill's fifteenth article, and goes back to the English Bill of Rights.[3] The Maryland minority was the first to propose an amendment on this subject.

ARTICLE II

A well regulated Militia, being necessary to the security of a free State, the right of the people to keep and bear Arms, shall not be infringed.

This article also goes back to the English Bill of Rights.[4] Madison's seventh item accepts the Virginia convention bill's seventeenth article (plus the nineteenth, regarding commutation by conscientious objectors). Article 13 of the Virginia Bill of Rights

[1] Warren, *Congress, the Constitution, and the Supreme Court*, 84. Italics in the original. A footnote on the next page in Warren quotes Article XII of the Pennsylvania Bill of Rights (see note 2 below) but that provision is overlooked by Warren when he makes his general statement that no state recognized the right to freedom of speech in 1788.

[2] *Conventions and Constitutions of Pennsylvania*, 56. Italics supplied.

[3] Interference with the right to petition was one of the grievances felt by colonists at the time of the Declaration of Independence. Dumbauld, *The Declaration of Independence and What It Means Today*, 104, 165.

[4] *Ibid.*, 166.

is the underlying source. The Pennsylvania minority was the first to propose an amendment dealing with this topic.

ARTICLE III

No Soldier shall, in time of peace be quartered in any house, without the consent of the Owner, nor in time of war, but in a manner to be prescribed by law.

This Article also goes back to the English Bill of Rights.[5] Madison's eighth item is derived from the Virginia convention bill's eighteenth article. The Maryland committee was the first to propose this provision.

ARTICLE IV

The right of the people to be secure in their persons, houses, papers, and effects, against unreasonable searches and seizures, shall not be violated, and no Warrants shall issue, but upon probable cause, supported by Oath or affirmation, and particularly describing the place to be searched, and the persons or things to be seized.

This article awakens memories of the eloquence of James Otis against the odious writs of assistance in 1761.[6] Madison's eleventh item is based on the Virginia convention bill's fourteenth article. The Pennsylvania minority was the first to propose an amendment on this subject.

ARTICLE V

No person shall be held to answer for a capital, or otherwise infamous crime, unless on a presentment or indictment of a Grand Jury, except in cases arising in the land or naval forces, or in the Militia, when in actual service in time of War or public danger; nor shall any person be subject for the same offence to be twice put in jeopardy of life or limb, nor shall be compelled in any

[5] *Ibid.,* 117, 164.
[6] *Ibid.,* 3.

criminal case to be a witness against himself, nor be deprived of life, liberty, or property, without due process of law; nor shall private property be taken for public use without just compensation.

With respect to the requirement of grand jury action, this Amendment is based on Madison's sixteenth item and the Massachusetts convention's sixth proposal.

Madison's ninth item treats the other topics covered. Except with respect to double jeopardy and eminent domain, the genesis of these rights is found in the Virginia convention bill's eighth and ninth articles, based on Article 8 of the Virginia Bill of Rights. With the same exceptions, the Pennsylvania minority was the first to assert these rights.

Possibly the prohibition against double jeopardy may have been taken by Madison from the prefatory declaration of rights contained in the New York act of ratification,[7] or from the Maryland committee's proposition "that there be no . . . second trial after acquittal."[8] Perhaps Madison himself may have been responsible for the requirement of just compensation in connection with the exercise of eminent domain.[9]

ARTICLE VI

In all criminal prosecutions, the accused shall enjoy the right to a speedy and public trial, by an impartial jury of the State and district wherein the crime shall have been committed, which dis-

[7] *Documentary History*, II, 192.

[8] Elliot, *Debates* (2d ed., 1881), II, 550. Madison may have had in mind also Blackstone's reference to "this universal maxim of the common law of England, that no man is to be brought into jeopardy of his life more than once for the same offence." Blackstone, *Commentaries*, IV, *335.

[9] Blackstone said that when property is taken for public use the legislature gives the owner "a full indemnification and equivalent for the injury thereby sustained." Blackstone, *Commentaries*, I, *139. The constitutions of Vermont (1777) and Massachusetts (1780) provided for just compensation, but Chancellor Kent regarded that requirement as based on "natural equity" even in the absence of specific language. J. A. C. Grant, "The Higher Law Background of Eminent Domain," *Wisconsin Law Review*, Vol. VI, No. 2 (February, 1931), 67, 70, 71–72. The provision for just compensation may be based on Magna Charta (Art. 28). Chafee, *How Human Rights Got Into the Constitution*, 45.

trict shall have been previously ascertained by law, and to be informed of the nature and cause of the accusation; to be confronted with the witnesses against him; to have compulsory process for obtaining witnesses in his favor, and to have the Assistance of Counsel for his defence.

Denial of the right to trial in the vicinage where the offense was committed was one of the grievances set forth in the Declaration of Independence.[10] Madison's sixteenth item refers to this topic,[11] and his insistence on its inclusion led to its reinsertion by the conference committee after the Senate had eliminated it.[12] His twelfth item covers the other rights enumerated in Article VI. All of these are specified in the Virginia convention bill's eighth article, and all except the right to counsel are found in Article 8 of the Virginia Bill of Rights. The origin of the right to counsel is undoubtedly to be found in the provisions contained in many state constitutions (but not that of Virginia) and statutes.[13] The Pennsylvania minority was the first to propose an amendment covering all the topics included in Article VI.

ARTICLE VII

In suits at common law, where the value in controversy shall exceed twenty dollars, the right of trial by jury shall be preserved, and no fact tried by a jury shall be otherwise re-examined in any Court of the United States, than according to the rules of the common law.

This article is based on Madison's fifteenth and seventeenth items. The latter of these goes back to the Virginia convention bill's eleventh article (Article eleven of the Virginia Bill of Rights), the Massachusetts convention's eighth proposal, and the

[10] Dumbauld, *The Declaration of Independence and What It Means Today*, 133.

[11] Madison's language resembles that found in the prefatory declaration of rights in the New York act of ratification. *Documentary History*, II, 192–93.

[12] See page 49.

[13] See page 22.

Pennsylvania minority's second proposition. Possibly the provision that facts tried by a jury shall not be re-examined otherwise than according to the rules of the common law may be based upon the prefatory declaration of rights contained in the New York act of ratification.[14] In substance this language deals with ground covered by the Maryland committee's third and fifth proposals, and the Virginia convention's fourteenth amendment.

ARTICLE VIII

Excessive bail shall not be required, nor excessive fines imposed, nor cruel and unusual punishments inflicted.

This Article goes back to the English Bill of Rights[15] by way of Madison's tenth item, and the Virginia convention bill's thirteenth article (Article 9 of the Virginia Bill of Rights). The Pennsylvania minority was the first to propose an amendment on this topic.

ARTICLE IX

The enumeration in the Constitution, of certain rights, shall not be construed to deny or disparage others retained by the people.

This Article represents, with modification of language, Madison's thirteenth item and the Virginia convention's seventeenth amendment.

ARTICLE X

The powers not delegated to the United States by the Constitution, nor prohibited by it to the States, are reserved to the States respectively, or to the people.

[14] *Documentary History*, II, 193, 194, which speaks of trial by jury "in the extent that it obtains by the Common law of England" and of appellate review "by writ of error and not otherwise" in cases determinable "according to the course of the common law." Adoption of civil law procedure was feared. Warren, "New Light on the History of the Federal Judiciary Act of 1789," *Harvard Law Review*, Vol. XXXVII, No. 1 (November, 1923), 102–103.

[15] Dumbauld, *The Declaration of Independence and What It Means Today*, 166.

This Article is based on Madison's nineteenth item. It is an emasculated version of Article II of the Articles of Confederation. The Pennsylvania minority was the first to propose such an amendment, and the topic headed the list of amendments recommended by the Massachusetts and Virginia conventions.

II

CURRENT JUDICIAL
INTERPRETATION OF THE
BILL OF RIGHTS

ONE of the important functions of a Bill of Rights, as Jefferson and Madison pointed out, is "the legal check which it puts into the hands of the judiciary."[1] Hamilton likewise stressed the importance of the courts in enforcing constitutional limitations upon governmental authority.[2]

Of course judicial power is not the sole bulwark which protects cherished constitutional rights.[3] A political barrier may be erected by public sentiment and the habits of the people which no ruler will dare to transgress. The structure of the government itself, if judiciously contrived, will thwart the encroachments of usurping ambition.[4] But even though it be the duty of the legislative

[1] Jefferson to Madison, March 15, 1789, Jefferson's *Works*, V, 461; *Writings of James Madison*, V, 385. A Bill of Rights also serves to "fix . . . for the people the principles of their political creed." Jefferson to Joseph Priestley, June 19, 1802, Jefferson's *Works*, IX, 381–82.

[2] "Limitations of this kind can be preserved in practice no other way than through the medium of courts of justice, whose duty it must be to declare all acts contrary to the manifest tenor of the Constitution void. Without this, all the reservations of particular rights or privileges would amount to nothing." *Federalist* (No. 78), 484–85.

[3] Justice Holmes admonishes that "it must be remembered that legislatures are ultimate guardians of the liberties and welfare of the people in quite as great a degree as the courts." *M., K. & T. Ry. Co.* v. *May*, 194 U.S. 267, 270 (1904).

[4] *Federalist* (No. 51), 323: "In framing a government which is to be administered by men over men, the great difficulty lies in this: you must first enable the government to control the governed; and in the next place oblige it to control itself." Madison had written to Jefferson, October 24, 1787, *Papers of Thomas*

branch and the executive to scrutinize the constitutionality of their own acts independently,[5] yet the temptation remains, when doubt exists in cases of importance, to cast upon the courts the final responsibility for protection of constitutionally guaranteed rights against infringement.[6] This means that, as Justice Robert H. Jackson declared, legal rights in the last analysis represent what some respected lawyer is willing to fight for.[7]

At any rate, the current judicial interpretation of the Bill of Rights is what determines the practical value of the contents of that venerated document in the life of American citizens today.[8] The real significance of the Bill of Rights is to be found, not in the history of the enshrined parchment, not in the doctrines of political philosophy which inspired our ancestors, but in the treatment that an unpopular victim can count on receiving in court today when hostile public officials are trying to make trouble for him. How much good do these much-vaunted prerogatives of American citizenship do for him in his time of travail?[9]

Jefferson, XII, 278–79: "The great desideratum in Government is, so to modify the sovereignty as that it may be sufficiently neutral between different parts of the Society to controul one part from invading the rights of another, and at the same time sufficiently controuled itself, from setting up an interest adverse to that of the entire Society." See also Dumbauld, *The Political Writings of Thomas Jefferson*, xxvi–xxviii.

[5] Corwin, *Court over Constitution*, 15, 69–79.

[6] Thus the President wrote in 1935 to a congressman that "the situation is so urgent and the benefits of the legislation so evident that all doubts should be resolved in favor of the bill, leaving to the courts, in an orderly fashion, the ultimate question of constitutionality. . . . I hope your committee will not permit doubts as to constitutionality, however reasonable, to block the suggested legislation." Franklin D. Roosevelt, *Public Papers and Addresses*, IV, 297–98; Corwin, *Constitutional Revolution, Ltd.*, 54.

[7] "Paper 'rights' are worth, when they are threatened, just what some lawyer makes them worth. Civil liberties are those which some lawyer, respected by his neighbors, will stand up to defend." *Proceedings . . . in Memory of Robert Houghwout Jackson*, 78.

[8] The Bill of Rights, like the rest of the Constitution, "is what the judges say it is." Charles Evans Hughes, *Addresses and Papers*, 139. Cf. Merlo J. Pusey, *Charles Evans Hughes*, I, 204.

[9] It must be remembered that the Bill of Rights affords protection only against action by public officials, not against grievances committed by private parties. Realistic appraisal requires recognition that "liberty is something which often

The actual scope of the Bill of Rights as applied in present-day litigation may be measured by analysis of the contemporary output of judicial decisions involving the first ten amendments to the Constitution.[10] What trends are observable in these pronouncements? How have the courts performed their task of translating this historic language into "current commands"?[11]

Examination of the pocket supplement to the volume of the *United States Code Annotated* covering these amendments will give a convenient survey of recent case law construing the Bill of Rights.[12]

Such scrutiny reveals that the different amendments vary widely with respect to the volume of litigation generated. Some are practically never passed upon by a court; others give rise to numerous rulings.

Analysis of the Bill of Rights with respect to contents leads to classification of its provisions into four groups, covering:

(1) Protection of the inner life of the individual citizen and preservation of democratic political processes: freedom of religion,

needs to be protected *by* government rather than *against* it." Corwin, *Court over Constitution*, 129. Government action is often the only method by which the people may resist the machinations of powerful private interests. "Our struggle has been one to restore effective government—the only means through which the will and opinion of the people can have any expression." Robert H. Jackson, *The Struggle for Judicial Supremacy*, xiii.

[10] A useful synopsis of Supreme Court decisions up to June 30, 1952, is contained in 82 Cong., 2 sess., Sen. Doc. No. 170, *The Constitution of the United States of America*, 749–921, edited by Edward S. Corwin.

[11] Robert H. Jackson, *The Supreme Court in the American System of Government*, 26. Liberty is "something which each age must provide for itself." *Ibid.*, 76.

[12] The bound volume, published in 1944, devotes 432 pages to the first ten amendments. The 290 pages in the 1955 pocket supplement thus embody the judicial output of approximately a decade, and disclose the trend of current doctrine on the topic. The number of pages devoted to each amendment is: First, 26; Second and Third, less than one; Fourth, 53; Fifth, 158; Sixth, 33; Seventh, 6; Eighth, 4; Ninth, less than one; Tenth, 7. In the Corwin volume cited in note 10, above, the corresponding figures are: First, 54; Second and Third, less than one; Fourth, 9; Fifth, 36; Sixth, 9; Seventh, 7; Eighth, 3; Ninth, less than one; Tenth, 7.

of speech, of the press; peaceable assemblage and petition for redress of grievances (Amendment I);

(2) Protection of the civilian population against military domination or oppression (Amendments II and III);

(3) Protection of the people against arbitrary or tyrannical acts of the civil government, particularly by establishment of safeguards with respect to procedure in criminal cases (Amendments IV, V, VI, and VIII), and by preservation of the right to jury trial in civil cases (Amendment VII); and

(4) Protection against undue extension of governmental powers, by establishment of rules for interpreting the Constitution restrictively so as to narrow the scope of such powers (Amendments IX and X).[13]

Litigation during the past decade has revolved primarily about the first and third groups of provisions. The First Amendment and the Fifth have been the most productive of controversy. It would seem that in the Supreme Court the profound philosophical issues arising out of the First Amendment have been most often elucidated; while in the lower courts practical problems arising under the Fourth, Fifth, and Sixth Amendments with regard to irregularities in criminal procedure and the use by the government of evidence improperly obtained have preponderated.

Unused Provisions

Group (2), relating to quartering of troops and the right of the people to bear arms,[1] did not contribute a single case, during the period covered, to the docket of the Supreme Court of the United States.[2] Writers regard Amendments II and III as "obsolete."[3]

[13] The Bill of Rights, in the language of Justice Jackson, delineates "the outlines of a free society." Jackson, *The Supreme Court in the American System of Government*, 76.

[1] It has always been understood that the right to bear arms does not authorize carrying concealed weapons. *Robertson* v. *Baldwin*, 165 U.S. 275, 281–82 (1897).

[2] Less than three pages suffices for the annotations to the Second Amendment in the bound volume, and no cases at all are cited under the Third Amendment. Only four cases (in lower or state courts) are listed under both amendments in the pocket supplement.

Earlier judicial decisions have contributed to the erosion of these amendments. The Supreme Court, in an effort to minimize the impact of "Reconstruction" after the war of 1861–65, struck down prosecution for interfering with the right of peaceable assembly and the right to bear arms by holding that those rights antedated the adoption of the Constitution, and hence were not rights "granted or secured . . . by the Constitution or laws of the United States."[4] The effect of the Bill of Rights was merely to declare the powerlessness of the federal government to infringe those pre-constitutional rights. To protect them against infringement by private individuals was a task for the state government to perform. The opposite tendency, inspired by ineffectiveness of local authorities in repressing gangsterism, led the Court at a later date to uphold federal legislation restricting interstate transportation of firearms.[5] The Court put forward the questionable proposition that the right to bear arms guaranteed in the Second Amendment was simply an implementation of the provisions in the Constitution relative to use of militia in the federal service,[6] and that in the absence of evidence to show that possession of a particular type of weapon would be of value in maintaining the

[3] Robert A. Rutland, *The Birth of the Bill of Rights 1776–1791*, 229. Roscoe Pound states more circumspectly that the right to bear arms has "a much altered significance under the conditions of popular uprising against oppression or under the conditions of military operations today." Bennett B. Patterson, *The Forgotten Ninth Amendment*, vi.

[4] *U. S.* v. *Cruikshank*, 92 U.S. 542, 551–53 (1875). If the indictment had specified that the conspiracy interfered with an assemblage *to petition Congress* it would have been valid. The prosecution was brought under section 6 of the Act of May 31, 1870, 16 Stat. 140, 141, penalizing conspiracy to "intimidate any citizen with intent to prevent or hinder his free exercise and enjoyment of any right or privilege granted or secured to him by the Constitution or laws of the United States." It would seem that the *Cruikshank* decision is wrong, since the rights involved are obviously "secured" by the Constitution, even though not "granted" by it, if "secure" is given the meaning it has in the Declaration of Independence and the Preamble to the Constitution. The word there means "safeguard" or "make secure," rather than "procure" or "obtain." Dumbauld, *The Declaration of Independence and What It Means Today*, 63. See also note 9, page 58.

[5] The National Firearms Act of June 26, 1934, 48 Stat. 1236–40.

[6] Art. I, sec. 8, cl. 15 and 16.

efficiency of a well regulated militia, the right to bear it was not constitutionally protected.[7]

That these amendments are defunct in practice is not due to diminishing importance of military affairs in modern society. In fact, since World War II no aspect of national life has assumed such overshadowing significance as has the burden of preparation for hostilities. Military demands have interrupted the education and civilian pursuits of every young man in America, saddled all taxpayers regardless of age with an unprecedented and well-nigh intolerable burden, brought an unhealthy semblance of prosperity to certain industries and institutions engaged in production or research for the armed services, and cast over the land a fatalistic foreboding of cosmic catastrophe and atomic annihilation.

But the armed services have not been guilty of the inconsiderate behavior which characterized the troops of George III in the colonial era. They have not put soldiers into the houses of citizens; they have simply removed the citizens from their houses and put them in the army, navy, and air force.

These constitutional guarantees were intended to ensure that the people would be more powerful than the government. The citizen militia was to be stronger than the standing armies in the pay of the sovereign. But modern weapons have irrevocably upset this balance. The feeble arms which a civilian group rebelling against oppression could wield today against the professionals in the service of the government would be as ineffective as the bare hands of the imprisoned Rhadames against the solid masonry enclosing him in the tomb to perish with Aida. Today there can no longer be a revolution, it has been observed, but only a *coup d'état*.[8]

The Second and Third Amendments stand simply as the empty

---

[7] *U.S. v. Miller*, 307 US. 174, 178 (1939). In *Tot* v. *U.S.*, 319 U.S. 463, 467–68 (1943), a provision of the Federal Firearms Act of June 30, 1938, 52 Stat. 1250, 1251, 15 U.S.C.A. 902 (f), creating a presumption that a weapon in the possession of a convict or fugitive from justice had been transported by such person in violation of the Act, was held invalid under the due process clause of the Fifth Amendment.

[8] Felix S. Cohen, *Ethical Systems and Legal Ideals*, 268.

symbol of what remains a living American ideal: the supremacy of the civil power over military. The deep-rooted dominance of this principle in the country's thinking was strikingly typified when President Truman relieved General MacArthur. Many people disagreed with the wisdom of the President's policies; but everyone agreed that he, and not the military commander, was the policy-making authority in the United States government, and that it was the duty of the armed services to accept and execute the policies formulated by the nation's civilian leadership.

Group (4) is likewise a dead letter in practice, not because of changed conditions, but because of the intrinsic nature of these amendments themselves. The Ninth Amendment was not intended to add anything to the meaning of the remaining articles in the Constitution. It was simply a technical proviso inserted to forestall the possibility of misinterpretation of the rest of the document. Alexander Hamilton and James Wilson had argued that a Bill of Rights, specifying that the federal government should not have particular powers (*e.g.*, to restrain freedom of the press) might be interpreted as implying that otherwise it would have had such powers, and hence that it did have certain powers not mentioned in the Constitution. Madison sought to preclude such an interpretation when adding the Bill of Rights to the Constitution.[9] A provision which he offered for this purpose became the Ninth Amendment. In other words the Ninth Amendment was designed to obviate the possibility of applying the maxim *expressio unius est exclusio alterius* in interpreting the Constitution. It was adopted in order to eliminate the grant of powers by implication as the result of any language in the Constitution which might contain a "negative pregnant."[10] It was

[9] An example of the type of interpretation which Madison intended to preclude is the argument that the *president* may abridge freedom of speech since the First Amendment only prohibits *Congress* from doing so. See page 104.

[10] Patterson, *The Forgotten Ninth Amendment*, 10, 12–13. This book contains a valuable appendix reprinting from the *Annals of Congress* the debates on the Bill of Rights. Unfortunately the original pagination is not indicated. *Ibid.*, 100–217.

intended to serve the same function as the modern draftsman's awkward expression "including but not limited to" when specifying some of the particular items embraced within a comprehensive category. It is destitute of substantive effect.

Hence there is no occasion for amazement when the fact comes to light that apparently there has never been a case decided which turned upon the Ninth Amendment. It has been invoked by litigants only ten times and in each instance without success.[11]

In a decision[12] upholding the Hatch Act's prohibitions of political activity by government employees, the Supreme Court discussed the Ninth Amendment as follows:

We accept appellant's contention that the nature of political rights reserved to the people by the Ninth and Tenth Amendments are involved. The right claimed as inviolate may be stated as the right of a citizen to act as a party official or worker to further his own political views. . . . The powers granted by the Constitution are subtracted from the totality of sovereignty originally in the States and the people. Therefore, when objection is made that the exercise of a federal power infringes upon rights reserved by the Ninth and Tenth Amendments, the inquiry must be directed toward the granted power under which the action of the Union was taken. If granted power is found, necessarily the objection of invasion of those rights, reserved by the Ninth and Tenth Amendments, must fail. . . . Congress and the President are responsible for an efficient public service. If, in their judgment, efficiency may be best obtained by prohibiting active participation by

[11] *Ibid.*, 2, 27, 29–33. Nevertheless, Patterson stresses the importance of this amendment as an enactment or recognition in our constitutional law of the "social contract" theory of inherent natural rights, pre-constitutional and pre-governmental in origin. *Ibid.*, 26, 41, 45. Undoubtedly the political philosophy underlying the Ninth Amendment is the same as that of the Declaration of Independence in this respect. See Dumbauld, *The Declaration of Independence and What It Means Today*, 58, 63–64, 69–71; and Dumbauld, *The Political Writings of Thomas Jefferson*, xxvi–xxix. According to Justice Jackson, Ninth Amendment rights are still a mystery. Jackson, *The Supreme Court in the American System of Government*, 3, 6, 74–75.

[12] *United Public Workers* v. *Mitchell*, 330 U.S. 75, 94–96, 99 (1947). The main question in this case was whether there was a violation of the freedom of speech provisions of the First Amendment. The Ninth Amendment, moreover, was discussed only in conjunction with the Tenth.

classified employees in politics as party officers or workers, we see no constitutional objection.

Similarly, the Tenth Amendment really adds nothing to the rest of the Constitution. It simply declares that powers not granted to the federal government are reserved; but this does not shed any light on the crucial question whether or not a particular power has been granted.[13]

It has been asserted by an eminent authority on constitutional law that the Supreme Court, in certain decisions now overruled, treated the Tenth Amendment as having a substantive effect and as withdrawing certain matters from federal control.[14] It is submitted, however, that the preferable explanation of those decisions is to regard them as being merely erroneous determinations of the scope of the granted powers rather than as holdings recognizing the existence of any substantive effect or independent operation on the part of the Tenth Amendment.[15]

The basic premise of these now-defunct cases, most of which construed the commerce power, was that "commerce succeeds to manufacture and is not a part of it."[16] A clearly-defined line was

[13] At most it might create a presumption in favor of construing a grant narrowly. In deciding whether a will should be construed to give a widow a life estate or a fee simple, it might make a difference whether, in case the widow did not get a fee, the remainder would go to the testator's children or escheat to the state for want of heirs. But the real question is what the testator in fact intended to grant. The same is true in determining the scope of a grant of power to the federal government. The Tenth Amendment merely makes plain that if a particular power is not conferred upon the federal government, it will not lapse into limbo, but there is an alternative recipient available to wield it.

[14] Corwin, *The Commerce Power versus States Rights*, 170–71; Corwin, *A Constitution of Powers in a Secular State*, 18.

[15] Typical of those decisions are *U.S. v. E. C. Knight Co.*, 156 U.S. 1, 12–13 (1895), holding that a monopoly of the manufacture of sugar was not a restraint of interstate trade or commerce in that article forbidden by the anti-trust laws; *Hammer v. Dagenhart*, 247 U.S. 251, 274–76 (1918), nullifying prohibition of interstate transportation of goods produced by child labor; *U.S. v. Butler*, 297 U.S. 1, 66, 68 (1936), overturning the first agricultural program of the Roosevelt administration; and *Carter v. Carter Coal Co.*, 298 U.S. 238, 289, 303 (1936), overthrowing the Guffey-Snyder bituminous coal Act. *U.S. v. Darby*, 312 U.S. 100, 113–15 (1941), upholding the Fair Labor Standards Act, is the leading case overruling the prior doctrine.

[16] 156 U.S. at 12.

drawn between commerce and production. The former was subject to federal regulation; the latter was not. It was subterfuge, the majority of the Supreme Court then believed, for Congress to enact laws which really aimed at regulating production, even though such laws on their face seemed to constitute a plain exercise of the commerce power or the taxing power.

It seems obvious that the Court was here doing nothing more than accepting too narrow an interpretation of federal power.[17] It was not holding that state power, or the Tenth Amendment, constituted an independent limitation upon federal power.

Jury Trial and Its Incidents

Group (3) of the classification of provisions contained in the Bill of Rights includes the guarantee of jury trial in civil cases which is embodied in the Seventh Amendment. Relatively little litigation arises under this article, not because it is obsolete, but because the principles involved are well settled, and trial courts have few difficulties in heeding its requirements.

Even here inroads have been made[1] on the rule that "jury trial" in this amendment means jury trial as it was understood at common law in 1791,[2] and that at common law when a verdict for the plaintiff was set aside by a court because not supported

[17] This is true whether the unduly narrow interpretation was applied to the term "commerce" (construed as excluding "production"), or to "regulate" (construed as not including power to prohibit), or to "taxes" (construed as not including those which would have a regulatory effect). In this connection it is interesting to note that (though no one now questions the legality of a protective tariff as against one for revenue only) the Supreme Court of a generation ago struck down an attempt to prevent child labor by use of the taxing power, and that Justices Frankfurter and Douglas displayed a similar vein of thought in their dissents when the Court recently upheld legislation requiring gamblers to register and pay a tax. *Bailey* v. *Drexel Furniture Co.*, 259 U.S. 20, 36, 38 (1922); *U.S.* v. *Kahriger*, 345 U.S. 22, 38 (1953). Justice Frankfurter characterized the presentation of the statute in the form of a revenue measure as nothing but "verbal cellophane."

[1] In *Baltimore & Carolina Line* v. *Redman*, 295 U.S. 654, 659 (1935). In *Galloway* v. *U.S.*, 319 U.S. 372 (1943), the court directed a verdict against a veteran whose evidence of disability did not cover five years of a twenty year period.

[2] *Dimick* v. *Schiedt*, 293 U.S. 474, 476, 487 (1935).

by evidence the court must order a new trial rather than render judgment *nonobstante veredicto* for the defendant.[3]

Group (3) also contains the Sixth Amendment, which safeguards jury trial in criminal cases.[4] Here too the constitutional requirements have been administered by the courts without much difficulty. The same is true of the Eighth Amendment, prohibiting excessive bail and fines, as well as the infliction of cruel and unusual punishments.

The Supreme Court in a recent case held that the Sixth Amendment prohibited the seizure of a Pittsburgh citizen and his being "transported beyond seas"[5] to be tried by a military court for an alleged murder committed in Italy while he was serving in the armed forces. He had since reverted to civilian status, and was no longer subject to the jurisdiction of military tribunals.[6]

An interesting question raised under the Sixth Amendment is whether the requirement of a "public trial" prevents the court from excluding curious spectators from the courtroom when scandalous matters are being aired.[7] Where testimony in a treason trial consisted of recordings of defendant's radio broadcasts, the fact that jurors listened over earphones instead of to an amplified broadcast audible throughout the court room did not keep the trial from being "public."[8]

[3] *Slocum* v. *N.Y. Life Ins. Co.*, 228 U.S. 364, 377, 380, 395 (1913); *Capital Traction Co.* v. *Hof*, 174 U.S. 1, 8, 13 (1899).

[4] On the legislative history of the Sixth Amendment, see Heller, *The Sixth Amendment to the Constitution of The United States*, 33. Jury trial is a "right" of the accused, which may be waived; it is not a mandatory feature of the functioning of the judicial system. *Ibid.*, 36–37; *Patton* v. *U.S.*, 281 U.S. 276, 296 (1930).

[5] Such transportation was one of the grievances complained of in the Declaration of Independence, which the Court cited in the *Toth* case. Dumbauld, *The Declaration of Independence and What It Means Today*, 133–37.

[6] *U.S. ex rel. Toth* v. *Quarles*, 350 U.S. 11, 16–17 (1955).

[7] *U.S.* v. *Kobli*, 172 F.(2d) 919, 921, 923 (C.A.3, 1949); *People* v. *Jelke*, 130 N.Y.S.(2d) 662, 675 (1954), affd. 308 N.Y. 56 (1954). The Supreme Court in *Re Oliver*, 333 U.S. 257, 268–70 (1948), held that a secret trial in Michigan violated the due process clause of the Fourteenth Amendment.

[8] *Gillars* v. *U.S.*, 182 F.(2d) 962, 977–78 (C.A.2, 1950).

Another unusual issue (but of considerable importance in the vicinity of the District of Columbia, where the seat of the national government is located) is whether the right to "an impartial jury" is violated when government employees serve as jurors. In several recent cases it has been held that such service is constitutional.[9]

The right to jury trial is inapplicable to proceedings before military tribunals.[10]

The right "to be informed of the nature and cause of the accusation" is infringed if the offense is charged in the indictment in a manner so vague as to be void for indefiniteness. This flaw vitiated the much-publicized prosecution of Owen Lattimore for alleged perjury in denying that he was a Communist "sympathizer" or "follower of the Communist line."[11]

An interesting application of the right "to be confronted" with adverse witnesses is found in the holding that the decision of a loyalty board, barring a government employee from service for a term of three years, constituted "punishment" and could not be inflicted without compliance with the Sixth Amendment.[12]

[9] *U.S. v. Wood*, 299 U.S. 123 (1936); *Frazier v. U.S.*, 335 U.S. 497 (1949); *Dennis v. U.S.*, 339 U.S. 162 (1950). In the last-named case Justice Jackson, dissenting, reaffirmed his disapproval of the *Frazier* ruling: "The right to fair trial is the right that stands guardian over all other rights. . . . The common instinct of men for fair dealing and the experience of trial lawyers alike reject this holding. . . . Whenever any majority can be mustered to overrule that weird and misguided decision, I shall be one of it." 339 U.S. at 173. See Heller, *The Sixth Amendment*, 73–88.

[10] *Ex parte Quirin*, 317 U.S. 1, 39 (1942).

[11] *U.S. v. Lattimore*, 112 F.Supp. 507, 519 (D.D.C. 1953); affd. 215 F.(2d) 847, 849 (D.C. App. 1954). No appeal to the Supreme Court was taken by the government. 125 F.Supp. 295, 296 (D. D.C. 1954). See also 127 F. Supp. 405 (D.D.C. 1955). Cf. *Boyce Motor Lines v. U.S.*, 342 U.S. 337, 342 (1952); *Gorin v. U.S.*, 312 U.S. 19, 26–27 (1941); and *Nash v. U.S.*, 229 U.S. 373, 377 (1913).

[12] *Bailey v. Richardson*, 182 F.(2d) 46, 55 (D.C. App. 1950), affd. 341 U.S. 918 (1951), by an equally divided court; cf. *U.S. v. Lovett*, 328 U.S. 303, 316–17 (1946), holding that such "punishment" of specified persons is a "bill of attainder," prohibited by Art. I, sec. 9, cl. 3, of the Constitution. The *Bailey* case (p. 57) held, however, that compliance with the Sixth Amendment is not a prerequisite to the *dismissal* of an employee from the government service. Justice Frankfurter, who disagreed with the characterization of the action of Congress in the Lovett case as a bill of attainder, also believes that "Dorothy

It is generally well understood that the right to counsel, guaranteed by the Sixth Amendment, must be scrupulously accorded in federal courts.[13] Judicial supervision by the Supreme Court of the administration of justice in federal courts enables a strict standard of fairness to be applied, regardless of constitutional commands or the requirements of due process of law.[14] In cases originating in state courts, however, federal intervention is permissible only if denial of counsel results in injury to a defendant which is so serious as to constitute a violation of the due process clause of the Fourteenth Amendment. Voluminous litigation has resulted in cases devoted to determination of that delicate issue.[15]

Bailey was not, to be sure, faced with a criminal charge and hence not technically entitled under the Sixth Amendment to be confronted with the witnesses against her." *Joint Anti-Fascist Refugee Committee* v. *McGrath*, 341 U.S. 123, 180 (1951). But the self-incrimination privilege in the Fifth Amendment, which by its language is limited to application "in any criminal case," just as the Sixth Amendment applies "in all criminal prosecutions," has been given a more extensive interpretation. See page 83. Why then should not the Sixth Amendment likewise be given a broader meaning? The Supreme Court recently in *Peters* v. *Hobby*, 349 U.S. 331, 338, 342 (1955), sidestepped the constitutional question involved in *Bailey* v. *Richardson* by holding that the action of the Loyalty Review Board exceeded its authority as conferred by Executive Order 9835.

[13] Thus in *Glasser* v. *U.S.*, 315 U.S. 60, 70 (1942), the defendant, himself a lawyer and represented by counsel, was held to have been deprived of his rights under the Sixth Amendment because his attorney was appointed by the court to represent a co-defendant.

[14] *McNabb* v. *U.S.*, 318 U.S. 332, 340-41 (1943). Not until *Johnson* v. *Zerbst*, 304 U.S. 458, 462-63, 467-68 (1938), had it been supposed that the Sixth Amendment required federal courts to *provide* counsel for defendants. The historical meaning of the constitutional provision was that the court must *permit* counsel, employed by defendants, to appear and participate in the proceedings. The odious English practice, which the Constitution outlawed, had required defendants to plead their own case without the assistance of counsel learned in the law.

[15] See *e.g.* *Betts* v. *Brady*, 316 U.S. 455, 461-62 (1942); *Uveges* v. *Pennsylvania*, 335 U.S. 437, 440-41 (1948); *Gallegos* v. *Nebraska*, 342 U.S. 55, 64-65 (1951); *Palmer* v. *Ashe*, 342 U.S. 134 (1951). This is one phase of the controversial issue as to the extent that the Bill of Rights is made applicable against the states by the due process clause of the Fourteenth Amendment. Differences of opinion among members of the Court on this question are based upon "fundamentally divergent conceptions of the judicial function," not upon conflicting interpretations of the terms of the Sixth Amendment itself. Heller, *The Sixth Amendment*, 137. See also note 13, page 74, and pages 132-38.

A recent Supreme Court decision has interpreted the prohibition of "excessive bail" in the Eighth Amendment as forbidding bail in an amount higher than is reasonably calculated to assure the appearance of the defendant for trial.[16]

This pronouncement was later offset by a harsh ruling that the attorney general could at his discretion, when Congress so empowered him, detain resident aliens without bail pending their deportation.[17] Under this interpretation, as Justice Black pointed out in his dissent, the Eighth Amendment "means just about nothing."[18] Influenced by its literal terms and by English cases, the Court held that it did not prohibit *denial* of bail, but merely prohibited *excessive* bail in cases where bail was permitted. To deny bail (especially in the case of a person who has been for many years a law-abiding citizen and is not even charged with any crime, as is the case in many deportation proceedings) is to violate a cherished principle of Anglo-American law. The function of bail, under the common law tradition, is to ensure that a defendant will not be punished by imprisonment before he has

[16] *Stack* v. *Boyle*, 342 U.S. 1, 5–6 (1951). The government's argument that because defendants in another case had forfeited bail it must be anticipated that all defendants accused of Communism would flee as pawns in a conspiracy at the command of a superior was characterized by the Supreme Court as an assumption which "would inject into our system of government the very principles of totalitarianism which Congress was seeking to guard against" when enacting the law which the defendants were indicted for violating.

[17] *Carlson* v. *Landon*, 342 U.S. 529, 538, 545 (1952).

[18] *Ibid.*, 556. "Maybe the literal language of the framers lends itself to this weird, devitalizing interpretation when scrutinized with a hostile eye." Justice Black's acute analysis deflated the government's timorous claims: "They are kept in jail solely because a bureau agent thinks that is where Communists should be. A power to put people in jail can not be derived from power to deport. . . . To put people in jail for fear of their talk seems to me to be an abridgement of speech in flat violation of the First Amendment." *Ibid.*, 551, 555. In similar vein is Justice Jackson's dissent in *Shaughnessy* v. *U.S.*, 345 U.S. 206, 218 (1953): "Fortunately it is still startling, in this country, to find a person held indefinitely in executive custody without accusation of crime or judicial trial. Executive imprisonment has been considered oppressive and lawless since John, at Runnymede, pledged that no free man should be imprisoned, dispossessed, outlawed, or exiled save by the judgment of his peers or by the law of the land."

been duly found guilty after a fair trial, and to enable him to prepare his defense without impediment.[19]

The definition of "cruel and unusual punishment" was also discussed in a recent case[20] where by reason of some defect in the apparatus the execution of a death sentence by electrocution was unsuccessful and the defendant survived. He resisted a second attempt to take his life, claiming that the psychological effect of the prolonged suspense would produce a "lingering death" which constituted cruel and unusual punishment. The Supreme Court rejected this contention, though conceding the principle invoked, namely that the Eighth Amendment prohibited unnecessary cruelty, such as burning at the stake, breaking on the wheel, crucifixion, torture, or a lingering death.[21]

Unreasonable Searches and Seizures

Group (3) also includes the Fourth Amendment, prohibiting unreasonable searches and seizures or the use of general search warrants.[1] Since this amendment, in conjunction with the cognate

[19] Blackstone, *Commentaries*, I, *135–36; IV, *296–300; *Stack* v. *Boyle*, 342 U.S. 1, 7–8 (1951).

[20] *Louisiana ex rel. Francis* v. *Resweber*, 329 U.S. 459, 463–64 (1947). The Court assumed, without deciding, that the Fourteenth Amendment made the Eighth applicable against the States. *Ibid.*, 462.

[21] In *Wilkerson* v. *Utah*, 99 U.S. 130, 135–36 (1879), it was held that torture or unnecessary cruelty was forbidden, but that shooting did not fall within that prohibition. In *Weems* v. *U.S.*, 217 U.S. 349, 373 (1910), a sentence of twelve to twenty years at hard labor with attendant indignities was regarded as excessive punishment for the offense of falsifying a public document in the Philippines, and the Court stated that the forms of punishment prohibited by the Eighth Amendment were not limited to those practiced by the Stuarts before adoption of the English Bill of Rights. During the debates in Congress on the Eighth Amendment, Representatives William Loughton Smith of South Carolina and Samuel Livermore of New Hampshire remarked that the language used was objectionably indefinite and meaningless. *Annals of Congress*, I, 754.

[1] General warrants were condemned under English law in the famous case of *Entick* v. *Carrington*, 19 Howell, *State Trials*, 1029, 1063–66 (1765). The odious "writs of assistance" used to repress smuggling in Massachusetts were of that type. They evoked the eloquent denunciation of James Otis in 1761, and in the opinion of John Adams "American independence was then and there born." *Works of John Adams*, X, 247.

privilege against self-incrimination in the Fifth Amendment,[2] has practical application in connection with the gathering of evidence for use in court, it naturally follows that this portion of the Bill of Rights is the most useful part of it insofar as the practicing lawyer is concerned, and that numerous adjudications have been made with respect to the precise scope of the protection which it affords.

The Supreme Court has established the rule that a subpoena *duces tecum*, ordering the production of papers for use as evidence in court or before a grand jury or other governmental agency, is invalid under the Fourth Amendment if it is unreasonable in extent.[3] Whether a health inspection can be made without a search warrant is undecided.[4]

A series of recent cases[5] has clarified (or confused) the state

[2] The interrelatedness of the protection afforded by the Fourth and Fifth Amendments was emphasized in the leading case of *Boyd* v. *U.S.*, 116 U.S. 616, 633 (1886), a landmark in the law. See also *Feldman* v. *U.S.*, 322 U.S. 487, 488–90 (1943).

[3] *Boyd* v. *U.S.*, 116 U.S. 616, 622, 630, 634–35 (1886); *Hale* v. *Henkel*, 201 U.S. 43, 76 (1906); *Federal Trade Commission* v. *American Tobacco Co.*, 264 U.S. 298, 305–306 (1924); *Oklahoma Press Pub. Co.* v. *Walling*, 327 U.S. 186, 196, 202–209 (1946).

[4] By holding that defendant's refusal, under claim of constitutional right, to open a locked door when a health inspector without a search warrant visited the premises, did not constitute the offense of "interfering" with the inspection, the Court avoided passing upon the constitutionality of such inspection under the Fourth Amendment. *District of Columbia* v. *Little*, 339 U.S. 1, 4, 6 (1950).

[5] *U.S.* v. *Jeffers*, 342 U.S. 48, 51 (1951); *U.S.* v. *Rabinowitz*, 339 U.S. 56, 60–66 (1950), where the Court said: "What is a reasonable search is not to be determined by any fixed formula. . . . The recurring questions of the reasonableness of searches must find resolution in the facts and circumstances of each case. . . . It is not disputed that there may be reasonable searches, incident to an arrest, without a search warrant. . . . The relevant test is not whether it is reasonable to procure a search warrant, but whether the search was reasonable. That criterion in turn depends upon the facts and circumstances—the total atmosphere of the case." Justice Frankfurter, dissenting, said: "It is a fair summary of history to say that the safeguards of liberty have frequently been forged in controversies involving not very nice people. . . . With all respect I suggest that it makes a mockery of the Fourth Amendment to sanction search without a search warrant merely because of the legality of an arrest." 339 U.S. at 69–71. Cf. *Trupiano* v. *U.S.*, 334 U.S. 699, 704–706, 708 (1948); *Harris* v. *U.S.*, 331 U.S. 145 (1947); *McDonald* v. *U.S.*, 335 U.S. 451 (1948); *Johnson* v.

of the law regarding the right to search without a warrant the person and premises of a defendant in connection with the making of a lawful arrest.[6] The general rule is that things connected with the crime as its fruits or evidences or means of its commission, or weapons or means to facilitate escape, may be seized if found at the time of his arrest on the person of the defendant or on the immediate premises where the arrest takes place.[7] An indiscriminate search of a more extensive area is not permitted, nor may a general exploratory search be made. However, in the course of a lawful search articles may be seized of whose existence the officers had no previous knowledge;[8] but a search which is unlawful when undertaken is not validated because it is successful in unearthing evidence of crime.[9]

There is considerable uncertainty as to the extent to which officers may extend their examination of the premises. Of course

U.S., 333 U.S. 10 (1948); *Davis* v. *U.S.*, 328 U.S. 582 (1946); *U.S.* v. *Lefkowitz*, 285 U.S. 452 (1932); *Agnello* v. *U.S.*, 269 U.S. 20, 30 (1925); *Weeks* v. *U.S.*, 232 U.S. 383, 392 (1914).

[6] If the arrest is not lawful, the seizure is of course also invalid. Thus, in a recent much-publicized espionage case, when Judith Coplon and Valentine Gubitchev were arrested in Central Park by F. B. I. agents without a warrant, two appellate courts differed with respect to the admissibility in evidence of papers found in her handbag. The question turned on the effect to be given an act of Congress empowering F. B. I. agents to make arrests without a warrant under certain circumstances not applicable in the Coplon case. Was the power to arrest without a warrant limited to the circumstances so specified, or was that statutory provision an additional grant of power, so that the agents retained the same authority to arrest without a warrant which a private citizen would have had? An arrest made by a private citizen would have been lawful under the circumstances of the Coplon case. *U.S.* v. *Coplon*, 185 F.(2d) 629, 636 (C.A. 2, 1950); *U.S.* v. *Coplon*, 191 F.(2d) 749, 753-54 (C.A.D.C., 1951). The Supreme Court denied review of both Court of Appeals decisions. After lengthy litigation, involving also questions relating to the use of evidence obtained by wire-tapping, the defendant apparently escaped punishment and married her lawyer.

[7] Items that are merely evidence may not be seized under a search warrant. *Gouled* v. *U.S.*, 255 U.S. 298, 309-11 (1921).

[8] *Harris* v. *U.S.*, 331 U.S. 145, 153-54 (1947).

[9] *Byars* v. *U.S.*, 273 U.S. 28, 29 (1927); *U.S.* v. *Di Re*, 332 U.S. 581, 595 (1948); *Johnson* v. *U.S.*, 333 U.S. 10, 16-17 (1948); *McDonald* v. *U.S.*, 335 U.S. 451 (1948).

the owner may voluntarily permit an unrestricted search, and many cases turn on their particular facts and the credibility of the testimony as to a defendant's waiver of his rights under the Fourth Amendment.[10]

In the federal courts evidence unlawfully obtained by a federal official is excluded.[11] This exclusionary rule is ordinarily[12] not enforced by the Supreme Court against the states; they are free to regulate as they please the rules of evidence applicable in their own courts.[13] However, in a recent case it was held that

[10] *Zap* v. *U.S.*, 328 U.S. 624, 629–30 (1946); *U.S.* v. *Di Re*, 332 U.S. 581, 594–95 (1948); *Johnson* v. *U.S.*, 333 U.S. 10, 13 (1948); *Davis* v. *U.S.*, 328 U.S. 582, 587 (1946).

[11] *Lustig* v. *U.S.*, 338 U.S. 74, 79 (1949); *Silverthorne Lumber Co.* v. *U.S.*, 251 U.S. 385, 391–92 (1920); *Weeks* v. *U.S.*, 232 U.S. 383, 398 (1914). Justice Holmes remarked that if use of evidence obtained unlawfully is not forbidden "it reduces the 4th Amendment to a form of words. The essence of a provision forbidding the acquisition of evidence in a certain way is that not merely the evidence so acquired shall not be used before the court, but that it shall not be used at all." 251 U.S. at 392. As observed by Justice Jackson, dissenting in *Brinegar* v. *U.S.*, 338 U.S. 160, 180–81 (1949): "Uncontrolled search and seizure is one of the first and most effective weapons in the arsenal of every arbitrary government. . . . But the right to be secure against searches and seizures is one of the most difficult to protect. Since the officers are themselves the chief invaders, there is no enforcement outside of court. . . . Courts can protect the innocent against such invasion only indirectly and through the medium of excluding evidence obtained against those who frequently are guilty. . . . We must therefore look upon the exclusion of evidence in federal prosecutions if obtained in violation of the Amendment as a means of extending protection against the central government's agencies. So a search against Brinegar's car must be regarded as a search of the car of Everyman." But the government may use illegally obtained evidence to rebut defendant's perjury. *Walder* v. *U.S.*, 347 U.S. 62, 65 (1954). See also note 13, above.

[12] However, where a defendant was compelled, by use of a stomach pump, to regurgitate two capsules of narcotics which state officers had seen him swallow, the Supreme Court's conscience was shocked to such a degree that it held that to permit the capsules to be used as evidence in the state court would be a denial of due process of law under the Fourteenth Amendment. *Rochin* v. *California*, 342 U.S. 165, 166, 172–73 (1952).

[13] *Wolf* v. *Colorado*, 338 U.S. 25, 27–28 (1949); *Irvine* v. *California*, 347 U.S. 128, 136 (1954). These cases furnish an excellent illustration of the quagmire of subtleties in which the Supreme Court is obliged to flounder since committing itself to the doctrine that the Fourteenth Amendment makes applicable to the states some but not all of the rights guaranteed (against the federal gov-

a federal agent could be enjoined from testifying in a state court and producing evidence obtained by means of a defective search warrant.[14]

Wire-tapping is prohibited by the force of a federal statute and not on constitutional grounds.[15] The statute (which forbids unauthorized persons to "intercept" and "divulge or publish" any communication by wire or radio) is not violated by listening "be-

ernment) by the Bill of Rights. Justice Black and others of his way of thinking would make a blanket application of the entire Bill of Rights against the states. But the majority of the Court limits the "incorporation" to basic rights "implicit in the concept of ordered liberty," denial of which by a state shocks the conscience of the Court. *Palko* v. *Connecticut*, 302 U.S. 319, 325 (1937); *Twining* v. *N.J.*, 211 U.S. 78, 101–102 (1908). The stomach-pump case, involving physical coercion (347 U.S. at 133) was so "repulsive" to the Court (347 U.S. at 144) that it departed from its usual view that the autonomy of the states with respect to procedure in their own courts should not be interfered with. But the deliberate and continued violation of defendant's rights by the police which the Court denounced strongly in the *Irvine* case did not shock the Court's conscience sufficiently to cause it to follow the *Rochin* principle. Instead, the Court adhered to the *Wolf* precedent. Justice Jackson commented on the impracticability of a rule which would depend upon whether state action shocked the Court's conscience only slightly or shocked it profoundly (347 U.S. at 134). Moreover, in the *Wolf* case the Court found that the right violated *was* one that was basic to a free society and implicit in the concept of ordered liberty, but that exclusion of the illegally obtained evidence was not an appropriate remedy. Even Justice Black agreed (338 U.S. at 40) that the exclusionary rule in federal courts was not compelled by the Fourth Amendment, but was a judicially created measure of supervision of the administration of justice under the *McNabb* principle. (See note 14, page 69.) And yet, as Justice Douglas observes, what other sanction than exclusion of evidence can the courts afford when constitutional rights are violated? (338 U.S. at 40; see also Justice Jackson's comment in the *Brinegar* case, note 11, page 74.)

[14] *Rea* v. *U.S.*, 350 U.S. 214, 216–17 (1956).

[15] 47 U.S.C.A. 605; *U.S.* v. *Coplon*, 185 F.(2d) 629, 636 (C.A.D.C. 1950); *Nardone* v. *U.S.*, 308 U.S. 338, 341 (1939); *Olmstead* v. *U.S.*, 277 U.S. 438, 464, 466 (1928). Justice Holmes, dissenting in the last-named case, spoke of the practice as "dirty business" and thought it "a less evil that some criminals should escape than that the government should play an ignoble part." *Ibid.*, at 470. Evidence obtained by wire-tapping is admissible (without violating the due process requirements of the Fourteenth Amendment) under a Texas statute excluding evidence obtained in violation of the Constitution of the United States. (Before amendment the statute had excluded evidence obtained in violation of the Constitution *and laws* of the United States.) *Schwartz* v. *Texas*, 344 U.S. 199, 202 (1952).

hind the arras," like Polonius in Hamlet, to the person talking by telephone; nor is it violated by use of a transmitting device "planted" where it will broadcast conversation in its vicinity.[16]

Grand Jury; Double Jeopardy

Group (3) also includes the Fifth Amendment, an extremely prolific breeder of litigation, which embodies three provisions of great practical importance relating to criminal cases. The first of these, requiring grand jury action before a civilian can be subjected to criminal prosecution for a capital or otherwise infamous crime, is a recognized feature of federal procedure.[1] The second, prohibiting "double jeopardy" (being tried more than once for the same offense), is likewise a maxim the application of which in practice gives rise to relatively few problems.[2] The third is the much-publicized privilege against self-incrimination ("nor

[16] *On Lee* v. *U.S.*, 343 U.S. 747, 753 (1952); *Goldman* v. *U.S.*, 316 U.S. 129, 133-34 (1942).

[1] A capital crime is one punishable by death; an infamous crime is one punishable by imprisonment for more than one year. A proposal by Congressman Burke of South Carolina which would have required indictment in all criminal cases was rejected by the Committee of the Whole on August 18, 1789. *Annals*, I, 760. In *Beavers* v. *Henkel*, 194 U.S. 73, 84 (1904), the Court pointed out that the Fifth Amendment requires only one indictment, not two, and that in removal proceedings an indictment found in another district is sufficient "probable cause" to warrant holding a defendant for trial. No grand jury is required in cases before military tribunals. *Ex parte Quirin*, 317 U.S. 1, 39-44 (1942).

[2] In *Wade* v. *Hunter*, 336 U.S. 684, 688-89 (1949), the Supreme Court refused to regard as double jeopardy a second court-martial, when the first had been interrupted because the army advanced such a great distance from the scene of the offense that it was impracticable, in the commanding officer's opinion, to proceed with the trial. This holding, as the dissenting opinion points out, sacrifices the defendant's rights for the sake of considerations of expediency. That it is not double jeopardy to convict for conspiracy to commit an offense and also for the substantive offense itself (fraudulent use of the mails, interstate transportation of stolen property) was held in *Pereira* v. *U.S.*, 347 U.S. 1, 5, 11 (1954), where a false Lothario and his confederate disappeared after obtaining a Cadillac and a check for $35,000 from a romantically inclined widow. In *Rex Trailer Co.* v. *U.S.*, 350 U.S. 148, 151 (1956), the Court found no double jeopardy when proceedings to collect a penalty in the nature of liquidated damages (such a penalty being regarded as civil, not criminal) were brought after there had been a plea of *nolo contendere* to an indictment involving the same transaction.

shall any person . . . be compelled . . . to be a witness against himself"), which in recent years has brought much grist to the judicial mill. The Fifth Amendment also contains the well-known "due process" clause ("nor be deprived of life, liberty, or property, without due process of law"), and the requirement of "just compensation" when private property is "taken for public use." While the privilege against compulsory incriminating testimony can be invoked only by natural persons,[3] the due process clause and the just compensation provision in eminent domain cases are beneficial also to corporations.[4]

Self-Incrimination

The privilege against self-incrimination is of ancient origin and when incorporated in the American constitution was hallowed by the traditions of the unremitting struggle in England against the tyranny of the Crown. The maxim *nemo tenetur seipsum prodere* (no one is bound to accuse himself) arose as a reaction against the ecclesiastical practice of inquisition, where the accused was required *ex officio* to take an oath to answer truly under inquisitorial interrogation.[1] Often in cases of heresy or other forms of "dangerous thoughts" in spiritual matters, no evidence to inculpate an individual could as a practical matter be obtained except

[3] *U.S.* v. *White*, 322 U.S. 694, 701 (1944).

[4] Like the Fourteenth Amendment, operative against the states, the Fifth Amendment requires both "procedural due process" and "substantive due process," the latter of which has proved very helpful in the past to corporate enterprise seeking to avoid the impact of public regulation (of rates, wages, and similar matters). *Santa Clara County* v. *Southern Pacific Railroad Co.*, 118 U.S. 394, 396 (1883); *Adair* v. *U.S.*, 208 U.S. 161 (1908); *Farrington* v. *Tokushige*, 273 U.S. 284 (1927); *Adkins* v. *Children's Hospital*, 261 U.S. 525 (1923); *St. Joseph Stock Yards Co.* v. *U.S.*, 298 U.S. 38 (1936). See also text at notes 17–19, page 93.

[1] The *ex officio* oath was administered to the accused even if no charge were pending against him. The victim's own testimony then became the basis of such a charge. Thus the *ex officio* oath was distinct from the oath of compurgation, which was a mode of trial employed to dispose of a pending charge during the era before trial by a petty jury became the established practice. Holdsworth, *A History of English Law*, I, 305.

by thus extorting his own evidence against himself.[2] Torture was standard practice in obtaining such confessions.

Courts of High Commission from the king took over from the mediaeval canon law this mode of procedure.[3] "The feature in its procedure which was the main object of attack was the *ex officio* oath, because that oath was the most efficient means of extracting information as to the policy of the opponents of the established church."[4] The suspected party was required to answer on oath a series of interrogations so comprehensive as to embrace the whole scope of religious orthodoxy, yet so precise and minute as to leave no room for evasion. Archbishop Whitgift, to whom the sixth High Commission was issued in 1583, became particularly obnoxious because of his active zeal in employing these methods, particularly against Puritan clergymen and other dissenters. The Court of Star Chamber was another odious tribunal which was authorized in 1487 to interrogate defendants upon oath.[5]

Sir Edward Coke, that renowned oracle of English law and hero of many struggles to exalt the common law courts against the king's prerogative and other tribunals dependent on the pleasure of the Crown,[6] attacked the inquisitorial procedure both while at the bar[7] and while on the bench.[8] The Court of High Com-

[2] There is a resemblance between the privilege against self-incrimination and the other Fifth Amendment privilege against being "held to answer for a . . . crime, unless on a presentment or indictment of a Grand Jury." The grand jury's action must be based on a *prima facie* case against the accused, proved by the testimony of witnesses other than himself.

[3] Courts of High Commission exercised the powers of the king as head of the Church of England. The first general commission was issued by Edward VI in 1549. In 1641 when the Long Parliament met, this type of court was abolished by the Act of 16 Charles I, c. 11. Holdsworth, *History*, I, 605–611; VI, 112. The English Bill of Rights in 1689 declared that "all other commissions and courts of like nature are illegal and pernicious."

[4] *Ibid.*, I, 609.

[5] By the Act of 3 Henry VII, c. 1. Holdsworth, *History*, I, 495. The Court of Star Chamber was abolished by the Long Parliament in 1641 by the Act of 16 Charles I, c. 10. Holdsworth, *History*, I, 515; VI, 112–13. On the use of torture in Star Chamber procedure see Holdsworth, *History*, V, 184–87.

[6] Frederick C. Hicks, *Men and Books Famous in the Law*, 59–105; *Prohibitions del Roy*, 12 Rep. 63 (1609).

[7] In *Cullier and Cullier*, Cro. Eliz. 201 (1589): "They were sued in the

mission and Star Chamber were finally abolished in 1641. It was cantankerous John Lilburne, however, whose undaunted determination was chiefly responsible for the establishment of the right to be free from compulsion to testify against oneself.

Lilburne was examined in the Star Chamber in 1637–38 for printing seditious books in Holland and importing them into England.[9] Declaring his innocence, he refused to take the oath to be interrogated generally: "Why do you ask me all these questions? these are nothing pertinent to my imprisonment, for I am

Spiritual Court for incontinency, and the Judges there would examine them upon their oath, if they did it.—But because *nemo tenetur prodere seipsum* in such cases of defamation, but only in causes testamentary and matrimonial, where no discredit can be to the party by his oath, Coke prayed a prohibition; and it was granted." Another report of the same case to the same effect is given in Moore 906; while in a third version in 4 Leonard 194 no decision was reached: "Between Collier and Collier the case was, that the plaintiff was sued for incontinence in the Spiritual Court, and there they would have him answer upon his oath if he ever had carnal knowledge of such a woman; upon which he prayed a prohibition: . . . but the Court would advise of it."

[8] 12 Rep. 26. Here Coke gave the opinion: "1. That the Ordinary cannot constrain any man, ecclesiastical or temporal, to swear generally to answer to such interrogatories as shall be administered to him; but ought to deliver him the articles upon which he is to be examined, to the intent that he may know whether by the law he ought to answer to them. . . . 2. No man ecclesiastical or temporal shall be examined upon secret thoughts of his heart, or of his secret opinion: but something ought to be objected against him what he hath spoken or done. No lay-man may be examined *ex officio*, except in two causes . . . [matrimonial and testamentary matters which] are many times secret; and they do not concern the shame and infamy of the party, as adultery, incontinency, usury, simony, hearing of mass, heresy, &c." Coke went on to say (p. 29) "that the law and custom of England is the inheritance of the subject, which he cannot be deprived of without his assent in Parliament."

[9] His own account of the case is reported in 3 Howell, *State Trials*, 1315–1367 (1637). The preceding case in that volume (p. 826) is the *Case of Ship-Money* (1637). This juxtaposition typifies Lilburne's place in history beside John Hampden as a pioneer of English liberties. Mention should also be made of the case of John Udall, 1 How. St. Tr., 1275–1316 (1590). This learned divine, of Presbyterian persuasion, was suspected (wrongly) of authorship of the "Martin Marprelate" tracts. He refused to take the *ex officio* oath. *Ibid.*, 1275. His case also involved denial of counsel, of confrontation with witnesses against him, and of the right to produce witnesses in his favor. *Ibid.*, 1277, 1302, 1304. He died in prison in 1592. See Chafee, *The Blessings of Liberty*, 192–97. As to Lilburne, see *ibid.*, 197–206.

not imprisoned for knowing and talking to such and such men, but for sending over Books; and therefore I am not willing to answer you to any more of these questions, because I see you go about this Examination to ensnare me: for seeing the things for which I am imprisoned cannot be proved against me, you will get other matter out of my examination: and therefore if you will not ask me about the thing laid to my charge, I shall answer no more: but if you will ask of that, I shall then answer you and do answer that for the thing for which I am imprisoned, which is for sending over books, I am clear, for I sent none."[10]

Persisting in his refusal to take the oath, he was sentenced to pay a fine of £500 and be whipped through the streets from the Fleet prison to a pillory placed between Westminster Hall Gate and the Star Chamber. This punishment took place on April 18, 1638. Tied to a cart and stripped from the waist upward, he received at least 500 lashes with a threefold knotted cord. He was then made to stand bareheaded in the pillory for two hours, the hole being a great deal too low for him, his "back being also very sore" and "the sun shining very hot." Nevertheless, he proceeded to make a lengthy speech to his "Christian Brethren." His discourse was interrupted by "a fat lawyer" who bade him hold his peace, but Lilburne refused to quit preaching. Soon the fat lawyer returned with the Warden of the Fleet prison, who caused Lilburne to be gagged "in such a cruel manner, as if he would have torn his jaws in pieces, insomuch that the blood came out of his mouth." After remaining in the pillory for an hour and a half gagged, he was returned to the Fleet.[11]

In his address he declared that the oath which he had refused to take was "a sinful and unlawful oath: it being the High Commission oath, with which the prelates ever have, and still do, so butcherly torment, afflict and undo the servants of God. It is an oath against the law of the land. . . . And also it is expressly against the Petition of Right. . . . Again, it is absolutely against the law of God; for that law requires no man to accuse himself;

[10] 3 How. St. Tr., 1318.
[11] *Ibid.*, 1328, 1337, 1340, 1349–50.

but if anything be laid to his charge, there must come two or three witnesses at least to prove it. It is also against the practice of Christ himself, who, in all his examinations before the high priest would not accuse himself. . . . Withal, this Oath is against the very law of nature, for nature is always a preserver of itself, and not a destroyer: But if a man takes this wicked oath, he undoes and destroys himself, as daily experience doth witness."[12]

Before being gagged, he had taken from his pocket and scattered among the crowd several copies of books by Dr. John Bastwick, who was the author of the books which Lilburne was charged with having distributed.[13] Incensed by his defiant behavior, the Court of Star Chamber on April 18, 1638, ordered that Lilburne be put in irons and kept in solitary confinement. Friends visiting him were denied access or beaten by the prison guards, and he would have died of starvation but for the help of fellow prisoners who conveyed food to him by stealth.[14]

On November 3, 1640, the first day that Parliament sat, he presented a petition and was released from prison. The House of Commons on May 4, 1641, resolved "That the Sentence of the Star-Chamber given against John Lilburn is illegal, and against the Liberty of the subject; and also bloody, cruel, wicked,

[12] *Ibid.*, 1332.

[13] *Ibid.*, 1338. On June 14, 1637, Bastwick, Henry Burton, and William Prynn were fined £ 5000 apiece and were condemned in Star Chamber to have their ears cut off for writing "seditious, schismatical and libellous Books against the Hierarchy." Prynn was also to be branded in the cheeks with the letters S and L as a seditious libeller. 3 How. St. Tr. 711, 725. The court treated the charges as confessed because no answers had been filed. Prynn and Bastwick had prepared answers but their counsel had refused to sign them for fear they would displease the court; and the court would not receive the answers without the signatures of counsel, though Prynn was himself a barrister. Burton's answer, though duly signed and filed, was rejected as "impertinent." 3 How. St. Tr. 719-20, 724. (Cf. *Hovey* v. *Elliott*, 167 U.S. 409, 413-19 [1897]). After execution of the sentence they were imprisoned for life in separate castles until released by the Long Parliament. 3 How. St. Tr. 755. Prynn had already four years previously lost his ears (though not completely, thanks to the executioner's mercifulness or clumsiness) and been disbarred for writing a book against stage plays, a diversion to which the queen and the court were addicted. 3 How. St. Tr. 561.

[14] 3 How. St. Tr. 1341, 1351-52.

barbarous, and tyrannical." The House of Lords after presentation of his case by his counsel, John Bradshaw and John Cook,
made an order on February 13, 1645, that the sentence of the
Star Chamber be vacated "as illegal, and most unjust, against
the liberty of the subject and law of the land, and Magna Charta,
and unfit to continue upon record: And that the said Lilburn shall
be for ever absolutely freed and totally discharged from the said
Sentence, and all proceedings thereupon as fully and amply as
though never any such thing had been."[15] Moreover, on December 21, 1648, by an ordinance of both houses of Parliament, he was
awarded £3,000 as reparation. However, "Lilburne, after great
trouble and much expense, got but little of the money ordered
him."[16]

The privilege against self-incrimination became firmly established in English law as the result of Lilburne's pertinacity in
vindicating his refusal to submit to inquisitorial interrogation.

In recent years this provision of the Fifth Amendment has
often been invoked by persons being questioned by Congressional
committees investigating "subversive" activities. Its frequent use
by Communist-tainted individuals has led some patriotic but un-
thinking zealots to regard it as a nuisance.[17] The expression "Fifth
Amendment Communist" has often been used by careless thinkers
as if the Fifth Amendment were merely a distinctive characteristic
identifying a particular species of Communist. (Actually, of
course, the person to whom this epithet is applied is so designated merely by reason of having invoked the Fifth Amendment,
and may or may not be a Communist at all.) Most Americans,
however, being mindful of the precious heritage of constitutional liberty won by the struggles of past generations, will agree
with Chief Justice Earl Warren's declaration that "the privilege
against self-incrimination is a right that was hard-earned by our
forefathers. The reasons for its inclusion in the Constitution—

15 *Ibid.*, 1340, 1359.
16 *Ibid.*, 1368. The money was to be paid out of the profits of the sequestered
estates of insurrectionists who had assisted in Lord Hamilton's invasion.
17 Justice Black, dissenting, in *Rogers* v. *U.S.*, 340 U.S. 367, 376 (1951).

and the necessities for its preservation—are to be found in the lessons of history. . . . To apply the privilege narrowly or begrudgingly—to treat it as a historical relic, at most merely to be tolerated—is to ignore its development and purpose."[18]

In keeping with this principle, the Supreme Court held that no particular form of words need be used in order to invoke the privilege.[19] Nor is it confined to a defendant on trial in a "criminal case"; it may be utilized by a witness as well as by a party, and in connection with an investigation by a legislative committee or executive agency as well as in a court proceeding of any kind. Likewise the question put to the witness need not be one the answer to which would directly disclose his guilt. It is enough if it may reasonably be regarded as constituting a link in the chain of evidence needed to prosecute him for a federal crime.[20] That

[18] *Quinn* v. *U.S.*, 349 U.S. 155, 161–62 (1955). "Such liberal construction is particularly warranted in a prosecution of a witness for a refusal to answer, since the respect normally accorded the privilege is then buttressed by the presumption of innocence accorded a defendant in a criminal trial." *Ibid.*, 162.

[19] *Ibid.*, 162, 164. It was thus sufficient for Quinn to adopt the statement of another witness, who referred to "the First and Fifth Amendments." The dissenting judges thought that this smacked of a "due process" claim under the Fifth Amendment, rather than one against self-incrimination. *Ibid.*, 183. The majority of the Court believed that "in popular parlance and even in legal literature, the term 'Fifth Amendment' in the context of our time is commonly regarded as being synonymous with the privilege against self-incrimination." *Ibid.*, 163. In a companion case, *Emspak* v. *U.S.*, 349 U.S. 190, 195–96 (1955), the Court held that waiver is not to be lightly inferred and that the privilege when once claimed was not waived even when the witness in answer to a particular question denied that revealing his knowledge of the persons under investigation would subject him to criminal prosecution. In another companion case, *Bart* v. *U.S.*, 349 U.S. 219, 223 (1955), it was held that a witness can not be prosecuted for failure to answer a pertinent question before a Congressional committee unless the committee makes a clear-cut ruling requiring him to answer and rejecting his claim of privilege.

[20] *Hoffman* v. *U.S.*, 341 U.S. 479, 486, 488 (1951). In this case the witness, a notorious underworld character with a twenty year police record, refused to answer when asked what his occupation was, when he last saw one William Weisberg, or whether he talked with Weisberg within the past week, or knew his present whereabouts. Weisberg was "hiding out" to avoid service of a subpoena to appear before the same grand jury before which Hoffman was testifying. The Supreme Court held that these questions might well have incriminated the witness.

his testimony may subject him to prosecution in state courts is not a peril against which the Fifth Amendment affords protection.[21] Nor will evidence be excluded in a federal prosecution which was extorted by compulsion in a state proceeding.[22]

The witness's own declaration "does not of itself establish the hazard of incrimination"; it is for the court to say whether his silence is justified, and to require him to answer if it clearly appears that there is no reasonable apprehension of prosecution.[23] Thus a witness may not refuse to answer if prosecution would be impossible, by reason of the statute of limitations, or the rule against double jeopardy, or a pardon,[24] or the protection of a statutory provision granting immunity.[25] Similarly, if the witness has voluntarily revealed incriminating facts, the privilege cannot be invoked in order to withhold details—a full disclosure must be made. There must be "a real danger of legal detriment

---

[21] *U.S.* v. *Murdock*, 284 U.S. 141, 149 (1931); *Hale* v. *Henkel*, 201 U.S. 43, 68–69 (1906); *Brown* v. *Walker*, 161 U.S. 591, 608 (1896). See also *U.S.* v. *Kahriger*, 345 U.S. 22, 32, 40 (1953); *Lewis* v. *U.S.*, 348 U.S. 419, 422–23 (1955). In *Brown* v. *Walker* the Court regarded the immunity statute as precluding state prosecution (161 U.S. at 607) and declared that there was no real or probable danger of prosecution in another jurisdiction (*ibid.*, 608); the implication being that if such a danger really existed the witness would be entitled to assert his constitutional privilege, which remains available unless superseded by a statutory immunity coextensive therewith. Later cases, beginning with *Hale* v. *Henkel*, treated *Brown* v. *Walker* as authority for the proposition that if the immunity granted precluded federal prosecution, it was immaterial whether the witness would be subject to prosecution elsewhere. Very recently, in *Ullmann* v. *U.S.*, 350 U.S. 422, 436, 439 (1956), the Court reaffirmed *Brown* v. *Walker* in its original form, and upheld a broad immunity provision affording protection against state prosecution. This result agrees with the views advocated by Professor Grant, and seems to be sound doctrine.

[22] *Feldman* v. *U.S.*, 322 U.S. 487, 493 (1944).

[23] 341 U.S. at 486. This rule (together with the rule as to "links in the chain of evidence") was announced by Chief Justice John Marshall during the course of the trial of Aaron Burr in Richmond for treason. *U.S.* v. *Burr*, Fed. Cas. No. 14,692e (1807); David Robertson, *Reports of the Trials of Colonel Aaron Burr*, I, 244–45.

[24] *Brown* v. *Walker*, 161 U.S. 591, 598–99 (1896).

[25] *U.S.* v. *Monia*, 317 U.S. 424, 428 (1943). The immunity must be coextensive in scope with the testimony compelled. *Counselman* v. *Hitchcock*, 142 U.S. 547, 585–86 (1892).

arising from the disclosure," and when the door has been opened questions must be answered unless to do so would *"further* incriminate" the witness.[26] Desire to protect other parties is not a valid justification for refusal to testify.[27] But privilege may be claimed with respect to inquiries about others if association with them might be made the basis of a prosecution against the witness charging conspiracy or other crime.[28]

Another important limitation on the protection afforded relates to production of *public* as distinguished from *private* records. If the law requires certain data to be kept in the course of business and made available for inspection by government agents as a means of facilitating enforcement of valid regulatory provisions (such as ration coupons, prescriptions for narcotic drugs, and the like), there is no violation of either the Fourth or the Fifth Amendments if information yielded by those sources is used as evidence in a prosecution against the party required to keep such records of his transactions.[29]

[26] *Rogers* v. *U.S.*, 340 U.S. 367, 373–74 (1951).

[27] *Ibid.*, 371; *Brown* v. *Walker*, 161 U.S. 591, 597, 600 (1896).

[28] *Blau* v. *U.S.*, 340 U.S. 159, 161 (1950). Patricia Blau was asked for the names of the persons having possession of the books and records of the Communist Party of Colorado, asked whether she had ever had possession of them herself, to whom she had given them, who were the officers of the organization, and similar questions. At the time she was asked these things, the Smith Act was in force, the effect of which was to make membership in the Communist Party a crime. 62 Stat. 808, 18 U.S.C.A. 2385. Her husband, Irving Blau, was not obliged to reveal her whereabouts, while she was "hiding out" from the grand jury. As his knowledge was derived from a telephone conversation with her, it was protected by marital privilege. *Blau* v. *U.S.*, 340 U.S. 332, 333 (1951).

[29] *Davis* v. *U.S.*, 328 U.S. 582, 593 (1946); *Shapiro* v. *U.S.*, 335 U.S. 1, 17, 33 (1948). Justice Frankfurter, dissenting, observed that "If Congress, by the easy device of requiring a man to keep the private papers that he has customarily kept can render such papers 'public' and non-privileged, there is little left to either the right of privacy or the constitutional privilege." Justice Jackson pithily observes: "The protection against self-incrimination, guaranteed by the Fifth Amendment, is nullified to whatever extent this Court holds that Congress may require a citizen to keep an account of his deeds and misdeeds and turn over or exhibit the record on demand of government inspectors, who then can use it to convict him." *Ibid.*, 70. As to the act of Congress requiring gamblers to register and pay federal tax, see the *Kahriger* and *Lewis* cases cited in note 21, page 84.

An interesting aspect of the indirect consequences of invoking the privilege against self-incrimination is illustrated by the fate of a physician who was drafted into the army but because in filling out a form he refused to answer questions about his "leftist" activities was denied the commission which all other draftees from the medical profession were granted.[30] There was no question about his right to claim privilege; but having done so could he compel the president to commission him as an officer in whose "patriotism, valor, fidelity and abilities" special trust and confidence was reposed? The majority of the Court answered that question with a resounding "No."[31] They gave the same response to his demand that he be assigned to duties in keeping with his professional status in the medical profession. Many soldiers dislike their assignments, "but judges are not given the task of running the army."[32]

Justice Black's dissent averred that Orloff was being kept in the army as a punishment for having asserted his constitutional rights, rather than because his services were needed as a medical practitioner: "I think the Government breaks faith with the Congress and with the doctors of America in drafting a doctor without granting him a commission. . . . And if there was any genuine question about his loyalty to our country, it seems unthinkable that any responsible person in the armed forces would be willing to let him have any part in the treatment of sick or wounded soldiers. If therefore Dr. Orloff is being used as a doctor, the Army must believe that he is dependable despite his failure to

[30] *Orloff* v. *Willoughby*, 345 U.S. 83 (1953).

[31] *Ibid.*, 91.

[32] *Ibid.*, 93. His assignment did involve medical work of a sort, but he was forbidden to administer drugs that might cause hypnosis, on the theory that officers being treated might betray military secrets. In the Supreme Court the government conceded that he must be given medical work, as distinguished from other tasks of a common soldier, but contended that under current regulations the medical corps was no longer composed entirely of officers. In the court below that obligation had not been admitted, but on appeal the parties "changed positions as nimbly as if dancing a quadrille." *Ibid.*, 87–88. Justice Frankfurter, dissenting, noted that the only undeviating purpose of the government was to keep this man in the army. *Ibid.*, 99.

answer the question about his past associations. If he is being used, the law entitles him to a commission.

"This record indicates to me, however, that Dr. Orloff is being held in the Army not to be used as a medical practitioner, but to be treated as a kind of pariah in order to punish him for having claimed a privilege which the Constitution guarantees. . . . And if some kind of punishment is to be imposed for asserting constitutional rights, it should not be imposed without a trial according to due process of law."[33]

The consequences of failure to invoke the privilege are shown by the Supreme Court's decision in the case of a policeman who in order to hold his job was required to sign a waiver of immunity. Later, after he was no longer on the police force, he was asked during a grand jury investigation the question whether he had ever received any bribes while on the force. The Court held that he could be punished for contempt for refusing to answer. In response to his claim that this amounted to punishment for exercising a legal right, the Court pointed to his waiver of that right. This was a valid and voluntary act, notwithstanding the fact that it was a condition upon which depended the continuance of his employment as a policeman.[34]

An important decision regarding the effect of immunity statutes was rendered in a recent case where the testimony of a witness was sought by the government under a broad immunity provision which afforded protection against both federal and state prosecution. The Court upheld the constitutional power of Congress to grant immunity against prosecution by a State.[35] But the Court

[33] *Ibid.*, 96–97.

[34] *Regan* v. *N. Y.*, 349 U.S. 58 (1955). These were state proceedings, and the Supreme Court's decision apparently involved the due process clause of the Fifth Amendment, not the self-incrimination provision. Perhaps this case invites a paraphrase of Justice Holmes's quip in *McAuliffe* v. *New Bedford*, 155 Mass. 216, 220 (1892), that "The petitioner may have a constitutional right to talk politics [or to refuse to testify], but he has no constitutional right to be a policeman."

[35] *Ullman* v. *U.S.*, 350 U.S. 422, 436 (1956). See note 21, page 84. The Immunity Act of 1954, 68 Stat. 745–46, provided that a witness whose testimony was required thereunder "shall not be prosecuted or subjected to any penalty

reaffirmed the rule that protection against criminal prosecution is all that a witness is entitled to under the Fifth Amendment. If that is adequately assured by the immunity provision he must testify. It is of no significance that his testifying might subject him to loss of employment, public ignominy, disabilities such as deprivation of the right to obtain a passport, and other detrimental consequences against which the immunity extended by Congress would afford no safeguard.[36]

Two weeks later the Supreme Court again had occasion to delineate the extent of Fifth Amendment protection. A faculty member of a college operated by the city of New York invoked the Fifth Amendment before a United States Senate subcommittee investigating matters dealing with national security which were unrelated to education or the professional qualifications or conduct of the witness. Thereupon he was notified of his dismissal, pursuant to a provision of the New York City charter which the state court construed as meaning that the assertion of the privilege against self-incrimination is automatically equivalent to a resignation. The Supreme Court held that this constituted denial of due process of law. "The privilege against self-incrimination would be reduced to a hollow mockery if its exercise could be taken as equivalent either to a confession of guilt or a conclusive presumption of perjury."[37]

According to the majority of the Court, "In practical effect the questions asked are taken as confessed and made the basis of dis-

---

or forfeiture for or on account of any transaction, matter or thing concerning which he is compelled, after having claimed his privilege against self-incrimination, to testify or produce evidence, nor his testimony so compelled be used as evidence in any criminal proceeding [except prosecution for perjury] against him in any court." Approval of the attorney general of the United States and a court order must be obtained before a witness can be compelled to testify under this statute.

[36] Justices Douglas and Black would have overruled *Brown* v. *Walker* and permitted the witness to refrain from testifying.

[37] *Slochower* v. *Bd. of Higher Education*, 350 U.S. 551, 557 (1956). Four Justices dissented.

charge." While perhaps upon proper inquiry the continued employment of the witness might be found inconsistent with the public interest, "there has been no such inquiry here."[38]

Since there was no actual investigation as to the official conduct of the witness, or inference of misconduct based upon refusal to answer questions in regard thereto, the only ground upon which the discharge could rest would be an untenable inference of "subversiveness" (which the Court brands as unwarranted, and which the state court in fact disavowed) or a ruling that the city would be justified in discharging an employee for refusing to co-operate with a public agency investigating matters unrelated to his official conduct. The precise question decided in this case therefore is that due process is denied by arbitrarily discharging an employee (otherwise entitled to tenure) for failure to comply with the general civic duty of testifying as a witness whenever called upon to do so by any duly authorized public agency inquiring into a matter within its jurisdiction. In other words, is one of the qualifications which a city may legitimately require of teachers a readiness to be a willing witness in any sort of local or federal investigation; or is that circumstance so remote from and irrelevant to the teaching function that it has no reasonable pertinence as a criterion of fitness to teach? It is this issue of "substantive due process" upon which the majority and minority of the Court differed; there was no disagreement regarding the proposition that no inference of guilt may be based upon exercise of the privilege against self-incrimination embodied in the Fifth Amendment.

[38] *Ibid.*, 558, 559. The dissenting Justices emphasized that the dismissal was not based upon any inference of "subversiveness," but upon the state's unwillingness to employ persons "who refuse to cooperate with public authorities when asked questions relating to official conduct." *Ibid.*, 566. However, the Senate investigation where Slochower refused to testify was not one relating to his "official conduct" as a city employee. The effect of the decision therefore is that it is arbitrary action violative of due process for an employee to be discharged for failure to perform a general testimonial obligation (incumbent upon all citizens equally) to furnish all information desired by any duly authorized public agency.

Even more prolific of litigation than the self-incrimination provision of the Fifth Amendment is its due process clause. This is perhaps to be expected, because of the vague nature of the criterion embodied in the words used. Due process is one of those inherently meaningless legal formulas (like "negligence," "reasonable rates," "sound judicial discretion," and similar shibboleths) which derive concrete significance only from their application in particular cases.[1]

The notion of due process of law is derived historically from Magna Charta.[2] The essence of its meaning was that no person could be punished by the king's government save for a violation of law (which the people participated in making) and after a jury trial (which the people participated in administering). These twin pillars of freedom were deemed essential features of American government by patriots such as Samuel Adams and Thomas Jefferson, who were at all times mindful of the unrelenting struggles against the arbitrary power of the crown which emblazoned the history of English constitutional practice.[3]

Purely procedural in origin,[4] the term came rather to mean "process of due law" in the course of judicial decisions. The concept of "substantive due process" was developed, alongside of the earlier "procedural due process." Legislative power was treated as non-existent if it was not reasonably exercised. The validity of legislation depended upon its content.[5] Laws were upheld only

---

[1] Some scholars denominate these vague criteria as legal "standards," distinguishing them from "rules," "principles," and "concepts," which are more definite. John Dickinson, *Administrative Justice and the Supremacy of Law in the United States*, 128.

[2] Griswold, *The Fifth Amendment Today*, 31–36; *Hurtado* v. *California*, 110 U.S. 516, 523–24 (1884); *Twining* v. *New Jersey*, 211 U.S. 78, 100 (1908).

[3] Dumbauld, *The Declaration of Independence and What It Means Today*, 8–9, 22, 73–74.

[4] See *Murray's Lessee* v. *Hoboken Land & Improvement Co.*, 18 How. 272, 276 (1856).

[5] This is essentially "natural law" doctrine. So is it when the Supreme Court applies the due process clause of the Fourteenth Amendment to invalidate state action which, in the Court's opinion, is not compatible with "the concept of

if they involved the use of rationally relevant means to effect a legitimate objective of governmental power.[6]

Procedural due process relates to the mode of proceeding which must be pursued by a governmental agency in order to take action which is legally valid and binding upon parties affected thereby. The prerequisites of such procedure vary according to the subject-matter involved. Thus in the case of an alien seeking to enter the United States, there is no right of entry. Inherent in national sovereignty is the right to exclude aliens at will. Hence any process that Congress prescribes is due process insofar as an alien seeking admission to the country is concerned.[7] This rule applies to a person who has lived in the United States twenty-five years as a law-abiding citizen but has made a short trip abroad and seeks to return. He is to be treated as an entrant, just like an alien who has never before set foot on the sacred soil of our shores.[8]

However, once an alien is inside the United States (even illegally) he "may be expelled only after proceedings conforming to traditional standards of fairness encompassed in due process

ordered liberty." Dumbauld, *The Declaration of Independence and What It Means Today*, 41. See notes 13, page 74, and 21, page 135.

[6] An example already noted of a legislative provision held invalid for want of rational connection with the legitimate objective aimed at is the presumption ordained by the Federal Firearms Act that any weapon in the possession of a convict or fugitive from justice had been illegally transported in interstate commerce. See note 7, page 62. On the other hand, Congress could validly dispense with proof that the Communist Party advocates overthrow of the United States government by violence. *Galvan* v. *Press*, 347 U.S. 522, 529 (1954). The earlier statute involved in *Harisiades* v. *Shaugnessy*, 342 U.S. 580, 534 (1952), did not contain that presumption, but required proof in each case.

[7] *Shaughnessy* v. *U.S.*, 345 U.S. 206, 212 (1953).

[8] *Ibid.*, 213, 219. In this case the alien was indefinitely detained on Ellis Island, for no other country would receive him. Justice Jackson picturesquely declared: "This man, who seems to have led a life of unrelieved insignificance, must have been astonished to find himself suddenly putting the Government of the United States in such fear that it was afraid to tell him why it was afraid of him. . . . Since we proclaimed him a Samson who might pull down the pillars of our temple, we should not be surprised if peoples less prosperous, less strongly established and less stable feared to take him off our timorous hands. . . . Realistically, this man is incarcerated." *Ibid.*, 219–20. A possible solution of the dilemma would be to set him adrift in a rowboat. *Ibid.*, 227.

of law."[9] In other words, he is then a "person" within the meaning of the Fifth Amendment.[10]

The basic ingredients of due process are reasonable notice and fair hearing. "When the Constitution requires a hearing, it requires a fair one, one before a tribunal which meets at least currently prevailing standards of impartiality."[11] Fair hearing includes the right to know the claims of the opposing party, and to a decision in accordance with the evidence in the record.[12] It does not always include opportunity for oral argument.[13] Nor need hearing be accorded at the outset, so long as it is ultimately available at some stage of the proceedings.[14] The mere fact that a wrong decision is rendered does not prove that the hearing was unfair.[15]

Soldiers, as well as aliens, are entitled to due process, the Supreme Court has held; but if the military tribunal has given con-

[9] *Ibid.*, 212. In *Kwong Hai Chew* v. *Colding*, 344 U.S. 590, 599–601 (1953), where a resident alien was returning to the country after having been employed on an American ship, the Court held that his status was not changed by his absence, and that his voyage abroad did not deprive him of the right to procedural due process. The Court therefore interpreted a regulation giving the attorney general power to deny a hearing as applicable only in cases of "exclusion" and not of "expulsion."

[10] *Galvan* v. *Press*, 347 U.S. 522, 530 (1954). "The essence of due process," said the Court in that case, is that it "bars Congress from enactments that shock the sense of fair play." *Ibid.*, 530. See also *Guessfeldt* v. *McGrath*, 342 U.S. 308, 318 (1952).

[11] *Wong Yang Sung* v. *McGrath*, 339 U.S. 33, 50 (1950). Fair hearing was a requirement of ancient Hebrew and Roman law. John 7:51; Acts 25:16.

[12] *Morgan* v. *U.S.*, 304 U.S. 1, 18–19 (1938); *Twining* v. *New Jersey*, 211 U.S. 78, 110–11 (1908). A predetermined decision, regardless of what the evidence demonstrates, would be considered as a denial of fair hearing. *U.S.* v. *Shaughnessy*, 347 U.S. 260, 267 (1954). But the Court after further proceedings in that case treated as credible the statements of subordinates in the Department of Justice that their decision had not been influenced by the attorney general's public pronouncement that certain specified "unsavory" individuals should be promptly deported. *Shaughnessy* v. *U.S.*, 349 U.S. 280, 283 (1955).

[13] *F.C.C.* v. *WJR*, 337 U.S. 265, 275–76 (1949).

[14] *Yakus* v. *U.S.*, 321 U.S. 414, 435–37, 442 (1944).

[15] *Bridges* v. *Wixon*, 326 U.S. 135, 156 (1945). Otherwise, even decisions of the Supreme Court would not be immune from challenge for unfairness. As Justice Jackson said, "We are not final because we are infallible, but we are infallible because we are final." *Brown* v. *Allen*, 344 U.S. 443, 540 (1953).

sideration to the constitutional question raised, the civil courts will not retry the issue.[16]

Substantive due process deals with the legitimacy of the regulation imposed rather than with the fairness of the procedure by which it is applied. Legislation unreasonably interfering with liberty or property is often challenged under the due process clause, occasionally with success. Thus a law (directed against Japanese) prohibiting operation of foreign-language schools in Hawaii was stricken down.[17] However, a war-time measure of even greater severity directed against American citizens of Japanese ancestry was upheld as permissible under the circumstances, although the Court stated that restrictions based on racial grounds are *prima facie* suspect.[18] Racial segregation in public schools of the District of Columbia has been condemned as a denial of due process in a widely-heralded decision.[19]

[16] *Burns* v. *Wilson,* 346 U.S. 137, 142, 144 (1953). Dissenting opinions disapproved the Court's decision giving "binding effect to the ruling of the military tribunal on the constitutional question, provided it has given fair consideration to it." *Ibid.,* 149, 154. In the case of civil administrative agencies, judicial review includes independent consideration of constitutional questions. *St. Joseph Stockyards* v. *U.S.,* 298 U.S. 38, 51-54 (1936); *B.&O. R.R. Co.* v. *U.S.,* 298 U.S. 349, 363-64 (1936); *Morgan* v. *U.S.,* 298 U.S. 468, 477 (1936); *Crowell* v. *Benson,* 285 U.S. 22, 60 (1932). But the majority view is supported by *Whelchel* v. *McDonald,* 340 U.S. 122, 124 (1950); *Gusik* v. *Schilder,* 340 U.S. 128, 132-33 (1950), and other cases.

[17] *Farrington* v. *Tokushige,* 273 U.S. 284, 299 (1927). Minimum wage legislation was stricken down in *Adkins* v. *Children's Hospital,* 261 U.S. 525 (1923), a decision now overruled.

[18] *Korematsu* v. *U.S.,* 323 U.S. 214, 216-18 (1944). Justice Jackson, in his dissent, pointed out that their race was the only circumstance that subjected these citizens to the harsh treatment which they received. *Ibid.,* 233. While willing to concede that "the armed services must protect a society, not its Constitution" and that the measure may have been reasonable from the military standpoint, nevertheless he believed that the courts should not share the responsibility of enforcing it "or they cease to be civil courts and become instruments of military policy." *Ibid.,* 244, 247.

[19] *Bolling* v. *Sharpe,* 347 U.S. 497, 500 (1954). *Brown* v. *Board of Education of Topeka,* 347 U.S. 483, 495 (1954), a companion decision based on the "equal protection" clause of the Fourteenth Amendment (a provision not found in the Fifth Amendment) and outlawing educational segregation by state action, has received even greater publicity.

No denial of due process was found in a statute authorizing deportation upon the ground of Communist Party membership prior to the enactment of the law. The Court rejected the contention that this *"ex post facto"* condemnation of subversive activity had "no reasonable relation to protection of legitimate interests of the United States."[20]

Retroactive application of legislation was likewise sustained when the Supreme Court held that the National Labor Relations Board could condemn as an "unfair labor practice," under a newly-enacted provision of law, a strike which had been called before (but continued after) the new statute took effect.[21] In like manner the laws governing renegotiation of unduly profitable wartime contracts for supplies and services vital to national defense could validly be applied to contracts entered into (but final payment on which had not been made) before the laws went into force.[22]

Lack of relevancy to a lawful governmental purpose was the reason which invalidated the attempt of a committee of Congress to require a "right-wing" propaganda organization to disclose the names of large contributors supplying funds used to distribute its publications.[23] In other cases where disclosure of information

[20] *Harisiades* v. *Shaughnessy*, 342 U.S. 580, 584 (1952). The Court pointed out that it had long been settled that the term *"ex post facto* law" was to be construed as applicable only to criminal matters and that deportation was not a criminal proceeding. *Ibid.*, 594. Since citizens might constitutionally be subjected to the hardships endured by the Nisei as described in the *Korematsu* case, or subjected to conscription, in order to combat Communism, the Court did not feel that the law was invalidated because of hardship to alien Communists. *Ibid.*, 591.

[21] *Local 74* v. *N.L.R.B.*, 341 U.S. 707, 714–15 (1951). Tax laws are often made applicable retroactively to transactions entered into while the legislation was pending in Congress, or under other circumstances where the tax does not unreasonably produce an unforeseeable burden. *U.S.* v. *Hudson*, 299 U.S. 498, 500–501 (1937); *Milliken* v. *U.S.*, 283 U.S. 15, 21 (1931).

[22] *Lichter* v. *U.S.*, 334 U.S. 742, 789 (1948).

[23] *U.S.* v. *Rumely*, 345 U.S. 41, 44–47 (1953). This decision did not involve the Fifth Amendment, and the Court avoided constitutional questions under the First Amendment by adopting a narrow interpretation of "lobbying," and holding accordingly that the questions asked the witness were beyond the lawful scope of the investigation. The committee was empowered to investigate "lobby-

94

by paid lobbyists[24] or transportation agencies was sought, the necessary rational connection with a legitimate objective was found to exist.[25] Thus a steamship company could be compelled to reveal the rates it charged,[26] and an oil company to furnish the Interstate Commerce Commission with data needed in connection with the valuation of its pipe-line facilities.[27] In like fash-

ing activities intended to influence, encourage, promote, or retard legislation." The Court construed "lobbying" as direct contact with Congress, not including manipulation of public opinion "to saturate the thinking of the community." After passage of the Regulation of Lobbying Act, requiring disclosure of the names of contributors of $500 or more to influence legislation, the organization employing Rumely treated all contributions over $490 as being for the purchase of literature, and hence did not report them. *Ibid.*, 50.

[24] *U.S.* v. *Harriss*, 347 U.S. 612, 624–25 (1954). As narrowly construed by the Court, the statute was upheld against challenge under both the Fifth and the First Amendments. The Court followed the *Rumely* case and limited the application of the act to persons in direct contact with Congress, who *received* compensation. (The language used by Congress would also have covered *expending* money to influence legislation.) Justice Jackson said, "The clearest feature of the Court's decision is that it leaves the country under an Act which is not much like any Act passed by Congress. Of course, when such a question is before us, it is easy to differ as to whether it is more appropriate to strike out or to strike down. But I recall few cases in which the Court has gone so far in rewriting an Act." *Ibid.*, 633.

[25] See also note 29, page 85.

[26] *Isbrandtsen-Moller Co.* v. *U.S.*, 300 U.S. 139, 146 (1937). The only Fifth Amendment issue decided by the Court was the carrier's claim of arbitrary discrimination, no other carriers having been ordered to furnish similar information, though they had in fact done so.

[27] *Champlin Refining Co.* v. *U.S.*, 329 U.S. 29, 35 (1946). The company was obliged to furnish valuation data only if it was a "carrier" subject to regulation under the Interstate Commerce Act. If it were such a "carrier" it was also obliged to file rates and transport oil for others; it had never transported anything but its own products. In *U.S.* v. *Champlin Refining Co.*, 341 U.S. 290, 296–300, 305 (1951), the Court held that the company was not required to comply with the rate requirements of the Act. The decision was reached by a tortured construction of the statute, not on constitutional grounds; but the Court did not state, as it often does, that it adopted a narrow construction in order to avoid passing upon a constitutional question. The company's claim that to impose upon a private carrier the obligations of a common carrier would violate the Fifth Amendment was untenable, since the pipe-line was built after the regulatory legislation was in force. As Justice Black's dissent noted, "the decision reflects either a hostility to the policy of the Act or an unarticulated belief that it is unconstitutional, if enforced as written." *Ibid.*, 313.

ion Congress could oblige interstate sellers of cigarettes to furnish the names of their customers to the tax authorities of the States into which shipments were made.[28]

Application of the same basic principle resulted in upholding loyalty oath legislation.[29] For Congress to protect labor unions from domination by Communists was as legitimate a legislative purpose as to protect them from domination by employers. An appropriate means to effect this aim was the imposition of a condition requiring that before a union could take advantage of the procedures prescribed by labor legislation there must be affidavits filed showing that the union officers were not Communist-connected. This requirement was sustained by the Supreme Court. "The fact that the statute identifies persons by their political affiliation and beliefs, which are circumstances ordinarily irrelevant to permissible subjects of government action, does not lead to the conclusion that such circumstances are never relevant."[30] The nature of the Communist Party and the differences between its activities and the normal functions of American political parties[31] justified the restrictive measures contained in the statute. They were reasonably related to the evil against which Congress was legislating.

Restrictions on the use of property by its owner have often been attacked as denying due process of law. Public utilities whose rates are subject to regulation by governmental agencies in order to prevent exaction of unreasonable charges have frequently complained that the rates prescribed were so low as to be "confisca-

[28] *Consumer Mail Order Assn. of America* v. *McGrath*, 94 F. Supp. 705, 711 (D.D.C. 1950), affd. 340 U.S. 925 (1951).

[29] *American Communications Assn.* v. *Douds*, 339 U.S. 382, 391 (1950). As to State laws requiring loyalty oaths, see *Wieman* v. *Updegraff*, 344 U.S. 183, 188 (1952).

[30] Such a standard would normally be *prima facie* suspect, like the racial test involved in the *Korematsu* case. See text at note 18, page 93. The main attack in the *Douds* case was based upon the First Amendment. See note 18, page 120.

[31] These differences were even more dramatically demonstrated in a concurring opinion by Justice Jackson. *Ibid.*, 422 *et seq.*

Courtesy Hirschl and Adler Galleries

Portrait of James Madison (1791), by Charles Wilson Peale

View of the Old City Hall, Wall Street, in the year 1789

tory." The rule is that there is no "confiscation" if the rate permits a "fair return" on the property devoted to the public service. Prolonged litigation is usually required in order to determine what constitutes a fair return and what is the proper "valuation" for the utility company's property. Should valuation be based on original cost, replacement cost, or "prudent investment" (which Justice Brandeis advocated)? The Supreme Court's present view is that none of these factors is controlling, but all may be taken into consideration by the rate-making agency, which will be accorded considerable leeway in making its determination of value.[32] Court review on the constitutional issue of confiscation is always in order, even though in other respects the administrative agency's findings of fact may be accorded finality.[33] In a remarkable recent decision the Court held that a railroad rate on a particular commodity could not be invalidated as confiscatory so long as the rate structure as a whole was yielding an adequately compensatory return on the road's total operations.[34]

Another type of interference with property rights which the Supreme Court has sustained is wartime control of rents and prices.[35] Another is divestiture as a remedy in case of monopolistic acquisitions violating the anti-trust laws.[36] Still another is taxation of one person upon property owned by someone else.[37] As a final instance of permissible restriction upon a property owner's prerogatives may be mentioned a decision holding that it was an

[32] *F.P.C.* v. *Hope Natural Gas Co.*, 320 U.S. 591, 601–602 (1944); *F.P.C.* v. *Natural Gas Pipe Line Co.*, 315 U.S. 575, 585–86 (1942).

[33] *B.&O. R.R. Co.* v. *U.S.*, 298 U.S. 349, 363–64 (1936). Cf. note 16, page 93.

[34] *B.&O. R.R. Co.* v. *U.S.*, 345 U.S. 146, 148 (1953). Cf. *Northern Pacific R.R. Co.* v. *North Dakota*, 236 U.S. 585, 595–96 (1915).

[35] *Bowles* v. *Willingham*, 321 U.S. 503, 516–18 (1944).

[36] *Standard Oil Co.* v. *U.S.*, 221 U.S. 1, 79 (1911); *U.S.* v. *American Tobacco Co.*, 221 U.S. 106, 187 (1911).

[37] *Fernandez* v. *Wiener*, 326 U.S. 340, 357–58 (1945). "The tax burden thus laid is not so unrelated to the privileges enjoyed by the taxpayers who are owners of the property affected that it can be said to be an arbitrary exercise of the taxing power." Cf. *Hoeper* v. *Wisconsin*, 284 U.S. 206, 215 (1931). See also *Helvering* v. *Clifford*, 309 U.S. 331, 334–35 (1940).

"unfair labor practice" to refuse the use of a company-owned hall to a union organizer.[38]

Just Compensation

Almost as prominent a feature of the Fifth Amendment as the due process clause is the provision prohibiting the taking of private property for public use without just compensation.[1] Four questions are constantly arising under the language of this clause: (1) What is "private property"? (2) When is property "taken"? (3) What is a "public use"? (4) What is "just compensation"?

In answering the first question, the Supreme Court has often enunciated the principle that not every economic advantage constitutes "property." Thus when Congress, in the exercise of its power to pre-empt the entire flow of water in a navigable river, deprives the riparian owners of their former use of the water, there is no vested claim belonging to such owners which can be recognized by the courts as constituting "private property."[2] Similarly, where public works result in raising the level of a river, so that a power company's "head" of water at its dam is reduced, there is no property right invaded.[3] Likewise there is no "property" taken when the aboriginal occupants of Indian lands are evicted by the onward march of the white man's civilization.[4]

---

[38] *N.L.R.B.* v. *Stowe Spinning Co.*, 336 U.S. 226, 228–29 (1949). The company had built the hall for use by a patriotic secret society, which had given permission to the organizer to use the premises. The company then intervened, forbidding use of the hall under a requirement never theretofore enforced permitting use of the hall only by the patriotic society. The majority of the Court stated that discrimination was the evil being condemned by the decision, not mere denial of facilities. *Ibid.*, 233. The majority regarded the hall as property used in the company's business, since it was important to have a meeting place in the town in order to attract employees and promote their morale. *Ibid.*, 230. Dissenters thought a serious problem was presented under the Fifth Amendment since the hall was not property connected with the business. *Ibid.*, 244.

[1] Aliens are entitled to the benefits of this provision. *Guessfeldt* v. *McGrath*, 342 U.S. 308, 318 (1952).

[2] *U.S.* v. *Twin City Power Co.*, 350 U.S. 222, 227 (1956).

[3] *U.S.* v. *Willow River Power Co.*, 324 U.S. 499, 502–503, 510 (1945).

[4] *Tee-Hit-Ton Indians* v. *U.S.*, 348 U.S. 272, 285 (1955). The Court here

Equally subtle niceties mark the Court's decisions on the question of what is a "taking." Thus, there is no taking when a railroad is required, by exercise of "police power" for the protection of public health and safety, to spend money to eliminate grade crossings.[5] But there is a taking when riparian property is flooded when the level of a river is raised by construction of a dam by the government. Formal condemnation proceedings are not necessary; the mere course of physical events can amount to a taking, and by virtue of the constitutional requirement there is an implied obligation resting upon the government under such circumstances to pay just compensation. The courts will take a practical rather than theoretical view of the matter in such cases and protect a property owner's substantial rights. "Property is taken in the constitutional sense when inroads are made upon an owner's use of it to an extent that, as between private owners, a servitude has been acquired either by agreement or in course of time."[6] Thus there is a taking when airplanes fly so low over a farm that the owner's chickens are frightened and the value of his land is substantially diminished.[7]

Although the Supreme Court asserts that it is a question for the courts to decide whether a particular taking of property is for a "public use," there has never been a case where the determination by Congress of that issue has been overruled. The Court's own language gives Congress practically unlimited leeway in deciding whether a particular use is for a "public" purpose.[8] Thus the "redevelopment" of land in the District of Columbia by con-

followed the "great case" of *Johnson and Graham's Lessee* v. *McIntosh*, 8 Wheat. 543, 573–74 (1823), decided by Chief Justice John Marshall. See Edward Dumbauld, "John Marshall and Treaty Law," *American Journal of International Law*, Vol. L, No. 1 (January, 1956), 69; Dumbauld, "John Marshall and the Law of Nations," *U. of Pa. Law Review*, Vol. CIV, No. 1 (August, 1955), 38, 54.

[5] *A.T.&S.F. Ry. Co.* v. *P.U.C. of California*, 346 U.S. 346, 349, 352 (1953).

[6] *U.S.* v. *Dickinson*, 331 U.S. 745, 748–49 (1947).

[7] *U.S.* v. *Causby*, 328 U.S. 256, 261 (1946).

[8] *U.S. ex rel. T.V.A.* v. *Welch*, 327 U.S. 546, 551–52 (1946). But the President has no power to take property without authority from Congress. *Youngstown Sheet & Tube Co.* v. *Sawyer*, 343 U.S. 579 (1952).

demning it and reselling it for use by private enterprise has recently been held to be a public use.[9]

The greatest volume of litigation is devoted to determination of what constitutes "just compensation." Here the basic principle is that the owner is to receive a "full and perfect equivalent" in money for the property taken.[10] Ordinarily the standard is "market value," but the Court "has refused to make a fetish even of market value, since it may not be the best measure of value in some cases."[11] Thus in the case of tugboats condemned during wartime, when their market value had increased by reason of shortage caused by previous condemnations by the government, the Court excluded from the measure of just compensation the value arising from the government's own special need, even though this was reflected in the market value.[12] Special or peculiar value to the owner is also excluded.[13] A similar rule excludes value derived from the owner's authority to exercise the power of eminent domain: it is *private* property, not the right to exercise a public power, for which compensation must be paid under the Fifth Amendment.[14] But proximity to previously condemned land is an element of value, and must be compensated for unless the

[9] *Berman* v. *Parker*, 348 U.S. 26, 34 (1954).

[10] *U.S.* v. *Miller*, 317 U.S. 369, 373 (1943); *Monongahela Navigation Co.* v. *U.S.*, 148 U.S. 312, 326 (1893). The Court in the latter case held (contrary to the terms of the act of Congress involved) that a franchise or right to take tolls, granted to a canal company by Pennsylvania, was part of the value of the property taken when the canal was condemned by the federal government. *Ibid.*, 328, 337.

[11] *U.S.* v. *Cors*, 337 U.S. 325, 332 (1949).

[12] *Ibid.*, 333. Four Justices dissented, contending that the enhanced market value was due to the need of other private tug operators, rather than that of the government. *Ibid.*, 343-44.

[13] *U.S.* v. *Miller*, 317 U.S. 369, 375 (1943). Compensation is made for the owner's loss, not the taker's gain. See also *Kimball Laundry Co.* v. *U.S.*, 338 U.S. 1, 5, 13 (1949).

[14] *U.S. ex rel. T.V.A.* v. *Powelson*, 319 U.S. 266, 276, 280 (1943). Four Justices dissented. In this case the Court noted that value need not be measured by the existing use of the land, but that potential use must be of reasonable probability in the reasonably near future if it is to be the measure of value. *Ibid.*, 275-76.

land being condemned was itself a part of the original project from the beginning.[15]

Requisition of articles subject to ceiling prices under wartime price control gave rise to peculiar problems in applying the formula of just compensation. Here there was no free market, and the criterion of market value had to be supplemented. In a case involving lard and pork chops, the Court held that the burden was on the owner to prove that the ceiling price was not "just compensation."[16] This burden was not met by showing the replacement cost of hogs (which were not price-controlled), since some of the products made from the hogs were not subject to price control, and there was no loss on total operations.[17] The majority of the Court relied upon the economic theory of "joint costs."[18]

Another case where in practice the owner received only the ceiling price, though the Court theoretically recognized the inapplicability of the market value test, involved black pepper.[19] The particular pepper requisitioned had cost the owner more than the ceiling price.[20] The owner acquired pepper as an investment, not for current trading purposes, in accordance with a plan which took into account fluctuations in price over a 75 year cycle. The lower court had allowed a "retention value" based upon potential profits obtainable after removal of wartime restrictions.[21] The Supreme Court rejected this element of value,[22] influenced by a desire to adhere to the ceiling price as just compensation whenever possible, since otherwise owners would be encouraged to refuse to sell, in order to obtain a higher price when the govern-

[15] *U.S.* v. *Miller*, 317 U.S. 369, 375–77 (1943).

[16] *U.S.* v. *John J. Felin & Co. Inc.*, 334 U.S. 624, 631 (1948).

[17] *Ibid.*, 640–41. Cf. note 34, page 97.

[18] *Ibid.*, 632. This was criticized by other Justices. *Ibid.*, 643.

[19] *U.S.* v. *Commodities Trading Corp.*, 339 U.S. 121, 123, 131 (1950).

[20] *Ibid.*, 130. But the government claimed that the owner supplied high-cost rather than low-cost pepper to fill the requisition when both were available.

[21] *Ibid.*, 123, 128.

[22] *Ibid.*, 126, 130.

ment was forced to resort to condemnation.[23] The Court also felt that to permit compensation for "retention value" would be a discrimination against owners of perishable articles which could not be withheld from the market.[24]

The Court had resorted to a similar artifice in finding that no damage was suffered by a government bond holder entitled to be paid in gold coin but paid in paper money. If the obligation had been paid in accordance with its terms the holder would have been required to turn the gold over to the treasury at the same rate of exchange; there was no free market in gold to which he could have lawful access. The constitutional question under the Fifth Amendment was therefore moot.[25]

In case of a temporary taking, incidental damages are allowed which would not be paid for if the taking were permanent. Thus when a coal mine was taken over by the government during a strike, operating losses due to wage increases were paid by the government as compensation.[26] Similarly a laundry, temporarily taken and operated by the government to meet the needs of service personnel, was compensated for the loss of trade routes and goodwill, although the government did not benefit in any manner by the laundry's loss of customers.[27] When a tenant holding under a long-term lease was temporarily evicted and the government took possession of the premises, the Court held that the tenant should be compensated for fixtures and equipment destroyed or depreciated in value, as well as for the expense of evacuating the premises.[28]

[23] *Ibid.*, 125. But, as Justice Jackson pointed out in his dissent, the price-control law did not compel sale (thereby avoiding constitutional problems). *Ibid.*, 141. He made the same point in the *Felin* case, 334 U.S. at 651.

[24] *Ibid.*, 127. But a perishable article would have no "retention value."

[25] *Nortz* v. *U.S.*, 294 U.S. 317, 329–30 (1935).

[26] *U.S.* v. *Pewee Coal Co.*, 341 U.S. 114, 117–18 (1951). Four dissenting Justices said there was no proof that the company could have operated its mine without paying the increased wages even if the government had not taken it over. *Ibid.*, 122.

[27] *Kimball Laundry Co.* v. *U.S.*, 338 U.S. 1, 11 (1949). The government did not serve any outside customers during its operation of the laundry, but merely handled the laundry needs of service personnel.

Another curious rule is that the government and the owner may by contract agree upon the price to be paid for the property taken, and effect will be given to such agreement even if the contract price is less than what the government would otherwise have been obliged to pay as just compensation under the Fifth Amendment.[29]

First Amendment Freedoms

Group (1), containing those provisions of the Bill of Rights which protect the inner life of citizens and the integrity of democratic political processes, gives rise to the greatest volume of activity by the Supreme Court. There has been in recent years a constant stream of litigation involving the application of the First Amendment, which guarantees freedom of religion, of speech, of the press, of assemblage, and of petition to the government for a redress of grievances.

The religious clause gave the greatest difficulty in 1789 when the amendments were being prepared in Congress. Several versions were offered, at various stages of the drafting process. That which finally became part of the Constitution reads:

"Congress shall make no law respecting an establishment of religion, or prohibiting the free exercise thereof."

Interpretation of this language, beginning with the first word, has been productive of controversy. At the outset, it should be noted that the prohibition which the clause contains is directed against *Congress*. Does this mean that the *president* is not subject to this prohibition? Even if he is not, he would have no authority with respect to establishment of religion if the federal government as a whole has no power to intermeddle in matters of re-

---

[28] *U.S.* v. *Gen. Motors Corp.*, 323 U.S. 373, 381–83 (1945). When the fee title to the premises is taken, no compensation is allowed for collateral or consequential damages such as moving costs, good will, loss of future profits, and the like. *Ibid.*, 378.

[29] *Albrecht* v. *U.S.*, 329 U.S. 599, 601–604 (1947).

ligion.[1] This seems to be the case, unless the president might have authority by virtue of the treaty-making power to take action, with respect to religion, which would be given legal effect as part of "the supreme Law of the Land."[2]

It seems likely that the reference to Congress was meant to contrast the powers of that body with those of the state governments, rather than with those of other branches of the federal government. For the prohibition against establishment of religion, like the rest of the Bill of Rights, was directed against the federal government, not against the states.[3] In fact, it must be borne in mind that in several New England states (as in Massachusetts until 1833) an established church was maintained long after the Bill of Rights went into force.[4]

Recognition of the rights of the several states to regulate religious matters may have influenced the choice of words used in the First Amendment. Congress is forbidden to make any law at all *"respecting"* an establishment of religion. In other words, even a law *prohibiting* establishment would be invalid. Perhaps the states which then had establishments desired to place their regime beyond all danger of interference by the federal government. In this field there was to be a total lack of legislative power insofar as Congress was concerned.[5]

[1] Professor Corwin emphasized the distinction between Congress and president in 1951 during discussion of President Truman's proposal to send an ambassador to the Vatican. Leo Pfeffer, *Church, State, and Freedom,* 115–17. Pfeffer's suggestion that the wording "No religion shall be established by law" was put into the active voice when Madison's proposal to prohibit violation of the rights of conscience by states was defeated is superficially plausible but contrary to the record (which Pfeffer himself quotes). *Ibid.,* 141. The rewording which mentions Congress and uses the active voice was adopted by the *House* on August 15, 1789; the restriction on states was not defeated until September 7, 1789, by the *Senate.* See pages 39, 46.

[2] Constitution, Art. II, sec. 2; Art. VI, cl. 2. See Dumbauld, "John Marshall and Treaty Law," *American Journal of International Law,* Vol. L, No. 1 (January, 1956), 69–70.

[3] *Barron* v. *Baltimore,* 7 Pet. 243, 247 (1833); *Permoli* v. *Municipality of New Orleans,* 44 U.S. 589, 609 (1845).

[4] See page 133.

[5] If this assumption is correct, the exertion of federal judicial power to make the First Amendment applicable to the states, by virtue of the Fourteenth Amend-

With regard to free exercise of religion by individuals, Congress is prevented from "prohibiting" it. In the case of the remaining First Amendment freedoms, no law "abridging" them is permissible.

Recalling a distinction elaborated in judicial decisions of a former day regarding the powers of Congress over interstate commerce,[6] may one assert that Congress could "regulate" free exercise of religion, so long as such regulation did not amount to prohibition? Or regulate freedom of speech, press, assembly, and petition, so long as those rights were furthered and promoted thereby, rather than abridged or curtailed?[7]

Of course, as stated above with regard to the powers of the president as distinguished from those of Congress, such authority to "regulate," even if not denied by the terms of the First Amendment, would have to be shown to be derivable from an affirmative grant in some other part of the Constitution. For neither the First Amendment nor any other part of the Bill of Rights operates as a grant of power, either expressly or by implication; rather it is a restriction upon the exercise of powers already granted elsewhere.[8]

Another verbal peculiarity may be noted. The clause prohibits legislation "respecting *an* establishment of religion." Does this

ment's due process clause, would undoubtedly have shocked the framers of the Bill of Rights. When the Supreme Court prohibits establishment of religion by a state (see pages 106–107), it is exercising a power which is wholly denied to Congress by the express terms of a constitutional prohibition. Exercise of federal judicial power in an area beyond the legislative authority of Congress was condemned in *Erie R. R. Co.* v. *Tompkins*, 304 U.S. 64, 78–80 (1938), as unconstitutional usurpation. Thomas Jefferson, a strong advocate of religious freedom against any type of governmental restraint, nevertheless did recognize a distinction between federal and state power in this field. As president he refused to proclaim holidays of religious thanksgiving, but did so while governor of Virginia. Proclamation of November 11, 1779, *Papers of Thomas Jefferson*, III, 177–79; to Levi Lincoln, January 1, 1802, *Works of Thomas Jefferson*, IX, 346.

[6] See Corwin, *The Commerce Power versus States Rights*, 55–112.

[7] "Regulation and suppression are not the same, either in purpose or result, and courts of justice can tell the difference." *Poulos* v. *New Hampshire*, 345 U.S. 395, 408 (1953).

[8] The Ninth Amendment precludes any grant of power by implication.

imply that only a *single* establishment is forbidden, but that a *multiple* establishment (if such a concept is not a contradiction in terms)[9] would not be forbidden? Is the meaning any different from what it would have been if the provision had read "respecting establishment of religion" or "respecting the establishment of religion"? Does "establishment" refer only to a concrete institution, not a process of governmental action?

This verbal nicety does not seem sufficiently significant to make the contentions convincing of those who criticize the interpretation of the First Amendment which the Supreme Court adopted in a recent case[10] involving payment from tax funds for transportation of pupils to a Roman Catholic parochial school. The Court held that such payment was permissible, on the theory that it was a benefit to the individual pupil, not to the school.[11] But Justice Black's majority opinion contained an elaborate dictum adopting the Jeffersonian interpretation of the First Amendment as "building a wall of separation between church and state."[12] The Court said:

The "establishment of religion" clause of the First Amendment means at least this: Neither a state nor the Federal Government can set up a church. Neither can pass laws which aid one religion, aid all religions, or prefer one religion over another. Neither can force nor influence

[9] Apparently this situation did exist in New York in the seventeenth century. Pfeffer, *Church, State, and Freedom*, 70. See also Corwin, *A Constitution of Powers in a Secular State*, vii. Corwin advocates the theory that "establishment" means "preferred status." *Ibid.*, 99. See notes 19, page 108, 27, page 111, and 25, page 136.

[10] *Everson* v. *Board of Ed. of Ewing Twp.*, 330 U.S. 1, 17–18 (1947).

[11] The "pupil benefit" theory was upheld with regard to supplying secular textbooks in *Cochran* v. *La. State Bd. of Educ.*, 281 U.S. 370, 375 (1930), in an opinion by Chief Justice Charles Evans Hughes. Similarly, a war veteran entitled to "G.I." educational benefits could doubtless use them for training at a theological seminary.

[12] To Danbury Baptist Association, January 1, 1802, *Writings of Thomas Jefferson*, XVI, 281–82. Of this statement the Supreme Court had said in *Reynolds* v. *U.S.*, 98 U.S. 145, 164 (1878): "Coming as this does from an acknowledged leader of the advocates of the measure, it may be accepted almost as an authoritative declaration of the scope and effect of the amendment thus secured."

a person to go to or remain away from church against his will or force him to profess a belief or disbelief in any religion. No person can be punished for entertaining or professing religious beliefs or disbeliefs, for church attendance or non-attendance. No tax in any amount, large or small, can be levied to support any religious activities or institutions, whatever they may be called, or whatever form they may adopt to teach or practice religion. Neither a state nor the Federal Government, can, openly or secretly, participate in the affairs of any religious organizations or groups and vice versa. In the words of Jefferson, the clause against establishment of religion by law was intended to erect "a wall of separation between Church and State." . . .

The First Amendment has erected a wall between church and state. That wall must be kept high and impregnable. We could not approve the slightest breach. New Jersey has not breached it here.[13]

Four of the nine Justices disagreed with the conclusion reached in this case. In a cogent dissent Justice Jackson stated the actual question decided by the Court in these terms: "Is it constitutional to tax this complainant to pay the cost of carrying pupils to Church schools of one specified denomination?"[14] After reviewing the pertinent provisions of canon law, he concludes that "the parochial school is a vital, if not the most vital, part of the Roman Catholic Church. . . . Catholic education is the rock on which the whole structure rests, and to render tax aid to its Church school is indistinguishable to me from rendering the same aid to the Church itself."[15] Disposing of the "pupil benefit" theory he says: "The State cannot maintain a Church and it can no more tax its citizens to furnish free carriage to those who attend a Church. . . . The

[13] 330 U.S. at 15–16, 18. Comparing this statement with the result reached, Justice Jackson in his dissent says: "The case which irresistibly comes to mind as the most fitting precedent is that of Julia who, according to Byron's reports, 'whispering "I will ne'er consent," consented.' " *Ibid.*, at 19.

[14] *Ibid.*, 21. Justice Jackson's statement of the precise question for decision is justified by the fact that the school board's resolution was actually drawn up in those terms, authorizing "transportation of pupils of Ewing to the Trenton and Pennington High Schools and Catholic Schools by way of public carrier as in recent years." *Ibid.*, 21, 62. Justice Jackson was noted for his belief that cases should be decided on their facts rather than to promote a policy.

[15] *Ibid.*, 24.

Court, however, compares this to other subsidies and loans to individuals. . . . Of course, the state may pay out tax-raised funds to relieve pauperism, but it may not under our Constitution do so to reward piety. It may spend funds to secure old age against want, but it may not spend funds to secure religion against skepticism. It may compensate individuals for loss of employment, but it cannot compensate them for adherence to a creed."[16]

Continuing, Justice Jackson points out that "the basic fallacy in the Court's reasoning which accounts for its failure to apply the principles it avows, is in ignoring the essentially religious test by which beneficiaries of this expenditure are selected. A policeman protects a Catholic, of course—but not because he is a Catholic; it is because he is a man and a member of our society. The fireman protects the Church school—but not because it is a Church school; it is because it is property, part of the assets of our society. Neither the fireman nor the policeman has to ask before he renders aid 'Is this man or building identified with the Catholic Church?' But before these school authorities draw a check to reimburse for a student's fare they must ask just that question, and if the school is a Catholic one they may render aid because it is such, while if it is of any other faith . . . the help must be withheld."[17] A lengthier dissenting opinion by Justice Rutledge emphasized that the object of the First Amendment was "to create a complete and permanent separation of the spheres of religious activity and civil authority by comprehensively forbidding every form of public aid or support for religion."[18]

The "wall of separation" doctrine was reaffirmed by the Court in the "released time" case a year later, and sufficed to invalidate the plan used in the schools of Champaign, Illinois.[19] Many re-

[16] *Ibid.*, 24-25.

[17] *Ibid.*, 25.

[18] *Ibid.*, 31-32. Justice Rutledge reviews in detail the labors of Madison and Jefferson for religious freedom. *Ibid.*, 33-43, 63-74.

[19] *Illinois ex rel. McCollum* v. *Bd. of Educ.*, 333 U.S. 203, 209-11 (1948). Counsel in this case sought to have the Court reconsider the *Everson* statement and hold that non-preferential support accorded to all religions equally was permissible. The Court rejected this attempt to weaken the "wall of separation"

ligious leaders of various denominations believe that the Roman Catholic position with regard to education is essentially sound: that religious instruction should be an integral, significant part of the educational process, and not merely an ornamental supplement consuming a short time on Sundays. The importance of religion requires that it be brought to the children's attention during their "business hours" on week-days.[20] One method of dealing with the problem is the "released time" plan, whereby public school pupils (upon request of their parents) are dismissed at certain periods during school hours for the purpose of attending religious instruction given by teachers supplied by the various participating churches. The plan adopted in Champaign permitted use of the public school premises for such teaching, and also the use of services of school personnel and supplies in keeping attendance records and the like. These features of the plan condemned it as being public financial support to religion,[21] when Mrs. Vashti McCollum, a militant atheist, brought suit because her son Terry was lonesome and became the butt of his classmates' gibes when he was obliged to endure the humiliation of sitting alone at a desk in the hall while the other pupils attended the religious instruction class.[22]

That it was the affirmative participation of the school in the religious teaching program which vitiated the Champaign plan was made clear four years later in a case upholding the constitutionality of a "released time" plan established in New York.[23]

and reaffirmed its former principle. *Ibid.*, 211. Strong support for the correctness of the Court's construction is to be found in the legislative history of the First Amendment. On two occasions the Senate rejected amendments embodying the non-preferential interpretation. Pfeffer, *Church, State, and Freedom*, 141; see page 45.

[20] 333 U.S. at 222.

[21] Justice Frankfurter, concurring, intimated that other forms of "released-time" plans might be acceptable. *Ibid.*, 231. Justice Reed, dissenting, pointed out the lack of clarity in the Court's opinion with regard to the features which condemned the Champaign plan. *Ibid.*, 240.

[22] Justice Jackson, in a concurring opinion, tartly observed that a nonconformist should not expect to enjoy all the comforts of conformity. *Ibid.*, 233.

[23] *Zorach* v. *Clauson*, 343 U.S. 306, 308–309 (1952).

Here there was no use made of school premises for religious instruction; and the participating religious organizations bore the entire cost of administration, including the preparation and distribution of application blanks to be signed by the pupils' parents. The school merely excused the pupils in order that they might leave school and go to the religious centre where the instruction was to be given. Under this plan, as the Court observed, "the public schools do no more than accommodate their schedules to a program of outside religious instruction."[24]

Dissenting Justices[25] contended that in fact the coercive apparatus of the public school system was being used to promote religious teaching.[26]

The First Amendment's provisions touching religious liberty are twofold. Not only is the individual free from all governmental coercion to participate against his will in the support of

[24] *Ibid.*, 315. "The government must be neutral when it comes to competition between sects. . . . It may not coerce anyone to . . . take religious instruction. But it can close its doors or suspend its operations as to those who want to repair to their religious sanctuary for worship or instruction. No more than that is undertaken here." *Ibid.*, 314.

[25] Of the eight Justices concurring in the *McCollum* decision, three (Black, Frankfurter, Jackson) dissented in *Zorach* v. *Clauson*. Two (Murphy and Rutledge) had died. Pfeffer, *Church, State, and Freedom*, 156–59, asserts that the *Zorach* case represents a "retreat" from the *McCollum* principle. But the distinction drawn by the majority of the Court between the two situations seems legitimate and convincing.

[26] Justice Black said: "Here the sole question is whether New York can use its compulsory education laws to help religious sects get attendants presumably too unenthusiastic to go unless moved to do so by the pressure of this state machinery. . . . The state thus makes religious sects beneficiaries of its power to compel children to attend secular schools. Any use of such coercive power by the state to help or hinder some religious sects or to prefer all religious sects over nonbelievers or vice versa is just what I think the First Amendment forbids." 343 U.S. at 318. Justice Frankfurter pointed out that: "The school system is very much in operation during this kind of released time. If its doors are closed, they are closed upon those students who do not attend the religious instruction in order to keep them within the school." *Ibid.*, 321. Justice Jackson noted that: "Here schooling is more or less suspended during the 'released time' so that the nonreligious attendants will not forge ahead of the churchgoing absentees. But it serves as a temporary jail for a pupil who will not go to church. It takes more subtlety of mind than I possess to deny that this is governmental constraint in support of religion." *Ibid.*, 324.

any religion (either directly, as by compulsion to attend cere-
monies, or indirectly, as by compulsion through taxation to make
contributions), but also is free from all governmental coercion
interfering with his participation in the support (direct or indirect) of any religion which he does choose of his own will to
embrace.[27]

Freedom to engage in the exercise of one's chosen religion has
been accorded extensive protection by the Supreme Court. In accordance with the Jeffersonian principle set forth in the Virginia
Act for Establishing Religious Freedom, that "it is time enough
for the rightful purposes of civil government for its officers to
interfere when principles break out into overt acts against peace
and good order,"[28] the Court has held that "Congress was deprived of all legislative power over mere opinion, but was left
free to reach actions which were in violation of social duties or
subversive of good order." Thus polygamy may be punished as
a crime, even when committed by Mormons in accordance with
their religious beliefs.[29] Similarly, a conscientious objector can
not escape on grounds of religious belief the military training
requirements of the curriculum at a state university.[30] Nor may
public health be endangered,[31] nor fraud be perpetrated,[32] "under
the cloak of religion."

[27] This double aspect of religious liberty, embodied in the language of the
First Amendment, has been noted by the Court and by commentators. *Cantwell*
v. *Connecticut*, 310 U.S. 296, 303 (1940); Pfeffer, *Church, State, and Freedom*,
121–24.

[28] For this statute, see Hening, *The Statutes at Large*, XII, 84–86 (1823).
Jefferson's draft, which was in some particulars amended in the legislature, is in
Works of Thomas Jefferson, II, 438–41. Jefferson regarded his authorship of
this law as one of the three outstanding achievements of his life, ranking with
his writing the Declaration of Independence and founding the University of
Virginia. *Ibid.*, XII, 483.

[29] *Reynolds* v. *U.S.*, 98 U.S. 145, 164 (1878); *Cleveland* v. *U.S.*, 329 U.S.
14, 20 (1946).

[30] *Hamilton* v. *Regents*, 293 U.S. 245, 262 (1934).

[31] Vaccination may be required. *Jacobson* v. *Massachusetts*, 197 U.S. 11, 29
(1905). Snake-handling may be prohibited. *State* v. *Massey*, 229 N.C. 734
(1949); appeal dismissed for want of a substantial federal question *sub nom.*
Bunn v. *North Carolina*, 336 U.S. 942 (1949).

[32] *Cantwell* v. *Connecticut*, 310 U.S. 296, 306 (1940); *U.S.* v. *Ballard*, 322

But, as was held in one of the thirteen Jehovah's Witness cases decided on May 3, 1943, freedom of religion includes the right to sell pamphlets on the streets, as well as to worship in a sanctuary in more conventional fashion.[33] It also includes the right to knock or ring the doorbell when leaving such literature at a householder's door.[34]

Justice Jackson voiced vigorous disagreement with the ludicrous excesses engendered by the Court's zeal in protecting the right to engage in religious proselytizing:[35]

In my view the First Amendment assures the broadest tolerable exercise of free speech, free press, and free assembly, not merely for religious purposes, but for political, economic, scientific, news, or informational ends as well. When limits are reached which such communications must observe, can one go farther under the cloak of religious evangelism? Does what is obscene, or commercial, or abusive, or inciting become less so if employed to promote a religious ideology? I had not supposed that the rights of secular and non-religious communications were more narrow or in any way inferior to those of avowed religious groups.

It may be asked why then does the First Amendment separately mention free exercise of religion? The history of religious persecution

---

U.S. 78, 86–88 (1944). Justice Jackson flatly asserted the futility of attempts to assess the *bona fides* of religious professions and experiences. "I would dismiss the indictment and have done with this business of judicially examining other people's faith." *Ibid.*, 95.

[33] *Murdock* v. *Pennsylvania*, 319 U.S. 105, 111 (1943). However, child labor restrictions may lawfully be applied to the sales activities of street vendors of tender age. *Prince* v. *Massachusetts*, 321 U.S. 158, 167–69 (1944).

[34] *Martin* v. *Struthers*, 319 U.S. 141, 147 (1943). The *Struthers* decision may be weakened by *Breard* v. *Alexandria*, 341 U.S. 622, 641–42 (1951), which sustained against challenge under the First Amendment an ordinance prohibiting commercial door-to-door solicitation to purchase magazines in the absence of invitation by the householder. The Court distinguished the *Struthers* case on the ground that it involved no commercial aspect. *Ibid.*, 642–43. The dissenting Justices complained that the *Struthers* holding was being overruled. *Ibid.*, 649. In *Dennis* v. *U.S.*, 341 U.S. 494, 540–41 (1951), Justice Frankfurter noted that the *Struthers* ordinance was specifically aimed at religious solicitation and did not impose the same restrictions upon commercial callers.

[35] *Douglas* v. *Jeannette*, 319 U.S. 157, 179, 181 (1943).

Reproduced from the Collections of the Library of Congress

George Mason

Richard Henry Lee

gives the answer. Religion needed specific protection because it was subject to attack from a separate quarter. It was often claimed that one was an heretic and guilty of blasphemy because he failed to conform in mere belief or in support of prevailing institutions and theology. It was to assure religious teaching as much freedom as secular discussion, rather than to assure it greater license, that led to its separate statement. . . .

For a stranger to corner a man in his home, summon him to the door and put him in the position either of arguing his religion or of ordering one of unknown disposition to leave is a questionable use of religious freedom. . . .[36]

This court is forever adding new stories to the temples of constitutional law, and the temples have a way of collapsing when one story too many is added.[37]

Indefatigable[38] exertions by Jehovah's Witnesses to obtain access to public school education without saluting the flag were likewise more successful than the efforts of California Methodists to secure a college education without participation in military training.[39] In striking down the flag salute requirement, the Court said, speaking through Justice Jackson, in spirited fashion: "It is now a commonplace that censorship or suppression of expression of opinion is tolerated by our Constitution only when the expression presents a clear and present danger of action of a kind the State is empowered to prevent and punish.[40] It would seem

[36] Justice Jackson also emphasizes the need of preventing disturbance in a community where many men work on night shift and where the householder has no servants to turn away unwelcome visitors. *Ibid.*, 174–75. See also Chafee, *Free Speech in the United States*, 406–407.

[37] "So it was with liberty of contract, which was discredited by being overdone." 319 U.S. at 181. In a later case where the Court refused to sanction regulation of sound trucks Justice Jackson expressed fear that the decision would "endanger the great right of free speech by making it ridiculous and obnoxious." *Saia* v. *New York*, 334 U.S. 558, 567–68 (1948). See note 6, page 128.

[38] In *Minersville School District* v. *Gobitis*, 310 U.S. 586, 597–98 (1940), a Pennsylvania flag salute requirement was upheld. A similar result was reached in four other cases.

[39] *West Virginia State Bd. of Education* v. *Barnette*, 319 U.S. 624, 633, 638, 642 (1943). See note 30, page 111.

[40] The "clear and present danger" rule in freedom of speech cases was enunci-

that involuntary affirmation could be commanded only on even more immediate and urgent grounds than silence. . . .[41] The very purpose of a Bill of Rights was to withdraw certain subjects from the vicissitudes of political controversy, to place them beyond the reach of majorities and officials and to establish them as legal principles to be applied by the courts. . . . If there is any fixed star in our constitutional constellation, it is that no official, high or petty, can prescribe what is orthodox in politics, nationalism, religion, or other matters of opinion or force citizens to confess by word or act their faith therein."[42]

This statement practically amounts to saying that the First Amendment prohibits an "establishment" in politics, as well as religion. "Authority here is to be controlled by public opinion, not public opinion by authority."[43] Such pronouncements empha-

---

ated by Justice Holmes in *Schenck* v. *U.S.*, 249 U.S. 47, 52 (1919). See note 3, page 116. For Justice Jackson's later views regarding this formula, see *Dennis* v. *U.S.*, 341 U.S. 494, 568–69 (1951), and *Beauharnais* v. *Illinois*, 343 U.S. 250, 302–304 (1952). In his *Barnette* opinion Justice Jackson also goes far toward acceptance of the "preferred position" doctrine (as to which see text at note 1, page 127) when he says: "The right of a State to regulate, for example, a public utility may well include, so far as the due process test is concerned, power to impose all of the restrictions which the legislature may have a 'rational basis' for adopting. But freedoms of speech and of press, of assembly and of worship may not be infringed on such slender grounds. They are susceptible of restriction only to prevent grave and immediate danger to interests which the state may lawfully protect." 319 U.S. at 639.

41 The Court treats the "compulsory rite" of flag salute as an interference with freedom of speech, rather than of religion. 319 U.S. at 634–35. Does this explain why a different result was reached in the case of military training? The Court draws a distinction based on the compulsory attendance at public school, as distinguished from college. *Ibid.*, at 632. But Justice Frankfurter points out that the option of attending a private school is constitutionally available (though perhaps not financially practicable). *Ibid.*, 656.

42 In *American Communications Assn.* v. *Douds*, 339 U.S. 382, 443–44 (1950), Justice Jackson reaffirmed his conviction "that our Constitution excludes both federal and local governments from the realm of opinions and ideas, beliefs and doubts, heresy and orthodoxy, political, religious, or scientific. . . . I think that under our system, it is time enough for the law to lay hold of the citizen when he acts illegally, or in some rare circumstances when his thoughts are given illegal utterance. I think we must let his mind alone." See also note 32, page 111.

114

size the close relation between the constitutional guarantees relating to religious liberty and those protecting "freedom of speech or of the press" against abridgement.[44]

In recent years, and particularly during World War II, the courts, government officials, and the general public have on the whole remained free from hysterical tendencies. The Supreme Court has adhered with commendable fidelity to the noble libertarian traditions of Milton, Jefferson, Mill, Holmes, Brandeis, and Chafee in protecting freedom of speech. According to this philosophy, truth in religion or science and the public good in politics are most effectively pursued and attained by means of free inquiry and discussion.

The "Clear and Present Danger" Test

Constitutional policy in the United States calls for protection of the right to enjoy freedom of speech. Yet this right is not absolute. Some words are the equivalent of acts. If horse-racing or prize-fighting were illegal, would the person signaling the beginning of the contest by shouting "Go" be immune from prosecution, whereas he could be punished if he fired a gun or rang a bell instead? Such "verbal acts" are subject to restraint under appropriate circumstances.[1] "There are certain well-defined and narrowly limited classes of speech, the prevention and punishment of which have never been thought to raise any Constitutional problem. These include the lewd and obscene, the profane, the libelous, and the insulting or 'fighting' word—those which by their very utterance inflict injury or tend to incite an immediate breach of the peace. It has been well observed that such

[43] *Ibid.*, 641. As stated by Justice Jackson on another occasion, "It is not the function of our Government to keep the citizen from falling into error; it is the function of the citizen to keep the Government from falling into error." *American Communications Assn.* v. *Douds*, 339 U.S. 382, 442–43 (1950).

[44] In *Thomas* v. *Collins*, 323 U.S. 516, 531 (1945), the Court said that "the First Amendment gives freedom of mind the same security as freedom of conscience." This view "is today open to doubt." Pfeffer, *Church, State, and Freedom*, 502. See pages 112, 117, and 122.

[1] *Gompers* v. *Buck's Stove and Range Co.*, 221 U.S. 418, 439 (1911).

utterances are no essential part of any exposition of ideas, and are of such slight social value as a step to truth that any benefit that may be derived from them is greatly outweighed by the social interest in order and morality."[2] Justice Holmes himself said: "The most stringent protection of free speech would not protect a man in falsely shouting fire in a theater, and causing a panic. . . . The question in every case is whether the words used are used in such circumstances and are of such a nature as to create a clear and present danger that they will bring about the substantive evils that Congress has a right to prevent."[3]

Such "clear and present danger" does not exist, according to a notable pronouncement by Justice Brandeis, if there is time to avert the impending evil by resort to rational processes. In situations where thorough discussion and intelligent criticism will suffice to forestall the advent of disaster, the drastic measure of suppressing speech is forbidden:

Those who won our independence by revolution were not cowards. They did not fear political change. They did not exalt order at the cost of liberty. To courageous, self-reliant men, with confidence in the power of free and fearless reasoning applied through the processes of popular government, no danger flowing from speech can be deemed clear and present, unless the incidence of the evil apprehended is so imminent that it may befall before there is opportunity for full discussion. If there be time to expose through discussion the falsehood and fallacies, to avert the evil by the processes cf education, the remedy to be applied is more speech, not enforced silence. Only an emergency can justify repression. Such must be the rule if authority is to be recon-

---

[2] *Chaplinsky* v. *New Hampshire,* 315 U.S. 568, 571–72 (1942). Although the defendant was a Jehovah's Witness, he was not engaged in preaching when he denounced the city marshal. "We cannot conceive that cursing a public officer is the exercise of religion in any sense of the term. . . . Argument is unnecessary to demonstrate that the appellations 'damned racketeer' and 'damned Fascist' are epithets likely to provoke the average person to retaliation, and thereby cause a breach of the peace." *Ibid.,* 571, 574. The observation regarding the "slight social value" of this type of utterance is from Chafee, *Freedom of Speech,* 170.

[3] *Schenck* v. *U.S.,* 249 U.S. 47, 52 (1919). In this case the conviction of the defendants was affirmed for obstructing recruiting during World War I by sending circulars to draftees urging resistance to conscription.

ciled with freedom. Such, in my opinion, is the command of the Constitution.

On the same occasion Justice Brandeis amplified the "clear and present danger" test by adding the requirement that the substantive evils themselves must be of grave and serious nature in order to warrant interference with freedoms protected by the First Amendment:

Moreover, even immediate danger cannot justify resort to prohibition of these functions essential to effective democracy, unless the evil apprehended is relatively serious. Prohibition of free speech and assembly is a measure so stringent that it would be inappropriate as the means of averting a relatively trivial harm to society.[4]

In later years the successors of Justices Holmes and Brandeis on the Supreme Court accepted completely and unreservedly the formula originated by those illustrious jurists. "What finally emerges from the 'clear and present danger' cases is a working principle that the substantive evil must be extremely serious and the degree of imminence extremely high before utterance can be punished."[5]

In other words, a restriction upon these valued freedoms can not be justified unless it is unavoidably necessary in order to prevent imminent peril to a public interest of comparable importance. Thus, distribution of religious or political literature on the streets can not be prohibited merely for the sake of keeping them clean and unlittered.[6] Nor can door-to-door canvassing be prohibited by city authorities, for the sake of protecting the repose and privacy of homeowners against intrusion and annoyance.[7] These are regarded as relatively trivial matters in comparison with religious

[4] Concurring opinion in *Whitney* v. *California*, 274 U.S. 357, 377 (1927).
[5] *Bridges* v. *California*, 314 U.S. 252, 262–63 (1941). Another leading case on "clear and present danger" and "preferred position" of First Amendment freedoms is *Thomas* v. *Collins*, 323 U.S. 516, 530 (1945). See notes 43, page 126, and 1, page 127.
[6] *Schneider* v. *Irvington*, 308 U.S. 147, 162–63 (1939).
[7] *Martin* v. *Struthers*, 319 U.S. 141, 418 (1943). See note 34, page 112.

liberty. Moreover, less drastic alternative means are available in those cases for dealing with the evils involved: prosecution of those who drop the pamphlets on the street, "no trespassing" signs on premises where occupants do not wish to be disturbed.

Overthrow of duly constituted government by force and violence (whether through "foreign levy" or "malice domestic") is obviously a "substantive evil," of primordial importance.[8] So is civil commotion, riot, disorder, and breach of the peace. "Civil liberties, as guaranteed by the Constitution, imply the existence of an organized society maintaining public order without which liberty itself would be lost in the excesses of unrestrained abuses."[9]

But when do the mouthings of agitators cease to be harmless froth or doctrinaire lucubrations and create a "clear and present danger" to established institutions? When do they become an "incitement" to riot or revolution? These are problems to which no definite and certain answers can be given. The pragmatic and empirical judgments which courts must formulate when those questions arise are productive of controversial and doubtful doctrines.

To some extent, as Justice Holmes observed, "Every idea is an incitement."[10] But as he also noted, exposure to the air is often the best way to let effervescence evaporate.[11]

The case in which Justice Holmes enunciated the "clear and present danger" test was one under a statute that did not forbid speech as such but merely prohibited certain acts such as obstructing recruiting or causing insubordination or mutiny in the armed forces.[12]

---

[8] *Dennis* v. *U.S.*, 341 U.S. 494, 509 (1951). See also *American Communications Assn.* v. *Douds*, 339 U.S. 382, 396, 401 (1950).

[9] *Cox* v. *New Hampshire*, 312 U.S. 569, 574 (1941).

[10] Dissent in *Gitlow* v. *New York*, 268 U.S. 652, 673 (1925).

[11] In 1920 Holmes ventured the reflection that "with effervescing opinions, as with the not yet forgotten champagnes, the quickest way to let them get flat is to let them get exposed to the air." Harry C. Shriver, *Justice Oliver Wendell Holmes: His Book Notices and Uncollected Letters and Papers*, 137. A favorite quotation by Justice Robert H. Jackson was Woodrow Wilson's statement that if a man is a fool or a rascal the best thing to do is to let him make a speech and demonstrate it publicly. See *Terminiello* v. *Chicago*, 337 U.S. 1, 36 (1949).

[12] Espionage Act of June 15, 1917, 40 Stat. 217; Chafee, *Freedom of Speech*,

In a later decision upholding New York's "criminal anarchy" law, the Court (Justices Holmes and Brandeis dissenting) said that the "clear and present danger" test was not applicable in a case where the legislation prohibited speech as such,[13] but was applicable only when some other type of conduct was forbidden and the defendant's utterances were merely the means of accomplishing the objective condemned by the statute in "non-speech terms."[14] During the "New Deal" period, the Court adopted the Holmes-Brandeis view, and even expanded the "clear and present danger" rule.[15] In a "non-speech" case arising during World War II under the Espionage Act of 1917, the Court ruled that in order to obtain conviction the government must prove "beyond a reasonable doubt" (presumably to the satisfaction of the jury) as an objective element of the offense "a clear and present danger that the activities in question will bring about the substantive evils which Congress has a right to prevent."[16]

Early in the present decade the Supreme Court rendered two decisions which indicated reluctance to apply the Holmes criterion in cases involving the Communist Party.[17] The first of these up-

42–56, 88. The *Abrams* case involved broader provisions of the Act of May 16, 1918, punishing certain types of speech. *Ibid.*, 154–56. In that case Justices Holmes and Brandeis dissented, arguing that the "clear and present danger" test should have been applied. See note 21, page 149.

[13] *Gitlow* v. *New York*, 286 U.S. 652, 667–78, 671–72 (1925). Holmes and Brandeis dissented. *Ibid.*, 672–73. This was the first case in which the Supreme Court assumed that any part of the Bill of Rights was applicable against the states. *Ibid.*, 666. The casual language to the contrary in *Prudential Insurance Co.* v. *Cheek*, 259 U.S. 530, 543 (1922), was regarded as not determinative of the question. See page 133.

[14] This expression is used in the analysis of the *Gitlow* case in *Dennis* v. *U.S.*, 341 U.S. 494, 505–506 (1951).

[15] *Ibid.*, 507, 541, 556–61. See note 5, page 117. As Justice Frankfurter said, concurring in *Kovacs* v. *Cooper*, 336 U.S. 77, 95 (1949): "The ideas now governing the constitutional protection of freedom of speech derive essentially from the opinions of Mr. Justice Holmes."

[16] *Hartzel* v. *U.S.*, 322 U.S. 680, 687 (1944).

[17] *Dennis* v. *U.S.*, 341 U.S. 494, 505, 510 (1951); *American Communications Assn.* v. *Douds*, 339 U.S. 382, 394 (1950). Justice Frankfurter had previously protested against use of the phrase as a dogmatic formula in lieu of critical analysis. *Pennekamp* v. *Florida*, 328 U.S. 331, 352–53 (1946); *West*

held the requirement of non-Communist affidavits from union officers, and has been previously discussed under the due process clause of the Fifth Amendment.[18] The differences between the Communist Party and the normal variety of political parties in the United States were elaborated at length, particularly by Justice Jackson in his concurring opinion. With regard to the "clear and present danger" criterion, the Court emphasized that it was not a "mechanical test" and that the statute involved did not endeavor to protect the public against the consequences (either present or remote) of the affiant's beliefs, but against "political strikes" and that to identify the type of persons who should be excluded from union office it was appropriate to determine their political affiliations and beliefs, although those matters are usually irrelevant criteria for government action.[19] For example, it would surely be proper to ascertain whether applicants for positions as secret service operatives guarding the president were anarchists who believed in assassination of all heads of state.[20] The Court concluded that the First Amendment "requires that one be permitted to believe what he will. . . . It does not require that he be permitted to be keeper of the arsenal."[21]

The other Communist case which weakened the sway of the "clear and present danger" test was the turbulent, nine-month trial of the leading New York Communists for violation of the Smith Act.[22] At the conclusion of this spectacle the trial judge was promoted to the Court of Appeals by President Truman, and

---

Virginia State Bd. of Educ. v. *Barnette,* 319 U.S. 624, 663 (1943); *Bridges* v. *California,* 314 U.S. 252, 295-96 (1941). See also *Craig* v. *Harney,* 331 U.S. 367, 389 (1947).

[18] See text at notes 29–31, page 96.

[19] 339 U.S. at 394, 396, 398.

[20] *Ibid.,* 408–409. A similar situation would be presented if an appointee to the Interstate Commerce Commission were to claim that the First Amendment justified his refusal to state his political affiliation: the law prohibits the appointment of more than six of the eleven Commissioners from the same political party.

[21] *Ibid.,* 412. See note 34, page 87.

[22] *Dennis* v. *U.S.,* 341 U.S. 494, 503–10 (1951). The act is 54 Stat. 670.

the defense attorneys sentenced for contempt of court.[23] The proof showed the formation of a disciplined party organization which systematically taught revolutionary doctrines as formulated in standard Communist textbooks. Apparently there was no immediate attempt to overthrow existing government in the United States, but the organization was to be in readiness to act at once to seize power whenever circumstances should become favorable. Meanwhile relations were maintained with Communists in other countries, especially Russia. The jury found that the defendants advocated seizure of power by force and violence as soon as practicable; this was a plan or program of future action, not an academic or philosophical exposition of Marxist views.[24]

How did these facts fit the pattern of "clear and present danger"? The important consideration was that the conspiracy constituted a continuing and substantial threat endangering the government, although there was no immediate likelihood of success. Five different opinions were rendered by members of the Court, six of whom joined in upholding the conviction of the defendants. Four of the six adhered to the "clear and present danger" rule as formulated by Judge Learned Hand in the court below. Under this standard the question is "whether the gravity of the 'evil,' discounted by its improbability, justifies such invasion of free speech as is necessary to avoid the danger."[25] Applying the test as so interpreted, they believed that sufficient danger existed as a result of the continuing conspiracy.[26] The majority of the Court also decided that application of the test was a matter for the judge, not the jury, to determine: "Whether the First Amendment protects the activities which constitute the violation of the statute must depend upon a judicial determination of the scope of the First Amendment applied to the circumstances of the case."[27] Two

[23] *Sacher* v. *U.S.*, 343 U.S. 1 (1952). The record covered 13,000 pages. Besides constant turmoil in the courtroom, Communists picketed the courthouse.
[24] 341 U.S. at 496, 498, 546–47, 564–67.
[25] *Ibid.*, 510. This formula does not require the government to await the successful consummation of the conspiracy before taking action against it.
[26] *Ibid.*, 511.
[27] *Ibid.*, 513. Cf. note 16, page 119.

of the six Justices did not believe that the "clear and present danger" rule should be applied in this type of case.[28] Two dissenting Justices believed that the rule should have been applied in this case and that doing so would have prevented conviction of these defendants.[29]

It seems an exaggeration to say, as one commentator does, that the "clear and present danger" standard is now bereft of significance in political cases.[30] Its essential features have been preserved, but adapted to the peculiar fact-situation presented by the menace of current Communist enterprise. In its new form the rule might be called the "electric eye" theory of clear and present danger. The danger is deemed to exist if there is a present and continuing mechanism which upon the occurrence of appropriate conditions will trigger into activity a future operation which constitutes a danger of substantial magnitude.

The same commentator who regards the "clear and present danger" test as moribund in political cases continues: "But it still possesses vitality in religious freedom cases. It is perhaps not without significance that on the same day the Supreme Court sustained a conviction against a young radical who in a street speech used derogatory language against the President and the American Le-

[28] Justice Frankfurter said: "To make validity of legislation depend on a judicial reading of events still in the womb of time—a forecast, that is, of the outcome of forces at best appreciated only with knowledge of the topmost secrets of nations—is to charge the judiciary with duties beyond its equipment." *Ibid.*, 550. Justice Jackson believed that to apply the test would be "to hold our Government captive in a judge-made verbal trap" as well as to require the Court to "appraise imponderables." *Ibid.*, 567–70. He would deal with the problem under the law of conspiracy. "The Constitution does not make conspiracy a civil right. . . . It is not to be supposed that the power of Congress to protect the nation's existence is more limited than its power to protect interstate commerce." *Ibid.*, 572, 574.

[29] Justice Black said that the *Dennis* decision "jettisons" the "clear and present danger" test and sanctions prior restraint on future utterance. *Ibid.*, 579–80. Justice Douglas emphasized that doctrines such as the defendants preached might have constituted a real danger during the depression when bread-lines existed, but did not under the circumstances under which defendants propagated them. *Ibid.*, 588. He also contended that the jury should apply the test, not the court. *Ibid.*, 587.

[30] Pfeffer, *Church, State, and Freedom*, 502.

gion, it reversed a conviction against a fiery Baptist street mission-
ary who used far more inflammatory language against the Catholic
Church."[31] Perhaps a better-grounded explanation for the difference in results reached in these two cases is that the one simply
involved a charge of "disorderly conduct" whereas the other dealt
with an ordinance requiring that a permit to speak be obtained
in advance. Prior restraint or censorship in advance has since
before Blackstone's time been regarded as a serious and unlawful
interference with freedom of speech.[32] An enactment of that sort,
unless it prescribes strict standards which prevent the official who
issues the permits from granting or denying them because he
favors or disfavors the contents of the speeches to be made, is
likely to be held void "on its face." But a licensing system which
regulates merely time, place, and manner of speaking (with no
possible control over the content) in a reasonable and nondis-
criminatory fashion having regard to public convenience will be
upheld as valid.[33] The same principle applies with regard to regulation of loudspeakers whose unrestricted use would render life
unbearable.[34] All media of communication, including moving pic-

[31] *Ibid.*, 502. The cases referred to are *Feiner* v. *New York*, 340 U.S. 315,
320–21 (1951), and *Kunz* v. *New York*, 340 U.S. 290, 293, 295 (1951).
Another companion case decided the same day was *Niemotko* v. *Maryland*, 340
U.S. 268, 271 (1951), where a requirement of prior license to speak in a park
was held invalid because no definite standards limited the discretionary power
to grant or deny the permit.

[32] *Patterson* v. *Colorado*, 205 U.S. 454, 462 (1907); Blackstone, *Commentaries*, IV, *151–52; Chafee, *Freedom of Speech*, 8–12.

[33] *Cox* v. *New Hampshire*, 312 U.S. 569, 575–76 (1941); *Poulos* v. *New
Hampshire*, 345 U.S. 395, 403–408 (1953). The latter case also held that wrong-
ful denial of a license was no defense to prosecution for speaking without a
license. *Ibid.*, 409. In Justice Jackson's view regulation of public address systems
is purely a question of time, place, and manner rather than censorship of contents.
See note 6, page 128.

[34] Thus in *Saia* v. *New York*, 334 U.S. 558, 559–60 (1948), an ordinance
which gave a chief of police power to grant or deny permits for the use of
sound trucks (without prescribing standards appropriately related to time, place,
and loudness) was held void because "it establishes a prior restraint on the right
of free speech." The ordinance upheld in *Kovacs* v. *Cooper*, 336 U.S. 77, 82
(1949), did not involve such a prior restraint. See also note 6, page 128.

tures,[35] radio and television,[36] are entitled to the protection which the First Amendment accords to freedom of speech.

The Baptist who proclaimed that Catholicism was "a religion of the devil" and that Jews were "Christ-killers" and "garbage" that "should have been burned in the incinerators" was speaking without a permit.[37] A previous permit had been revoked because of complaints about his attacks on other religions. There was no evidence of any disorder or likelihood of violence on the particular occasion when defendant was arrested for speaking without a permit. The Court held that the ordinance which defendant was charged with violating created a prior restraint without specifying adequate standards to control the discretion of the officer issuing the permits.[38]

The youth who said "President Truman is a bum,"[39] was not

[35] *Burstyn* v. *Wilson*, 343 U.S. 495, 501–502 (1952).

[36] *N.B.C.* v. *U.S.*, 319 U.S. 190, 226–27 (1943). As only a limited number of radio and television channels are available, regulation in the public interest is permissible, provided it is not discriminatory, arbitrary, or capricious.

[37] 340 U.S. at 296. Justice Jackson, with memories of the war crimes trials at Nürnberg, recognized that "Jews, many of whose families perished in extermination furnaces of Dachau and Auschwitz, are more than tolerant if they pass off lightly the suggestion that unbelievers in Christ should all have been burned. Of course, people might pass this speaker by as a mental case, and so they might file out of a theatre in good order at the cry of 'fire.' But in both cases there is a genuine likelihood that someone will get hurt." *Ibid.*, 299. "It would be interesting if the Court would expose its reasons for thinking that Kunz's words are of more social value than those of Chaplinsky." *Ibid.*, 303; see note 2, page 116.

[38] 340 U.S. at 293, 295. In the *Niemotko* case the same situation existed. Justice Jackson regarded this holding as "hypocritical," since the Court itself had established no standards for the guidance of local legislators. Even the regulations for maintaining decorum in the Supreme Court building display an "exalted artistry" in the use of vague language. *Ibid.*, 309. Similarly the loudspeaker ordinance held void in *Saia* v. *New York*, 334 U.S. 558, 559–60 (1948), established "previous restraint on the right of free speech"; while the one upheld in *Kovacs* v. *Cooper*, 336 U.S. 77, 82 (1949), did not.

[39] He also said "The American Legion is a Nazi Gestapo" and that "colored people don't have equal rights and ought to rise up in arms and fight for them." The testimony was not clear that he used the expression "in arms," which gave color to the Court's view that his language was an "incitement to riot." A man accompanied by his wife and children told the officers "that if they did not take that 'S.O.B.' off the box he would." Thereupon the police arrested the speaker, rather than protecting him from his heckler. 340 U.S. at 324, 330.

charged with violation of an ordinance requiring him to obtain a permit in advance. He had been permitted to continue speaking for a considerable time. The police officers at the scene were at first merely concerned with obstruction to traffic. They interrupted the speaker only after threats of violence against him had been made by a listener. The basis of his conviction was "incitement to riot" and refusal to obey the commands of the policemen when they finally ordered him to quit speaking.

In theory, therefore, this case falls within the category of "fighting words" or incitement to a breach of the peace. In such cases, as Justice Jackson has observed, considerable latitude should be given to the local law enforcement agencies.[40] Just as in the case of Communists plotting overthrow of the government the government need not stand idle until the conspiracy is crowned with success, so in a case of incitement to riot the police need not withhold action until an outbreak of violence actually occurs and people are killed or injured.

Nevertheless it is difficult to avoid agreeing with the dissenting Justices that as a practical matter there was no need to interfere with the Syracuse youth's speech. For the most part he was simply urging the crowd to attend a meeting held in a nearby hotel, where O. John Rogge, a former assistant attorney general of the United States, was to deliver an address on civil liberties. The irate listener who profanely threatened to silence the speaker if the police did not was accompanied by his wife and children. If their presence did not dissuade him from violence, the police officers could readily have arrested him rather than the speaker. In short, it does not seem as if the police in this instance did all they could have done to protect free speech without permitting an outbreak of violence.[41]

[40] See note 2, page 116. *Terminiello* v. *Chicago*, 337 U.S. 1, 33–34 (1949). Justice Jackson places a high value on prevention of disorder or breach of the peace. If necessary for this purpose, he favors permitting the police to ask the speaker to desist, though this "is like dynamiting a house to stop the spread of a conflagration." *Kunz* v. *New York*, 340 U.S. 290, 301 (1951).

[41] Compare the action of the New York City police described in Chafee, *Free Speech in the United States*, 156–57, 425.

A case where the rule of "fighting words" provoking a breach of the peace might have been more plausibly applied had occurred two years before in Chicago when an associate of Gerald L. K. Smith required a police escort in order to enter and leave the hall through the midst of cursing crowds outside. Rocks were thrown and windows broken. The doors had to be locked and were in danger of succumbing to the repeated assaults against them. The speech was inflammatory, and insultingly referred to Mrs. Eleanor Roosevelt and other public figures. Without police protection the meeting could not have been held at all. The Illinois courts tried the case as one involving the "fighting words" principle. The majority of the Supreme Court, however, seized upon a sentence in the trial court's charge permitting conviction if defendant's speech "invites dispute" or "causes a condition of unrest." This was held violative of the First Amendment, the Court pointing out that "the function of free speech under our system of government is to invite dispute" and that "speech is often provocative and challenging."[42]

Chicago's racial tension furnished the background for a later dispute in which the Supreme Court relied upon that part of the "fighting words" rule which excludes "libelous" utterances from the protection of the First Amendment. The defendant was prosecuted under a so-called "group libel" statute for distributing a circular, couched in the form of a petition to the mayor and council to protect white neighborhoods against encroachment, but which also contained an appeal to join and contribute financially to defendant's organization for the advancement of white people. Holding that libel was not constitutionally protected speech, the Court concluded that it was unnecessary to consider the "clear and present danger" rule.[43] Four Justices dissented.

[42] *Terminiello* v. *Chicago*, 337 U.S. 1, 4–5 (1949). Justice Jackson in his dissenting opinion, after a dramatic recital of the facts, exclaimed: "There is danger that, if the Court does not temper its doctrinaire logic with a little practical wisdom, it will convert the constitutional Bill of Rights into a suicide pact." *Ibid.*, 14–16, 37.

[43] *Beauharnais* v. *Illinois*, 343 U.S. 250, 266 (1952). Justice Jackson, dissenting, thought that this was the type of case where the rule did apply. Cf. note

The Doctrine of "Preferred Position"

Somewhat akin to the "clear and present danger" standard is the doctrine that First Amendment freedoms have a "preferred position" in the hierarchy of constitutional values.[1] According to Justice Frankfurter, who repudiates it, "This is a phrase that has uncritically crept into some recent opinions of this court. I deem it a mischievous phrase, if it carries the thought, which it may subtly imply, that any law touching communication is infected with presumptive invalidity."[2] The term originated with Chief Justice Harlan F. Stone,[3] and did not, as he used it, imply that

28, page 122. Moreover he believed that the due process concept of "ordered liberty" required that a statute punishing libel must admit truth as a defense. *Ibid.*, 299. Justice Black contended that the right of petition was being denied, and that the majority opinion "degrades First Amendment freedoms to the 'rational basis' level." *Ibid.*, 268–69. He declared that "The majority is giving libel a more expansive scope and more respectable status than it was accorded even in the Star Chamber." *Ibid.*, 273. Justice Reed emphasized that the statute curtailed the traditional function of the jury in libel cases. *Ibid.*, 278. Justice Douglas reaffirmed his adherence to the "preferred position" doctrine. *Ibid.*, 285. See note 2, below.

[1] Besides Justice Frankfurter, Justice Jackson has also spoken critically of the "preferred position" concept: "When this Court recently has promulgated a philosophy that some rights derived from the Constitution are entitled to a 'preferred position,' . . . I have not agreed. We cannot give some constitutional rights a preferred position without relegating others to a deferred position; we can establish no firsts without thereby establishing seconds. Indications are not wanting that Fourth Amendment freedoms are tacitly marked as secondary rights, to be relegated to a deferred position." *Brinegar* v. *U.S.*, 338 U.S. 160, 180 (1949).

[2] *Kovacs* v. *Cooper*, 336 U.S. 77, 90–96 (1949). Justice Frankfurter's dissertation on "preferred position" is comparable to his similar exposition on "clear and present danger" in *Dennis* v. *U.S.*, 341 U.S. 494, 527–46 (1951). For cases previously mentioned where the notion of "preferred position" was accepted by various members of the Court, see notes 40, page 114; 5, page 117; and 43, above.

[3] The thought was first put forward in a footnote in *U.S.* v. *Carolene Products Co.*, 304 U.S. 144, 152 (1938); the expression itself appeared in *Jones* v. *Opelika*, 316 U.S. 584, 608 (1942). Thereafter it was employed in various cases, which are reviewed by Justice Frankfurter in his discussion. Justice Frankfurter at one time accepted the notion, for which Justice Stone found a basis in language used by Chief Justice John Marshall. Mason, "The Core of Free Government, 1938–40: Mr. Justice Stone and 'Preferred Freedoms,' " *Yale Law Journal*, Vol. LXV, No. 5 (April, 1956), 600, 615.

all "legislation touching matters related to liberties protected by the Bill of Rights" was presumably unconstitutional, but merely indicated that such legislation should be "subjected to more exacting judicial scrutiny" since there is a narrower scope for the operation of the presumption of constitutionality under those circumstances.[4] Justice Frankfurter concedes that there is a valid idea behind the notion of "preferred position": the thinking of Justice Holmes is the source of current opinions on freedom of speech, and "for him the right to search for truth was of a different order than some transient economic dogma. . . . Accordingly, Mr. Justice Holmes was far more ready [and so, presumably, the Court today should be] to find legislative invasion where free inquiry was involved than in the debatable area of economics."[5] Nevertheless the current catchword embodying this notion should be eschewed. "The objection to summarizing this line of thought by the phrase 'the preferred position of freedom of speech' is that it expresses a complicated process of constitutional adjudication by a deceptive formula."[6]

[4] In other words, the whole question is a matter of degree. Under ordinary due process standards, a statute is sustained if it employs rationally relevant means to effect a proper governmental purpose. See note 6, page 91. The legislative judgment is normally supported by a presumption of constitutionality. But this "rational basis" level (see note 43, page 127) is not enough in a First Amendment case; for how can there be a presumption that legislation is constitutional which on its face conflicts with the Constitution (to wit, the First Amendment)? Something more is needed. How much? That seems to be the difference between Justice Frankfurter's view and that of the Justices who accept the "preferred position" formula.

[5] 336 U.S. at 95. Cf. Chafee, *Free Speech in the United States*, 359–61.

[6] 336 U.S. at 96. In the case which evoked this discussion, regarding regulation of loud-speakers, Justice Frankfurter finds that the "mechanical" formula of "preferred position" causes its adherents to overlook the difference between freedom of speech by means of the human voice and by means of mechanical apparatus. *Ibid.*, 96. Justice Jackson even finds no question of freedom of speech at all in a case involving use of sound equipment which if unregulated would make life intolerable: "No . . . infringement of freedom of speech arises until such regulation or prohibition undertakes to censor the contents of the broadcasting," as distinguished from the apparatus used. *Ibid.*, 97. See also *Saia* v. *New York*, 334 U.S. 558, 567–68 (1948). Dissenting in that case, Justice Jackson feared that the decision prohibiting regulation of sound trucks would "endanger the great right of free speech by making it ridiculous and obnoxious." *Ibid.*, 566.

Yet inevitably some symbol must be employed to mark the effect which must be given to the Bill of Rights. If the Bill of Rights has any legal value at all, the status of a law which conflicts with a specific constitutional prohibition must be different in some respect from one which is enacted without violating such a prohibition.

If both statutes are treated identically (as by the "rational basis" standard) in order to determine their constitutionality, no effect whatever is being given to the Bill of Rights. This is obviously an untenable procedure. In some fashion the Court must give recognition to the solemn prohibitions contained in the Constitution. To say that a statute relating to a matter concerning which Congress clearly has no power to legislate at all shall be accorded the same presumption of constitutionality as a statute relating to a matter clearly falling within the enumerated powers conferred upon Congress is an irrational mode of interpretation which the Court could not possibly accept without doing violence to basic principles of popular government "implicit in the concept of ordered liberty."

If the "preferred position" doctrine, or the "clear and present danger" test are not deemed to be satisfactory formulations of the fundamental concept that the commands of the Bill of Rights must be given legal effect, perhaps the thought could be expressed by saying that when laws are enacted which infringe upon freedoms protected by the Bill of Rights[7] they are valid only if they represent a necessary (not merely a proper or rationally relevant) means of attaining a legitimate and important governmental purpose, comparable in significance with the precious interests protected by the Bill of Rights.

A little-known feature of the "preferred position" doctrine is that it did not originate with Justice Black and the "activist" wing

---

[7] The "preferred position" doctrine is usually invoked in connection with First Amendment freedoms. That is because the First Amendment contains an explicit denial of congressional power. But the privileges conferred by other provisions in the Bill of Rights can also be construed as negating the exercise of legislative power by Congress, and hence as protected by the "preferred position" doctrine.

of the Court who have most ardently espoused it. One of the earliest statements of the doctrine was made by Justice Owen J. Roberts.[8] A still earlier adumbration of the doctrine was voiced by Justice George Sutherland and other conservative dissenters who believed that labor laws restricting the right to discharge for union activity should not be applicable to editorial employees of the Associated Press because freedom of speech should be "put in a category apart."[9]

Labor strife has given rise to one curious aspect of freedom of speech. The Court has held that "picketing" constitutes a mode of publishing information concerning labor disputes and hence is constitutionally protected as an exercise of the right to freedom of speech.[10] The applicability of this notion has been limited by recognition of the qualification that violence or other unlawful conduct is not protected merely because "speech" is an integral part of such conduct.[11] An employer's freedom of speech is likewise restricted if it amounts to "coercion" of employees, interfering with their free choice of collective bargaining representatives, or constitutes an "unfair labor practice."[12]

Likewise a "company town," whether privately-owned[13] or

[8] "In every case, therefore, where legislative abridgment of the rights is asserted, the courts should be astute to examine the effect of the challenged legislation. Mere legislative preferences or beliefs respecting matters of public convenience may well support regulation directed at other personal activities, but be insufficient to justify such as diminishes the exercise of rights so vital to the maintenance of democratic institutions." *Schneider* v. *Irvington*, 308 U.S. 147, 161 (1939).

[9] *Associated Press* v. *N.L.R.B.*, 301 U.S. 103, 135 (1937). Justices Vandevanter, McReynolds, and Butler joined in this dissent. Similarly, the antitrust laws may be enforced against newspaper interests without violation of freedom of the press. *Associated Press* v. *U.S.*, 326 U.S. 1, 7 (1945); *Lorain Journal* v. *U.S.*, 342 U.S. 143, 155–56 (1951). Newspapers are not exempt from burdens of citizenship in general, which do not restrict freedom as to the contents of the publications or establish censorship thereof.

[10] *Thornhill* v. *Alabama*, 310 U.S. 88, 102 (1940): "In the circumstances of our times the dissemination of information concerning the facts of a labor dispute must be regarded as within the area of free discussion that is guaranteed by the Constitution."

[11] *Giboney* v. *Empire Storage & Ice Co.*, 336 U.S. 490, 498, 502 (1949).
[12] *N.L.R.B.* v. *Va. Electric & Power Co.*, 314 U.S. 469, 477 (1941).

government-owned,[14] will be treated as if it were an ordinary community like other localities when the validity of restrictions upon door-to-door solicitation is under consideration. The fact that legal title to streets and other public places is vested in a single owner does not prevent their being treated as a suitable place for constitutionally protected discussion. Parks and streets are recognized as being traditionally appropriate for that purpose; though apparently, if adequate and suitable facilities for speaking are provided in one part of a park system, the public authorities may prohibit speaking in other parks and set them aside for recreation, meditation, and restful enjoyment, free from noisy interruptions and turmoil.[15]

Possibly because of historical reasons, rooted in popular usage and custom, parks and streets are treated as falling within an entirely different category from public buildings when it comes to their use for purposes of religious exhortation.[16] This paradox was strikingly exhibited by Justice Jackson, dissenting in the case where the majority of the Court refused to permit public regulation of loud-speakers operated by Jehovah's Witnesses in a park used for family picnicking and recreation: "I cannot see how we can read the Constitution one day to forbid and the next day to compel use of public tax-supported property to help a religious sect spread its faith."[17] In the case of the Baptist who denounced

[13] *Marsh* v. *Alabama*, 326 U.S. 501, 505 (1946).
[14] *Tucker* v. *Texas*, 326 U.S. 517, 519 (1946).
[15] *Poulos* v. *New Hampshire*, 345 U.S. 395, 399 (1953).
[16] Perhaps the English custom of permitting all sorts of discussion in Hyde Park has made such places of congregation seem to serve as a suitable forum for exercise of free speech. Public buildings, on the other hand, usually are constructed for the specific purpose of transacting a particular type of public business. See Chafee, *Free Speech in the United States*, 417–22; *Hague* v. *C. I. O.*, 307 U.S. 496, 515 (1939).
[17] *Saia* v. *New York*, 334 U.S. 558, 570 (1948). Justice Jackson was referring to the *McCollum* case, see text at note 19, page 108. Of the *Saia* case Corwin, *A Constitution of Powers in a Secular State*, 95–96, says: "The proposition for which the case seems to stand is that when a municipality establishes a public park it thereby renders the park a potential forum for any blatherskite politician or whirling dervish who wishes to peddle his doctrinal wares over a public address system, and that a park for quiet use, to serve the amenities of civilized living, is unconstitutional."

Roman Catholics and Jews, Justice Jackson said: "Do we so quickly forget that one of the chief reasons for prohibiting use of 'released time' of school students for religious instruction was that the Constitution will not suffer tax-supported property to be used to propagate religion? How can the Court now order use of tax-supported property for the purpose? In other words, can the First Amendment today mean a city cannot stop what yesterday it meant no city could allow?"[18]

Application of the Bill of Rights against the States

In concluding discussion of the various kinds of "freedom" guaranteed by the First Amendment, it remains to inquire whether there is any difference between such "freedom" and the "liberty" which is protected by the "due process of law" provisions of the Fifth and Fourteenth Amendments.

The Bill of Rights was enacted solely in order to limit the powers of the federal government. Madison had desired to include a provision prohibiting infringement by the states of certain basic rights (jury trial, freedom of religion, speech, and press), but this proposal was rejected in the Senate.[1] The ten amendments which went into force in 1791 did not bind the states. This was expressly decided by the Supreme Court in 1833, in an opinion written by Chief Justice Marshall.[2] The correctness of this

[18] *Kunz* v. *New York*, 340 U.S. 290, 311 (1951). See note 37, page 124. Justice Jackson also pointed out that a speaker in a place where other people are lawfully going about their own business is intruding himself upon a "captive audience." *Ibid.*, 298. But in *P.U.C.* v. *Pollak*, 343 U.S. 451, 463 (1952), the Court held that the captive audience riding Capital Transit vehicles in Washington were not entitled to "freedom from speech" inflicted upon them by broadcasts arranged for by the company through a local radio station. Justice Frankfurter, apparently the only member of the Court patronizing that plebeian mode of transportation, acknowledged that he was himself a victim of the company's practice and hence he could not trust himself sufficiently to decide the issue with impartiality if he participated in the case. He therefore abstained. *Ibid.*, 467.

[1] See pages 37, 41, 46. The Pennsylvania minority also sought protection against state action. See page 12.

view is shown by the fact that in several New England states (as in Massachusetts until 1833) an established church was maintained long after the First Amendment went into force.[3] This would have been impossible if the prohibition against "an establishment of religion" had been binding upon the states.

Was the situation changed by the adoption of the Fourteenth Amendment? The phrase "due process of law" in that amendment, addressed to the states, should have the same meaning as in the Fifth Amendment addressed to the federal government. The Fifth Amendment should not be considered as repetitious and covering the same ground as the First Amendment. If the "due process" clause embodies the subject matter of the other articles in the Bill of Rights, those other specific guarantees would be rendered superfluous.[4]

Indeed as late as 1922, the Supreme Court took the view that the Fourteenth Amendment did not make the First binding on the states. In 1925, however, it ventured the tentative assumption that the "freedom" of speech protected by the First Amendment was included in the "liberty" which the Fourteenth Amendment required the states to respect.[5] Thus began what Charles Warren called "the new liberty."

As time went on, every aspect of First Amendment freedoms was made available against the states under this "incorporationist"

[2] *Barron* v. *Baltimore*, 7 Pet. 243, 247 (1833). See also *Permoli* v. *Municipality of New Orleans*, 3 How. 589, 609 (1845).

[3] Dumbauld, *The Declaration of Independence and What It Means Today*, 62.

[4] *Ibid.* See also Roberts, *The Court and the Constitution*, 74–77; *Adamson* v. *California*, 332 U.S. 46, 66 (1947); *Twining* v. *New Jersey*, 211 U.S. 78, 107 (1908).

[5] *Prudential Insurance Co.* v. *Cheek*, 259 U.S. 530, 543 (1922); *Gitlow* v. *New York*, 286 U.S. 652, 666 (1925). Justice Holmes participated in both cases. See note 13, page 119. Since the "new liberty" originated under the "old court" (see notes 8, page 130, and 9, page 130), it may have been intended as a harmless gesture of impartiality at a time when "freedom of contract" was being magnified as a protection to "big business" interests. See notes 15, page 65, and 4, page 77. Chafee regards the "new liberty" as a "sharp sword with which to defend the ideals of Jefferson and Madison against local intolerance." Chafee, *Free Speech in the United States*, 325.

133

philosophy. Religion,[6] speech,[7] press,[8] assembly,[9] and petition[10] were all given protection against state action violative of the First Amendment.

Possibly in view of the trend toward incorporationism, every lawyer having a client sufficiently "rich and scared,"[11] would be justified in seeking to bring before the Supreme Court any action by a state which infringes the language of the Bill of Rights. However, a long series of cases has enumerated many provisions of the Bill of Rights which according to past decisions of the Court are not applicable against the states.

Thus, the Second Amendment, regarding the right to bear arms, does not bind the states.[12] No case can be found under the Third Amendment (relating to quartering troops), an obsolete provision which has apparently given rise to no litigation of any sort.[13]

The Fourth Amendment (unreasonable searches and seizures) does not apply to state action.[14] The same is true of those provisions of the Fifth Amendment which deal with the requirement of grand jury indictment,[15] double jeopardy,[16] and self-incrimination.[17] The "due process" clause is of course made effective against the states by the direct terms of the Fourteenth Amendment, and not by the incorporation method. The "just compensation clause"

[6] *Cantwell* v. *Connecticut*, 310 U.S. 296, 303 (1940).

[7] Freedom of speech was involved in the *Gitlow* case, where the doctrine of "incorporationism" first appeared. A recent leading case is *W. Va. State Bd. of Educ.* v. *Barnette*, 319 U.S. 624, 633 (1943). See note 39, page 113.

[8] *Near* v. *Minnesota*, 283 U.S. 697, 707 (1931).

[9] *De Jonge* v. *Oregon*, 299 U.S. 353, 364 (1937).

[10] *Bridges* v. *California*, 314 U.S. 252, 277 (1941). See also *Beauharnais* v. *Illinois*, 343 U.S. 250, 268 (1952).

[11] These qualities in a client were particularly prized, according to report, by a former president of the American Bar Association, Frank J. Hogan of Washington, D. C.

[12] *Presser* v. *Illinois*, 116 U.S. 252, 265 (1886).

[13] See pages 60–61.

[14] *Weeks* v. *U.S.*, 232 U.S. 383, 398 (1914). But cf. pages 74–75.

[15] *Hurtado* v. *California*, 110 U.S. 516, 538 (1884).

[16] *Palko* v. *Connecticut*, 302 U.S. 319, 326 (1937).

[17] *Twining* v. *New Jersey*, 211 U.S. 78, 102 (1908); *Adamson* v. *California*, 332 U.S. 46, 52–54 (1947).

does bind the states, according to the most recent Supreme Court decision on the subject.[18] But that decision was based on a direct interpretation of the Fourteenth Amendment in the light of "natural law" concepts of inherent and immutable principles of justice rather than upon the notion that the Fifth Amendment had become applicable to the states.[19]

At this point it will be helpful to explain the difference between the two schools of "incorporationists" on the Court. The "whole hog" theory, held by Justices Black and Douglas, maintains that all the prohibitions contained in the Bill of Rights are literally obligatory upon the states. This theory at least has the merit of being clear, simple, and direct.[20]

The "ordered liberty" theory, of which Justice Frankfurter is perhaps the chief expounder, rests upon the principle that the Fourteenth Amendment does not incorporate by reference the Bill of Rights *in toto*, but that by direct operation of the Fourteenth Amendment's due process requirements any state action is stricken down which does not measure up to the basic principles of justice and fair play which lie at the foundation of a free society and are "implicit in the concept of ordered liberty."[21]

[18] *C.B.&Q.R.R. Co.* v. *Chicago*, 166 U.S. 226, 241 (1897). A contrary earlier holding in *Davidson* v. *New Orleans*, 96 U.S. 97, 105 (1877) is supported by the legislative history of the Fourteenth Amendment, whose framers deliberately excluded the "just compensation" provision of the Fifth. 332 U.S. at 80. See also Roberts, *The Court and the Constitution*, 73.

[19] In Justice Frankfurter's phrase, the Fourteenth Amendment's "independent potency" operates to compel observance by the states of the same standard of behavior which the Bill of Rights would require if applicable. 332 U.S. at 66. See Heller, *The Sixth Amendment*, 124.

[20] Justice Black first expounded this theory of incorporation in *Adamson* v. *California*, 332 U.S. 46, 71–72, 75 (1947). It has never been accepted by the Court. Its unsoundness, as a matter of historical intention on the part of the framers of the Fourteenth Amendment, has been demonstrated by Professor Charles Fairman's careful examination of the evidence. See Roberts, *The Court and the Constitution*, 74, and note 21, below.

[21] This phrase, from Justice Cardozo's opinion in *Palko* v. *Connecticut*, 302 U.S. 319, 323, 325 (1937), sums up a principle laid down earlier in *Twining* v. *New Jersey*, 211 U.S. 78, 101–102 (1908). See also *Hebert* v. *Louisiana*, 272 U.S. 312, 316 (1926). The "ordered liberty" theory is akin to the natural law notions expressed in cases such as *Loan Association* v. *Topeka*, 29 Wall. 655, 663 (1874).

It thus becomes necessary for the Court to determine, when-ever any particular right enumerated in the Bill of Rights is claimed as constitutionally protected against state infringement, whether that right is sufficiently basic and important to be "of the very essence of a scheme of ordered liberty." This means that the Court must, in substance, to use the phrase of Justice Jackson, determine whether the state's action shocks the Court's conscience profoundly or only slightly.[22] It is difficult to deny Justice Black's charge that the Court is forced to render what are essentially "natural law" judgments declaring whether or not the right claimed is one the denial of which would be intolerably unjust.[23]

In his dissent in the Illinois group libel case,[24] Justice Jackson applied the "ordered liberty" theory, and drew a distinction be-tween "liberty" in the Fourteenth Amendment and "freedom" in the First.[25] He concluded that the requirements of "ordered liberty" included the principle that truth is a defense in a criminal libel prosecution.[26] That principle indeed looms large in the stir-ring history of English and American liberty.[27]

Unquestionably notice and hearing are fundamental requisites of fairness in exercising a state's jurisdiction.[28] But trial by a jury

[22] See notes 12 and 13, pages 74 and 75. The stomach-pump case shocked the Court's conscience so profoundly that it deviated from its rule of traditional deference to state power over judicial procedure in state courts.

[23] *Adamson* v. *California*, 332 U.S. 46, 70, 75, 90 (1947).

[24] See note 43, page 127.

[25] 343 U.S. at 288. Rejecting Justice Black's incorporationist theory, he ac-cepted the dissenting opinion in the *Gitlow* case and the *Palko* rule as the stand-ards to be followed. *Ibid.*, 294–95. Corwin, *A Constitution of Powers in a Secular State*, 113–14, argues that the Fourteenth Amendment protects only "liberty." States can establish religions, he asserts, "provided they do not deprive anybody of religious liberty." Corwin concedes that his contention conflicts with what was said in *Cantwell* v. *Connecticut*, 310 U.S. 296, 303 (1940). Obviously his argument ignores the dual aspect of religious liberty, which includes not only the right to worship without molestation by the state, but also the right to be free from taxation for the support of a religion established by the state. See note 27, page 111.

[26] 343 U.S. at 299.

[27] See Chafee, *Freedom of Speech*, 23–25; Chafee, *Free Speech in the United States*, 499–505; Stryker, *For the Defense*, 119–36, 152–60.

[28] *Twining* v. *New Jersey*, 211 U.S. 78, 110–111 (1908).

of twelve, as at common law, and as required by the Sixth Amendment, is not: a state may authorize trial and conviction by a smaller number of jurors without inflicting an injury shocking to one's sense of justice.[29] Under the "ordered liberty" theory, in this instance, as in the case of indictment by a grand jury, the law can be flexible and give room for experiment by the several states in reforming and modernizing their governmental procedures.[30]

Presumably the right of a defendant "to be informed of the nature and cause of the accusation" would be, like notice and hearing, a fundamental requirement with which state procedure must comply, although there seem to be no cases dealing with the applicability of this portion of the Sixth Amendment.[31]

However, the right "to be confronted with the witnesses against him" has been held not to be "of the very essence of a scheme of ordered liberty." The Court recognized that the procedure of taking testimony by depositions in writing, which Louisiana inherited from the French civil law, might well serve as a useful method of obtaining probative and trustworthy evidence.[32] The English common law procedure of oral testimony subject to cross-examination was not indispensable to the due administration of justice.

But it would seem that a defendant's right "to have compulsory process for obtaining witnesses in his favor" should be regarded as

[29] *Maxwell* v. *Dow*, 176 U.S. 581, 587 (1900). But as to secret trials see note 7, page 67.

[30] This theory accords with the familiar tenet of Justice Holmes: "There is nothing that I more deprecate than the use of the Fourteenth Amendment beyond the absolute compulsion of its words to prevent the making of social experiments that an important part of the community desires, in the insulated chambers afforded by the several States, even though the experiments may seem futile or even noxious to me and to those whose judgment I most respect." *Truax* v. *Corrigan*, 257 U.S. 312, 344 (1921). It was likewise Jefferson's belief "that laws and institutions must go hand in hand with the progress of the human mind. . . . We might as well require a man to wear still the coat which fitted him when a boy as civilized society to remain ever under the regimen of their barbarous ancestors." Dumbauld, *The Political Writings of Thomas Jefferson*, 124.

[31] Compare the rule set forth in *Morgan* v. *U.S.*, 304 U.S. 1, 18–19 (1938). See text at note 12, page 92.

[32] *West* v. *Louisiana*, 194 U.S. 258, 262 (1904).

a fundamental feature of a fair trial, although it was not a right enjoyed in England, and although no direct decision on the point by the Supreme Court is at hand.[33]

The right "to have the assistance of counsel" has caused voluminous litigation under the "ordered liberty" theory. The Court holds that a state is not required to furnish counsel to a defendant in all cases, but only where the crime is a serious one and injustice would result from lack of counsel.[34] The vagueness of the rule enforced by the Supreme Court leads to continual attempts by convicts to claim they were unfairly tried, and a multitude of habeas corpus proceedings are engendered by the opportunity for reflection which prison walls afford.

That the provisions of the Seventh Amendment regarding jury trial in civil cases[35] and of the Eighth Amendment (regarding excessive bail or fines and cruel or unusual punishment[36]) do not apply to the states seems well settled. Yet it appears certain that the Court would afford a remedy if confronted with a genuine instance of unusually cruel punishment.[37]

The Ninth and Tenth Amendments, being reservations for the benefit of the states, of course give no occasion for raising the question whether they are made applicable against the states by the Fourteenth Amendment.[38]

The preceding account of present trends in judicial interpreta-

[33] See *Tompsett* v. *Ohio*, 146 F.(2d) 95, 98 (C.C.A. 6, 1944), certiorari denied 324 U.S. 869. In England it was not until after the "Glorious Revolution" of 1688 that defendants were permitted to call witnesses. Heller, *The Sixth Amendment*, 9.

[34] See text at note 15, page 69 and cases there cited.

[35] *Walker* v. *Sauvinet*, 92 U.S. 90 (1875); *Hawkins* v. *Bleakly*, 243 U.S. 210, 216 (1917).

[36] *In re Kemmler*, 136 U.S. 436, 446 (1890).

[37] *Louisiana ex rel. Francis* v. *Resweber*, 329 U.S. 459, 464 (1947). See note 20, page 71.

[38] Patterson, *The Forgotten Ninth Amendment*, 41–42, argues that "unenumerated" pre-constitutional natural rights recognized by the Ninth Amendment must be protected against state governments as well as federal, and that "there could be no constitutional objection to any national legislation" enacted for the purpose of protecting such natural rights against infringement by the states.

tion of the Bill of Rights discloses a conscientious (even if sometimes eccentric) effort on the part of the Supreme Court to give
current meaning to the time-honored language which has been
part of the Constitution since 1791. Many provisions of this venerated document are landmarks of an even earlier era, when the
English Bill of Rights of 1689 (just a century before Madison
offered his amendments in Congress) went into force as the embodiment of "the true, ancient, and indubitable rights and liberties
of the people" who had triumphed in a "glorious revolution"
after many years of eventful struggle against the arbitrary power
of the Crown. This legacy of history, enshrined in constitutional
commands which outrank ordinary acts of state, stands as an ever-
lasting symbol of those principles of liberty and justice which lie
at the root of all free government. And by this touchstone those
who hold supreme judicial office in the land must daily measure
and appraise the deeds of men who wrestle with the problems of
a world where human speech shrieks with a panoply of mechan-
ized devices, and tree-lined avenues have been transformed into
an unabating bedlam of unmanageable traffic, and tyranny has
many new techniques at its disposal, but freedom still is prized
above all earthly things.

III

VALUE OF

THE BILL OF RIGHTS

AFTER the foregoing survey of the origin and scope of these amendments so strongly insisted upon by patriots of the Revolutionary generation, there remains the inquiry: What is the practical significance of the Bill of Rights in the atomic age? Does the present importance of these ten constitutional provisions warrant the apotheosis they enjoy in American public esteem, and justify the expenditure of eloquence and emotion devoted to them by politicians and commentators and bar association orators?

"Now the important fact about these ten Amendments," as Charles Warren observes, "is that *they* are the *essential portion* of the Constitution . . . the portion without which the Constitution itself would never have been accepted by the American people."[1]

It was the acceptance of the Bill of Rights as part of the fundamental law of the newly established government that gave to proponents of the Constitution framed at Philadelphia "the opportunity of proving . . . that they were as sincerely devoted to liberty and a Republican Government as those who charged them with wishing the adoption of this Constitution in order to lay the foundation of an aristocracy or despotism."[2]

Thereafter, the Constitution as amended ceased to be a mere political contrivance, a piece of governmental machinery that could be used for good or for ill, and came to be regarded as a symbol of the American way of life, as an embodiment of the trium-

[1] Warren, *Congress, the Constitution, and the Supreme Court*, 85. Italics in the original.
[2] *Writings of James Madison*, V, 374.

phant achievement of a self-governing and liberty-loving people. Through the adoption of the Bill of Rights the spirit of the Declaration of Independence was infused into the Constitution; and the American argosy, having been put upon her republican tack, could "show by the beauty of her motion the skill of her builders."[3] The Constitution became an instrument of democracy.

It is therefore understandable if Americans today cherish fervently this monument of a time of greatness and of splendor in their national life. One who reads the Bill of Rights may fittingly exclaim with the poet: "Of ancient love I felt the mighty spell."[4] It does not matter that the archaic language awakens reminiscences of long-vanished grievances that flourished centuries ago, of royal practices resisted by the men of Runnymede, or by those who slew one sovereign and deposed another for contemning "the true, ancient, and indubitable rights and liberties of the people." It does not matter that the evils which the framers feared and guarded against were injuries that had been suffered in former times and had been exposed to public condemnation out of "a decent respect to the opinions of mankind." These circumstances are as little significant as the outmoded garb of youth in the portrait of a beloved.

Moreover, even if the wrongs against which these safeguards afford protection are of a sort now extinct in this country, there is more than an antiquarian interest in the prohibitions thus established. A state in which such tyrannous practices are banned is, and continues to be, a different kind of state from one in which they are permitted to exist. The characteristics of America today are therefore what they are because of what the Bill of Rights abolished forever. A dike or sea-wall constructed generations ago is still important to the dry land which has not been inundated for centuries. The land would not be dry land if the protecting wall had not been there, or if it were to be removed.

[3] Jefferson to John Dickinson, Washington, March 6, 1801. *Works of Thomas Jefferson*, IX, 201. "It was Jefferson who taught the American people to regard the Constitution as an instrument of democracy." Walter Lippmann, *Public Opinion*, 282.

[4] "*D'antico amor sentì la gran potenza.*" Dante, *Purgatorio*, xxx, 39.

Besides this, the experience of the present age with totalitarian despotisms of one sort and another serves as a constant reminder that tyranny is not necessarily an obsolete and extinct evil, which need no longer be feared or guarded against. Indeed, it could spring up in the United States at any moment in full panoply if the people ceased to cherish vigilantly the traditions crystallized in the venerable Bill of Rights.

Thoughtful citizens of the United States will therefore beware of any tendency to belittle the value of the Bill of Rights. It would be easy to speak slightingly of these ten time-honored articles, and to minimize the present utility of the four groups of provisions they contain.

Is it important, a scoffer might plausibly ask, in an age when the world is faced with the possibility of destruction through man's own scientific ingenuity and political perversity, to set store by a constitutional requirement which on the one hand prohibits public school children from receiving religious instruction in the faith of their fathers, for fear that the young son of a female Illinois atheist will feel lonely and neglected and forlorn when his classmates are engaged in a pursuit in which he is forbidden by his parent to share, and which on the other hand, allegedly in the name of that freedom of religion which in Jefferson's words proclaimed that "to compel a man to furnish contributions of money for the propagation of opinions which he disbelieves and abhors is sinful and tyrannical," permits a New Jersey Presbyterian to be taxed for the purpose of delivering pupils to a Roman Catholic school?[5]

Is it rational, the scoffer might continue, to eulogize a provision of law that authorizes citizens to bear arms, when the puny pistol,

[5] *Illinois ex rel. McCollum* v. *Bd. of Education*, 333 U.S. 203 (1948); *Everson* v. *Bd. of Education*, 330 U.S. 17, 19–21, 25–26, 62 (1946); Jefferson's draft of Statute of Virginia for Religious Freedom, Jefferson's *Works*, II, 439. The theory accepted by the majority of the Supreme Court in the *McCollum* case is that the "released time" program there under consideration involved the use of *school property* and personnel for religious instruction; while in the *Everson* case it was not the *school* whose program of instruction was receiving benefit from public funds but the *pupils* as individuals. See pages 106–10.

rifle, dagger, or pitchfork which they might carry pursuant to this permission would be confronted by jet aircraft, tear gas bombs and atomic weapons? Of what value is it to a citizen today to bear arms, unless he be a gangster of the Capone ilk? Is the right to keep soldiers from living in one's home important to a citizen the largest part of whose income is taken from him to support armed forces in countless camps with PX privileges, government issue supplies, and medical care far superior to what is available in most civilian homes?

Why should a respectable citizen feel elated, the scoffer might ask, because of the existence of various provisions relating to criminal procedure? Are these requirements helpful except to members of the so-called "criminal classes"? Should it be a matter for pride that the premises where a bootlegger or dope-peddler operates can not be searched by the police without a warrant?

Is the provision for jury trial in civil cases involving over $20 of any practical value? By encouraging legal technicalities, is it not a hindrance to the establishment of efficient judicial procedure for the collection of small claims and to the creation of effective administrative agencies?

And who but a Philadelphia lawyer or an unreconstructed rebel cares whether restrictive language in the Constitution is to be interpreted as an implied grant by way of negative pregnant or as a particularization for the sake of precaution, or whether powers not delegated to the federal government are reserved to the states? Is this latter maxim any more meaningful than to say that money in bank which is not checked out remains on deposit? The question is always whether or not a particular power has been granted, and an argument based on the Tenth Amendment never amounts to more than an elegant or eloquent *petitio principii*.

Finally, what about the famous Fifth Amendment? It is perhaps the best-known part of the Bill of Rights today. A person's privilege not to be "compelled in any criminal case to be a witness against himself" has been expanded by the courts to cover self-incrimination in other proceedings besides criminal prosecutions. It is enough that the testimony elicited might serve as the basis for a future criminal prosecution. Why should the law be so solicitous for the welfare of "criminals" (some of whom may be Communists) so as to shield them from the obligation of telling the truth about their activities? Is there any reason why such tenderness should be exhibited in criminal proceedings, when the modern tendency in civil cases is to require, through "discovery," that every litigant should help his opponent prove the latter's case?[6]

A perhaps less publicized feature of the Fifth Amendment is the "due process" clause. The effect of this provision has been expanded by its inclusion in the Fourteenth Amendment as a restriction against state action. (The Fourteenth Amendment has also been construed by the Supreme Court in recent years as incorporating some, but not all, features of the federal Bill of Rights as part of the restrictions applicable against state action.)[7]

While the desirability of "procedural due process" may be conceded, as a means of requiring fair hearing and other basic procedural safeguards as a prerequisite to governmental action affecting private rights, is "substantive due process" anything but a means of imposing as a constitutional requirement the private notions of Supreme Court Justices as to what they consider socially desirable?

In reply to these inquiries, it must be emphasized that the importance of the restrictions upon the power of government contained in the Bill of Rights is to be found, not in the particular specific types of action prohibited, but in the general principle that keeps alive in the public mind the doctrine that *governmental power is not unlimited*. So long as limited government continues to exist, the distinctive characteristics of American polity as contrasted with totalitarianism will be preserved.

Submission to a government of unlimited powers was regarded by Thomas Jefferson as the greatest of all political evils.[8] He laid

[6] *Hickman* v. *Taylor*, 329 U.S. 495, 507 (1947).

[7] Dumbauld, *The Declaration of Independence and What It Means Today*, 62. See pages 132–38.

[8] Dumbauld, *The Political Writings of Thomas Jefferson*, 156, 161, 167–68.

great stress upon constitutional limitations and the doctrine of separation of powers. "The first principle of a good government is certainly a distribution of its powers into executive, judiciary, and legislative, and a subdivision of the latter into two or three branches." Hence "the English constitution, acknowledged to be better than all which have preceded it, is only better in proportion as it has approached nearer to this distribution of powers." It is then easy to show "by a comparison of our constitutions with that of England, how much more perfect they are."[9] In Jefferson's opinion, anything less than a basic or fundamental law binding upon all branches of the government and unalterable by them would not deserve to be called a constitution. In fact he regarded the British constitution, which can be changed by any act passed by Parliament, as being for that reason in truth "no constitution at all."[10]

The social compact philosophy and doctrines of natural law which were entertained by Jefferson and his contemporaries also contributed to the recognition of constitutional limitations upon governmental power. Under that theory individuals living in a "state of nature" prior to the establishment of civil society enjoyed certain unalienable "natural rights" with which they were endowed at their creation. Governments were established by consent of the governed in order to protect and secure such pre-existent rights. Since "the purposes of society do not require a surrender of all our rights to our ordinary governors," there remains reserved to the people after the government is formed an area of unsurrendered natural rights. Accordingly, a Bill of Rights, specifying the boundaries of this area which the government has no authorization to invade, is an important feature of every constitution.[11]

Freedom of religion, freedom of the press, trial by jury, habeas corpus, and a representative legislature were enumerated by Jefferson when specifying what he regarded as "the essentials con-

[9] *Ibid.*, 134.
[10] *Ibid.*, xiii, 119.
[11] *Ibid.*, xxvi–xxvii.

stituting free government."[12] He declared that "There are rights which it is useless to surrender to the government, and which governments have yet always been found to invade. These are the rights of thinking, and publishing our thoughts by speaking or writing; the right of free commerce; the right of personal freedom. There are instruments for administering the government [such as trial by jury] so peculiarly trustworthy that we should never leave the legislature at liberty to change them. . . . There are instruments [such as a standing army] so dangerous to the rights of the nation, and which place them so totally at the mercy of their governors, that those governors, whether legislative or executive, should be restrained from keeping such instruments on foot, but in well defined cases."[13] It will be observed how closely Jefferson's notions as to the contents of a Bill of Rights parallel the proposals which were made for amendments to the Constitution after the Philadelphia convention failed to include such a declaration of fundamental freedoms belonging to the citizens.[14]

Besides "the legal check which it puts into the hands of the judiciary" (witness the lengthy array of decisions of the United States Supreme Court which have been reviewed above), Jefferson and Madison believed that a Bill of Rights would be of value because it would "fix . . . for the people the principles of their political creed."[15]

The United States Bill of Rights has been extremely important in thus crystallizing the basic features of American polity. It has incorporated principles of freedom and self-government as an integral part of the nation's fundamental law. It has established democratic habits of thought and a code of political morality which cannot be obliterated no matter how violently the storms of controversy may rage. It has perpetuated and preserved the traditions of constitutional liberty which originated in English

[12] *Ibid.*, 59, 120.
[13] *Ibid.*, xxvi–xxvii.
[14] *Ibid.*, 140.
[15] *Ibid.*, 126, 128. See pages 8–9, 57.

experience and which animated the patriots and statesmen by whose labors were laid the foundations for American greatness. This philosophy of freedom which became part of the American "political creed" by reason of being embodied in the Bill of Rights has served to liberate the latent energies of a mighty people and to evoke achievements unmatched in human history. In every branch of science, in every field of endeavor, the individual's right to seek truth without interference by political edicts has been the means of promoting the advancement of learning, and the attainment of objectives beneficial to the public welfare.

Nowhere more forcefully than in John Milton's *Areopagitica* has the value of freedom of the mind been voiced. This plea to Parliament in behalf of freedom of the press, written in 1644 in opposition to restrictive legislation, proclaimed: "I cannot praise a fugitive and cloistered virtue. . . . Give me the liberty to know, to utter, and to argue freely according to conscience, above all liberties. . . . And though all the winds of doctrine were let loose to play upon the earth, so Truth be in the field, we do injuriously, by licensing and prohibiting, to misdoubt her strength. Let her and Falsehood grapple: who ever knew Truth put to the worse in a free and open encounter?"[16]

More than a century later, an equally classical exposition of the case for freedom to think and to speak was set forth by Thomas Jefferson. In the widely known Virginia Act for Establishing Religious Freedom he declared that "truth is the proper and sufficient antagonist to error and has nothing to fear from the conflict unless by human interposition disarmed of her natural weapons, free argument and debate; errors ceasing to be dangerous when it is permitted freely to contradict them." In another often-quoted affirmation he proclaimed: "I have sworn upon the

[16] *The Works of John Milton*, IV, 311, 346, 347. Milton regarded the system of licensing as "the greatest affront and discouragement that can be offered to learning and to learned men." *Ibid.*, 323. The Dutch scholar Hugo Grotius, whose acquaintance Milton made in Paris, wrote in 1609 in the preface to his treatise on *Freedom of the Seas* that truth is never so unlikely to be discovered as when agreement is compelled (*"nusquam minus inveniri veritatem quam ubi cogitur assensus"*). *Anthologia Grotiana*, 72.

altar of God eternal hostility against every form of tyranny over the mind of man." And speaking of his dearly-cherished University of Virginia he averred: "This institution will be based upon the illimitable freedom of the human mind. For here we are not afraid to follow truth wherever it may lead, nor to tolerate any error so long as reason is left free to combat it."[17]

John Stuart Mill, in a succeeding generation, asserted the same principle: "The only freedom which deserves the name, is that of pursuing our own good in our own way, so long as we do not attempt to deprive others of theirs. . . . If all mankind minus one were of one opinion, and only one person were of the contrary opinion, mankind would be no more justified in silencing that one person, than he, if he had the power, would be justified in silencing mankind. . . . We can never be sure that the opinion we are endeavoring to stifle is a false opinion; and if we were sure, stifling it would be an evil still. . . . Truth gains more even by the errors of one who . . . thinks for himself, than by the true opinions of those who only hold them because they do not suffer themselves to think. . . . In this age, the mere example of nonconformity, the mere refusal to bend the knee to custom, is itself a service."[18]

Mill emphasized in fourfold fashion the desirability of free inquiry: (1) Any opinion silenced by force may be true; (2) Or it may be partly true, and the full truth will emerge only from the clash of opposing views; (3) But even if the orthodox opinion is the whole truth, it does not deserve to be called knowledge unless it has been tested by the mental processes employed in argument and controversy; (4) And it will lose its vitality as a genuine conviction, becoming merely an irrational prejudice, ac-

[17] Dumbauld, *Political Writings of Thomas Jefferson*, 35, 76. In another noteworthy statement Jefferson asserted: "No government ought to be without censors: & where the press is free, no one ever will. If virtuous, it need not fear the fair operation of attack and defence. Nature has given to man no other means of sifting out the truth either in religion, law, or politics." Jefferson to George Washington, September 9, 1792, Jefferson's *Works*, VII, 146–47.

[18] Mill, *On Liberty*, 72–73, 75, 79, 94, 124.

cepted as an authoritarian pronouncement or upon the basis of custom or habit.[19]

In our own day Justice Holmes delivered an eloquent formulation of the philosophy of freedom which "will live as long as English prose has power to thrill."[20] He said:

Persecution for the expression of opinions seems to me perfectly logical. If you have no doubt of your premises or your power and want a certain result with all your heart you naturally express your wishes in law and sweep away all opposition. To allow opposition by speech seems to indicate that you think the speech impotent, as when a man says that he has squared the circle, or that you do not care wholeheartedly for the result, or that you doubt either your power or your premises. But when men have realized that time has upset many fighting faiths, they may come to believe even more than they believe the very foundations of their own conduct that the ultimate good desired is better reached by free trade in ideas—that the best test of truth is the power of the thought to get itself accepted in the competition of the market, and that truth is the only ground upon which their wishes safely can be carried out. That, at any rate, is the theory of our Constitution.[21]

Justice Brandeis likewise emphasized the importance of free discussion as an essential feature of democratic political processes. Effective operation of the American system of government requires participation by the people and the maintenance of an informed public opinion:

The right of a citizen of the United States to take part, for his own or the country's benefit, in the making of Federal laws and in the conduct of the government, necessarily includes the right to speak or write about them; to endeavor to make his own opinion concerning laws existing or contemplated prevail; and, to this end, to teach the truth as he sees it. . . . Full and free exercise of this right by the citizen is ordinarily also his duty; for its exercise is more important to the

[19] *Ibid.*, 111–12.
[20] Felix Frankfurter, *Mr. Justice Holmes*, 72.
[21] *Abrams* v. *U.S.*, 250 U.S. 616, 630 (1919).

149

nation than it is to himself. Like the course of the heavenly bodies, harmony in national life is a resultant of the struggle between contending forces. In frank expression of conflicting opinions lies the greatest promise of wisdom in governmental action; and in suppression lies ordinarily the greatest peril.[22]

In another eloquent summary of the American political creed he declared:

Those who won our independence believed that the final end of the state was to make men free to develop their faculties; and that in its government the deliberative forces should prevail over the arbitrary. They valued liberty both as an end and as a means. They believed liberty to be the secret of happiness and courage to be the secret of liberty. They believed that freedom to think as you will and to speak as you think are means indispensable to the discovery and spread of political truth; that without free speech and assembly discussion would be futile; that with them, discussion affords ordinarily adequate protection against the dissemination of noxious doctrine; that the greatest menace to freedom is an inert people; that public discussion is a political duty; and that this should be a fundamental principle of the American government.[23]

In similar vein, one of the foremost authorities on freedom of speech, Professor Zechariah Chafee, Jr., of the Harvard law school, emphasizes that the First Amendment expresses an important public policy as well as a legal limitation upon the powers of Congress. It is "much more than an order to Congress not to cross the boundary which marks the extreme limit of lawful suppression. It is also an exhortation and a guide for the action of Congress inside that boundary. It is a declaration of national policy in favor of the public discussion of all public questions. . . . The true meaning of freedom of speech seems to be this. One of the most important purposes of society and government is the

[22] Dissenting opinion in *Gilbert* v. *Minnesota*, 254 U.S. 325, 337–38 (1920).
[23] Concurring opinion in *Whitney* v. *California*, 274 U.S. 357, 375 (1927). For a good statement of similar sentiments by a contemporary journalist, see Elmer Davis, *But We Were Born Free*, 1, 81, 157, 175–79.

150

discovery and spread of truth on subjects of general concern. This is possible only through absolutely unlimited discussion. . . . Nevertheless, there are other purposes of government, such as order, the training of the young, protection against external aggression. Unlimited discussion sometimes interferes with these purposes, which must then be balanced against freedom of speech, but freedom of speech ought to weigh very heavily in the scale. The First Amendment gives binding force to this principle of political wisdom."[24]

These venerable precepts rest upon more than American experience and the lessons of English history. The same message is taught by memorable utterances of Hebrew prophets and Greek philosophers. Time after time the importance of free speech has been demonstrated. It is more beneficial to the welfare of the people that thinkers and seers should be free to seek and to speak the truth than that what they say should prove palatable to the rulers of the nation at the moment. Exile, imprisonment, and death have often been the fate of public benefactors. Yet Socrates avowed to the Athenians that "as long as I have breath and strength I will not cease from philosophy, and from exhorting you, and declaring the truth to every one of you"; and in like manner Christians of the apostolic age proclaimed: "We are not able to refrain from speaking about what we have seen and heard."[25] The framers of the First Amendment were guided by the teachings of ancient wisdom when they recognized the signifi-

[24] Chafee, *Free Speech in the United States*, 6, 31. Chafee emphasizes, as does Justice Brandeis, the benefit to the public which freedom of speech brings about. *Ibid.*, 33–35, 155. "The real value of freedom of speech is not to the minority that wants to talk, but to the majority that does not want to listen." *Ibid.*, ix. Chafee points out, however, that: "The First Amendment has never resulted in a decision declaring an Act of Congress unconstitutional or reversing a federal conviction." Chafee, *The Blessings of Liberty*, 323.

[25] Plato, *Apology*, 29 D (Translated by F. J. Church, London, 1886, 57–58); Acts 4:20. See also Amos 7:13–14; Numbers 22:37–38, 23:12; 2 Chron. 18:12–13, 26; Jer. 38:4. It is also recorded that after a debate at the court of Darius whether wine, women, or the king were strongest, the conclusion reached was: "Great is the truth, and stronger than all things. . . . As for the truth, it endureth, and is always strong; it liveth and conquereth for evermore. . . . Great is Truth and mighty above all things." 1 Esdras 4:35, 38, 41.

cance of free speech as a means of promoting the welfare of the nation.

But the value of the Bill of Rights is not to be measured merely by the importance of the general principle that governmental power is not unlimited and that freedom is desirable and beneficial to the public welfare. The specific provisions embodied in the Bill of Rights are themselves rules of practical utility tested by the experience of many generations of freedom-loving peoples. They cannot properly be dismissed as trivialities.

For example, when considering the emphasis on criminal procedure in the Bill of Rights, it must be borne in mind that strict observance of requirements of this sort is itself a basic feature of the American type of government.[26] Neglect of these rules would quickly result in the establishment of despotism. Where penalties may be incurred without specific violation of a legal rule, proved in accordance with due process of law, anyone who is the object of the displeasure of the government will soon find himself to be a "criminal."

The existence of safeguards utilized by "criminals" is thus a protection to all citizens, just as the availability of hospitals and medical research benefits persons who are healthy as well as those who are sick.

Moreover, the religious liberty enjoyed in America is genuine. In spite of the annoying cases involving "fringe" groups, it is obvious that the situation in the United States is much more desirable than in Spain[27] or in Iron Curtain countries.[28]

[26] The importance of procedure as a safeguard of substantive liberties has often been emphasized. "The history of liberty has largely been the history of observance of procedural safeguards." *McNabb* v. *U.S.*, 318 U.S. 332, 347 (1943). See also Brandeis, dissenting with Holmes in *Burdeau* v. *McDowell*, 256 U.S. 465, 477 (1921): "And in the development of our liberty, insistence upon procedural regularity has been a large factor."

[27] Regarding conditions in Spain, the New York *Times* of June 3, 1956, reports: "On April 24 the Spanish Ministry of Information ordered the seizure of 36,189 volumes stored in Madrid premises of the British and Foreign Bible Society. . . . Among the literature confiscated were 9,000 copies in Spanish of the New Testament. . . . Roman Catholicism is the state religion. Non-Catholics

The Fifth Amendment, likewise, is of real utility in many instances.[29] It serves as an effective barrier against inquisitorial practices. American principles of fair play discountenance attempts to condemn a person by compelling him to disclose his own transgressions. Law enforcement agencies should be encouraged to gather independent evidence by exercising an appropriate degree of resourcefulness and industry.[30] One should always feel uneasiness when people are penalized for exercising a privilege which a venerated provision of the Constitution affords them.

The privilege against self-incrimination in the Fifth Amendment is just as much a part of the Constitution as the provisions prescribing how members of Congress shall be chosen. If every person who utilized those provisions of the Constitution by becoming a candidate for Congress were to be subjected to penalties such as loss of employment, public ignominy, refusal of a passport, and similar disabilities, the unsoundness of such a policy would be obvious to all. Yet public opinion is apparently willing to tolerate legislation and practices inflicting those consequences upon persons who similarly utilize another portion of the Constitution. This is as irrational as if a university were to take pride in and expend great effort and sacrifice in establishing a magnificent library; but then were to expel any student who read a book.

Similarly, the "due process" clause is of indubitable value to those to whom it affords succor. When the Supreme Court interpreted it as prohibiting minimum wage laws,[31] it was certainly of

are forbidden to proselytize and stage external manifestations of worship; they are permitted to practice their faith only behind closed doors."

[28] The fate of Cardinal Mindszenty in Hungary and the harrowing experiences that befell many missionaries in China are typical of the persecution of religion under totalitarian regimes.

[29] The value of the Fifth Amendment has been recently demonstrated in a thoughtful treatment of the subject by Dean Erwin Griswold of the Harvard law school. Griswold, *The Fifth Amendment Today*, 7, 35, 39, 73, 82.

[30] As British authorities in India learned, with regard to coerced confessions: "It is far pleasanter to sit comfortably in the shade rubbing pepper into a poor devil's eye than to go about in the sun hunting up evidence." Sir James Fitzjames Stephen, *A History of the Criminal Law of England*, I, 442.

[31] *Adkins* v. *Children's Hospital*, 261 U.S. 525 (1923).

very great practical benefit to the corporations which found shelter under its provisions. When it is now interpreted as prohibiting racial segregation,[32] it is surely of immense practical advantage to the groups protected. That different policies and emphases are applied during different periods in giving specific content to the "vague contours"[33] of the clause is simply an inevitable incident of life. All law is mutable and expresses the standards of the time. *Tempora mutantur et nos in illis.* Constitutional rules, no less than other rules of law, are subject to this inherent infirmity. Because the evils against which a Bill of Rights affords protection vary from epoch to epoch, it must not be supposed that such protection is therefore valueless today. On the contrary, the remedy must be as flexible as the evil guarded against. The Bill of Rights is a part of the Constitution; hence, when speaking of the Bill of Rights, as Chief Justice Marshall observed, "We must never forget that it is a *constitution* that we are expounding . . . intended to endure for ages to come, and consequently to be adapted to the various crises of human affairs."[34]

Transformation is merely evidence of vitality. That which is alive cannot remain static and unchanged. Out of the old fields must come new corn. When yeasty bubbles swell and burst and are succeeded by others in a constant ferment, it is because there is life in the leavened mass of dough. Only in a dead language do words retain unaltered meaning from century to century. In like fashion new solutions must be sought and new remedies devised when new problems emerge in the realm of constitutional liberty. Such developments should cause no concern; they simply prove that the nation is not moribund, but viable, that its constitution is capable of displaying the vigorous adaptability of a healthy organism in response to the challenges of its environment, that the Bill of Rights continues to be a living and vital feature of the American body politic.

[32] *Bolling* v. *Sharpe*, 347 U.S. 497 (1954).
[33] 261 U.S. at 568 (Holmes, J., dissenting).
[34] *McCulloch* v. *Maryland*, 4 Wheat. 316, 407, 415 (1819).

It would be well, perhaps, if even greater changes were to occur than have already been experienced or can now be anticipated. In the dynamic world created by modern science, law (and particularly constitutional law) must not become a laggard; adequate protection for basic human needs under present-day conditions must be afforded by the legal and political institutions of contemporary society.

The time may come, for example, when the right of the people to be secure in their persons and homes will be effectively safeguarded not only against searches and seizures by police agencies of their own government, but also against attack by foreign armies and atomic weapons threatening a global holocaust. The destructive consequences of warfare (or starvation resulting from inadequate nutrition) may be treated by the judicial tribunals of that age as a deprivation of life without due process of law.

Even now the peculiar problems of particular localities require the use of varying modes of protecting by law the fundamental right to life. In a society where the inhabitants of vast cities like New York would soon die of hunger if transportation were cut off, or where the welfare of a region depends upon dams or irrigation, the legal system can not operate with the same techniques which would be suitable in an agrarian paradise where every family can provide for its own needs. Conditions are conceivable where there would be need for constitutional rights designed to *compel* the government to do things *for* the people, rather than to *prohibit* the government from doing things *to* the people.

The unfolding mysteries of atomic energy, when liberated for constructive peaceful uses, may place in the hands of every citizen untold prerogatives more wonderful than the marvels wrought by legendary magic carpets. These developments will doubtless constitute the subject matter of an ever-enlarging concept of "liberty" and "property," entitled to protection as a basic constitutional right.

The day may come, too, when the right to freedom of speech will be recognized effectively on a world-wide basis, and no rulers anywhere will have power to suppress discussion or to insulate their populations by any sort of an "iron curtain" from the voice of world opinion and the benefits of civilized society.

But these bright prospects for the future growth of constitutional liberty will prove unattainable, and even the maintenance of existing hard-won rights will be jeopardized, unless each citizen of the United States accepts the responsibility of sharing in the task of preserving, unimpaired, the long-cherished traditions of freedom which have given shape and substance to the Bill of Rights.

APPENDICES

INTRODUCTION

THE English Bill of Rights and the Virginia Bill of Rights are printed in this Appendix as given in Dumbauld, *The Declaration of Independence and What It Means Today*, 164–67, 168–70. The state proposals are from McMaster and Stone, *Pennsylvania and the Federal Constitution*, 421–23; Elliot, *Debates*, (2nd ed.), II, 550–53; *Documentary History of the Constitution*, II, 94–95; 139–40; 142–43; 190–203; 266–75; 377–84. Madison's are from Hunt, *Writings of James Madison*, V, 376–80. The others are from documents preserved in the Rare Book Room of the Library of Congress and the National Archives, Washington, D. C. The Select Committee's report of July 28, 1789, together with the seventeen articles passed by the House of Representatives on August 24, 1789, and the twelve articles passed by the Senate on September 9, 1789, are from the Library of Congress (Madison Papers, Vol. 76, p. 34). The printer in each case was Thomas Greenleaf, and the documents are described in Vincent L. Eaton's valuable article. The twelve articles finally agreed to by the House on September 24, 1789, and by the Senate on September 25, 1789, are from National Archives Publication No. 53–14, which reproduces in facsimile the enrolled resolution which is on permanent display in the shrine along with the Constitution and the Declaration of Independence. Only the last ten of these twelve articles were ratified and went into force as amendments to the Constitution on December 15, 1791. No official document renumbering the amendments which were ratified is known to exist.

1. TABLE FOR SOURCES

OF THE PROVISIONS

OF THE BILL OF RIGHTS

THE following table facilitates convenient reference to the sources for any particular provision of the Bill of Rights. Topics in capital letters were ultimately included in the ten amendments ratified. The first thirty-three topics were included in Madison's proposals to Congress. The other topics in the table were proposed by one or more states but not considered in Congress.

Figures in the first column refer to the substantive items in Madison's proposals as discussed in my text;* those in the second column to his proposals as numbered when offered in Congress.† The next five columns refer to the Select Committee's report (as numbered in the *Annals of Congress*), the seventeen articles adopted by the House, the twelve articles adopted by the Senate, the twelve articles agreed to after conference, and the ten amendments ratified, respectively. Then follow references to the English Bill of Rights, the Virginia Bill of Rights, and the proposals of the eight states which formulated amendments. The last column shows the number of states favoring a particular proposal.

* See pages 36–38.
† See pages 206–209.

Sources of the Provisions of the Bill of Rights

N Number	Subject	Madison Item	Madison N numbers	Select Committee	House	Senate	Conference	Ratified	English Bill of Rights	Virginia Bill of Rights	Va. Convention Bill of Rights	Va. Convention Amendments	Pennsylvania	Massachusetts	Maryland Majority	Maryland Minority	So. Carolina	New Hampshire	New York Bill of Rights	New York Amendments	No. Carolina Bill of Rights	No. Carolina Amendments	Number of States Favoring
1	Power from people	1	1(1)	1	d					2	2								1		2		3
2	Government for people	1	1(2)	1	d					3	3								1		3		3
3	Right to change govt.	1	1(3)							3	3					15			3		3		2
4	Representation	2	2	2	1	1	1a	NR				2	10	2				2				1	6
5	Compensation	3	3	3	2	2	2	NR				18								13		19	3
6	RELIGIOUS FREEDOM	4	4(1)	4(1)	3	3	3a	1		16	20		1			12		11	4		20		6
7	SPEECH & PRESS	5	4(2)	4(2)	4	3	3	1		12	16		6	12					16†		16		5
8	ASSEMBLY & PETITION	6	4(3)	4(2)	4	3	3	1	5		15					14			16		15		4
9	BEAR ARMS	7	4(4)	4(3)	5	4	4	2	7	13	17,19							12	12		17,19		5
10	QUARTERING SOLDIERS	8	4(5)	4(4)	6	5	5	3	3 pr. 5		18					10		10	8		18		5

† Press only.

Explanation of Symbols

a = amended in conference

d = defeated in House or Senate

M = from Magna Carta

pr. = preliminary recital in English Bill of Rights

NR = not ratified by three-fourths of the States

e = eliminated by the method adopted of adding amendments as supplementary articles.

Sources of the Provisions of the Bill of Rights

Number	Subject	Madison Item	Madison Numbers	Select Committee	House	Senate	Conference	Ratified	English Bill of Rights	Virginia Bill of Rights	Va. Convention Bill of Rights	Va. Convention Amendments	Pennsylvania	Massachusetts	Maryland Majority	Maryland Minority	So. Carolina	New Hampshire	New York Bill of Rights	New York Amendments	No. Carolina Bill of Rights	No. Carolina Amendments	Number of States Favoring
11	DOUBLE JEOPARDY	9	4(6)	4(5)	8	7	7	5							2				10				2
12	SELF INCRIMINATION	9	4(6)	4(5)	8	7	7	5		8	8		3	3							8		3
13	DUE PROCESS	9	4(6)	4(5)	8	7	7	5	M	8	9		3	3					9		9		4
14	JUST COMPENSATION	9	4(6)	4(5)	8	7	7	5															0
15	EXCESSIVE BAIL	10	4(7)	4(6)	13	10	10	8	10	9	13		4						12		13		4
16	SEARCHES & SEIZURES	11	4(8)	4(7)	7	6	6	4		10	14		5		8				15		14		5
17	SPEEDY & PUBLIC TRIAL	12	4(9)	7(1)	9	8	8	6		8	8		3						13		8		4
18	CAUSE & NATURE	12	4(9)	7(1)	9	8	8	6		8	8		3								8		3
19	CONFRONTATION	12	4(9)	7(1)	9	8	8	6		8	8		3								8		3
20	WITNESSES	12	4(9)	7(1)	9	8	8	6		8	8		3								8		3
21	COUNSEL	12	4(9)	7(1)	9	8	8	6		8	8		3								8		3
22	RETAINED RIGHTS	13	4(10)	4(8)	15	11	11	9				17							3			18	3
23	State violations	14	5	5	14	d																	0
24	Minimum value	15	6(1)	6(1)	11	d		7				14			7 3,4			7					3
25	RE-EXAMINATION OF FACTS	15	6(2)	6(2)	11	9	9	7				15			3,5			20				15	4
26	JURY OF VICINAGE	16	7(1)	7(2)	10	7	8a	6	11	8	8		3		2				13		8		5
27	GRAND JURY	16	7(2)	7(2)	10	7	7	5							6			6	13				3
28	Place of trial	16	7(3)	7(2)	10	d												13					1

29 Outside county	16																	1
30 JURY TRIAL (CIVIL)	17	7(4) 7(5)	7(2) 7(3)		d	9	9	7		11 11	5	2	8	3,5	13	8 14	11	7
31 Separation of powers	18	8(1)	7(3) 8	16	d	12			5 5		12					5	3
32 RESERVATION OF POWERS	19	8(2)	9	17	12	12	10	1 15	1 1	2 1	3		1	8
33 Renumber Article VII		9	10	e									1	3
34 Regulation of elections								16 10 3	2 1 3	2 1	3	4	17	8
35 Curb taxing power								3 9 4	3,9	3 9 4	2,3,15	3	8
36 No monopolies								5	5	6	22	4
37 No titles of nobility								9	9	30	3
38 No other religious test								4	1
39 No standing army			6 13 17	9 7	4	10	7 17	9	6
40 Ineligibility to office				4	8	17	4	4
41 Publish journals				5		14	5	3
42 Publish accounts				6		6	2
43 Commercial treaties				7		7	2
44 Navigation laws				8	7	8	3
45 Time of enlistment				10	9	10	3
46 Control of militia			11 11	13	1	6 29	11	5
47 Government of district			12		13	2
48 Term of president			13		17	14	3
49 Judicial power			14 14		22 24,28	15	4
50 Challenging jury			15		16	2
51 Impeachment of senators			19		20	2
52 Salaries of judges			20		21	2
53 Natural rights		1			2	1	3

Sources of the Provisions of the Bill of Rights

Number	Subject	Madison Item	Madison Numbers	Select Committee	House	Senate	Conference	Ratified	English Bill of Rights	Virginia Bill of Rights	Va. Convention Bill of Rights	Va. Convention Amendments	Pennsylvania	Massachusetts	Maryland Majority	Maryland Minority	So. Carolina	New Hampshire	New York Bill of Rights	New York Amendments	N.C. Bill of Rights	N.C. Amendts.	Number of States Favoring
54	No hereditary office									4	4											4	2
55	Frequent elections								8	6	6										6	6	2
56	Suspension of laws								1	7	7										7	7	2
57	Habeas corpus										10								11		10	10	3
58	Right to remedy										12										12	12	2
59	Right to hunt and fish												8										1
60	Executive council												12			11							2
61	Collusive jurisdiction														6				23				2
62	Mutiny bill														11								1
63	Tax credit to States															13							1
64	State districts																		18				1
65	Ex post facto laws																		19				1
66	Appeals and error																		20				1
67	Suits against States																		21				1
68	Effect of treaties												13			6			24		23	23	4
69	Disabilities of foreign born																			5			1
70	Borrowing money																			8			1
71	Declaring war																			9			1

No.	Item			
72	Suspending habeas corpus		10	1
73	District legislation		11	1
74	State laws in District		12	1
75	Recall of Senators		16	1
76	Vacancies in Senate		18	1
77	Bankruptcy		19	1
78	No third term		20	1
79	Pardons		21	1
80	Command of army	5	22	2
81	Writs in name of people		23	1
82	Impeachments		25	1
83	Correction of errors		26	1
84	No other office for judge	7	27	2
85	Respect States' rights		31	1
86	Residence requirements		32	1
87	Declaring rebellion		12	1
88	Vessels		24	1
89	Paper money		25	1
90	Foreign troops		26	1

2. ENGLISH BILL OF RIGHTS

[*The declaration of rights presented by the Lords and Commons to William and Mary on February 13, 1689, was formally enacted into law on December 16, 1689 (1 Wm. and Mary, 2nd sess., c. 2. See also* Journals of the House of Commons, *X, 28–29;* Journals of the House of Lords, *XIV, 373.)*]

WHEREAS the late King *James* the Second, by the assistance of divers evil counsellors, judges, and ministers employed by him, did endeavour to subvert and extirpate the protestant religion, and the laws and liberties of this kingdom.

1. By assuming and exercising a power of dispensing with and suspending of laws, and the execution of laws, without consent of parliament.

2. By committing and prosecuting divers worthy prelates, for humbly petitioning to be excused from concurring to the said assumed power.

3. By issuing and causing to be executed a commission under the great seal for erecting a court called, *The court of commissioners for ecclesiastical causes.*

4. By levying money for and to the use of the crown, by pretence of prerogative, for other time, and in other manner, than the same was granted by parliament.

5. By raising and keeping a standing army within this kingdom in time of peace, without consent of parliament, and quartering soldiers contrary to law.

6. By causing several good subjects, being protestants, to be

disarmed, at the same time when papists were both armed and employed, contrary to law.

7. By violating the freedom of election of members to serve in parliament.

8. By prosecutions in the court of King's bench, for matters and causes cognizable only in parliament; and by divers other arbitrary and illegal courses.

9. And whereas of late years, partial, corrupt, and unqualified persons have been returned and served on juries in trials, and particularly divers jurors in trials for high treason, which were not freeholders.

10. And excessive bail hath been required of persons committed in criminal cases, to elude the benefit of the laws made for the liberty of the subjects.

11. And excessive fines have been imposed; and illegal and cruel punishments have been inflicted.

12. And several grants and promises made of fines and forfeitures, before any conviction or judgment against the persons, upon whom the same were to be levied.

All which are utterly and directly contrary to the known laws and statutes, and freedom of this realm.

And whereas the said late king *James* the Second having abdicated the government, and the throne being thereby vacant . . . the said lords spiritual and temporal, and commons . . . do in the first place (as their ancestors in like case have usually done) for the vindicating and asserting their ancient rights and liberties, declare;

1. That the pretended power of suspending of laws, or the execution of laws, by regal authority, without consent of parliament, is illegal.

2. That the pretended power of dispensing with laws, or the execution of laws, by regal authority, as it hath been assumed and exercised of late, is illegal.

3. That the commission for erecting the late court of commissioners for ecclesiastical causes, and all other commissions and courts of like nature are illegal and pernicious.

4. That levying money for or to the use of the crown, by pretence of prerogative, without grant of parliament, for longer time, or in other manner than the same is or shall be granted, is illegal.

5. That it is the right of the subjects to petition the King, and all committments [*sic*] and prosecutions for such petitioning are illegal.

6. That the raising or keeping a standing army within the kingdom in time of peace, unless it be with consent of parliament, is against law.

7. That the subjects which are protestants, may have arms for their defence suitable to their conditions, and as allowed by law.

8. That election of members of parliament ought to be free.

9. That the freedom of speech, and debates or proceedings in parliament, ought not to be impeached or questioned in any court or place out of parliament.

10. That excessive bail ought not to be required, nor excessive fines imposed; nor cruel and unusual punishments inflicted.

11. That jurors ought to be duly impanelled and returned, and jurors which pass upon men in trials for high treason ought to be freeholders.

12. That all grants and promises of fines and forfeitures of particular persons before conviction, are illegal and void.

13. And that for redress of all grievances, and for the amending, strengthening, and preserving of the laws, parliaments ought to be held frequently.

And they do claim, demand, and insist upon all and singular the premisses, as their undoubted rights and liberties; and that no declarations, judgments, doings or proceedings, to the prejudice of the people in any of the said premisses, ought in any wise to be drawn hereafter into consequence or example.

[*The Lords and Commons then went on, in their declaration, to express confidence in the Prince of Orange as protector of these rights; resolved that William and Mary be declared king and queen for life; and proposed new oaths to be taken in lieu of the oaths of allegiance and supremacy theretofore used.*

After a recital of this declaration in full, and a recital of the acceptance of the crown by the Prince and Princess of Orange "according to the resolution and desire of the said lords and commons contained in the said declaration," the act of December 16, 1689, contained, among other things, the following provisions:]

VI. Now in pursuance of the premisses, the said lords spiritual and temporal, and commons, in parliament assembled, for the ratifying, confirming and establishing the said declaration, and the articles, clauses, matters, and things therein contained, by the force of a law made in due form by authority of parliament, do pray that it may be declared and enacted, That all and singular the rights and liberties asserted and claimed in the said declaration, are the true, ancient, and indubitable rights and liberties of the people of this kingdom, and so shall be esteemed, allowed, adjudged, deemed, and taken to be, and that all and every the particulars aforesaid shall be firmly and strictly holden and observed, as they are expressed in the said declaration; and all officers and ministers whatsoever shall serve their Majesties and their successors according to the same in all times to come.

XI. All which their Majesties are contented and pleased shall be declared, enacted, and established by authority of this present parliament, and shall stand, remain, and be the law of this realm for ever; and the same are by their said Majesties, by and with the advice and consent of the lords spiritual and temporal, and commons, in parliament assembled, and by the authority of the same, declared, enacted, and established accordingly.

3. VIRGINIA BILL OF RIGHTS

Adopted June 12, 1776

[Proceedings *of the Convention, 100–103;
Hening,* Statutes at Large, *IX, 109–12.*]

A DECLARATION OF RIGHTS *made by the representatives of the good
people of Virginia, assembled in full and free Convention; which
rights do pertain to them, and their posterity, as the basis and foundation of government.*

1. THAT all men are by nature equally free and independent,
and have certain inherent rights, of which, when they enter
into a state of society, they cannot, by any compact, deprive or
divest their posterity; namely, the enjoyment of life and liberty,
with the means of acquiring and possessing property, and pursuing and obtaining happiness and safety.

2. That all power is vested in, and consequently derived from,
the people; that magistrates are their trustees and servants, and
at all times amenable to them.

3. That government is, or ought to be, instituted for the common benefit, protection, and security, of the people, nation, or
community; of all the various modes and forms of government
that is best, which is capable of producing the greatest degree of
happiness and safety, and is most effectually secured against the
danger of mal-administration; and that whenever any government shall be found inadequate or contrary to these purposes, a
majority of the community hath an indubitable, unalienable, and

indefeasible right, to reform, alter, or abolish it, in such manner as shall be judged most conducive to the publick weal.

4. That no man, or set of men, are entitled to exclusive or separate emoluments or privileges from the community, but in consideration of publick services; which, not being descendible, neither ought the offices of magistrate, legislator, or judge, to be hereditary.

5. That the legislative and executive powers of the state should be separate and distinct from the judicative; and that the members of the two first may be restrained from oppression, by feeling and participating the burthens of the people, they should, at fixed periods, be reduced to a private station, return into that body from which they were originally taken, and the vacancies be supplied by frequent, certain, and regular elections, in which all, or any part of the former members, to be again eligible, or ineligible, as the laws shall direct.

6. That elections of members to serve as representatives of the people, in assembly, ought to be free; and that all men, having sufficient evidence of permanent common interest with, and attachment to, the community, have the right of suffrage, and cannot be taxed or deprived of their property for publick uses without their own consent, or that of their representatives so elected, nor bound by any law to which they have not, in like manner, assented, for the publick good.

7. That all power of suspending laws, or the execution of laws, by any authority without consent of the representatives of the people, is injurious to their rights, and ought not to be exercised.

8. That in all capital or criminal prosecutions a man hath a right to demand the cause and nature of his accusation, to be confronted with the accusers and witnesses, to call for evidence in his favour, and to a speedy trial by an impartial jury of his vicinage, without whose unanimous consent he cannot be found guilty, nor can he be compelled to give evidence against himself; that no man be deprived of his liberty except by the law of the land, or the judgment of his peers.

9. That excessive bail ought not to be required, nor excessive fines imposed, nor cruel and unusual punishments inflicted.

10. That general warrants, whereby any officer or messenger may be commanded to search suspected places without evidence of a fact committed, or to seize any person or persons not named, or whose offence is not particularly described and supported by evidence, are grievous and oppressive, and ought not to be granted.

11. That in controversies respecting property, and in suits between man and man, the ancient trial by jury is preferable to any other, and ought to be held sacred.

12. That the freedom of the press is one of the great bulwarks of liberty, and can never be restrained but by despotick governments.

13. That a well regulated militia, composed of the body of the people, trained to arms, is the proper, natural, and safe defence of a free state; that standing armies, in time of peace, should be avoided, as dangerous to liberty; and that, in all cases, the military should be under strict subordination to, and governed by, the civil power.

14. That the people have a right to uniform government; and therefore, that no government separate from, or independent of, the government of *Virginia*, ought to be erected or established within the limits thereof.

15. That no free government, or the blessing of liberty, can be preserved to any people but by a firm adherence to justice, moderation, temperance, frugality, and virtue, and by frequent recurrence to fundamental principles.

16. That religion, or the duty which we owe to our CREATOR, and the manner of discharging it, can be directed only by reason and conviction, not by force or violence; and therefore all men are equally entitled to the free exercise of religion, according to the dictates of conscience; and that it is the mutual duty of all to practice Christian forbearance, love, and charity, towards each other.

4. STATE PROPOSALS

Amendments Proposed by Pennsylvania Convention Minority
December 12, 1787

1. The rights of conscience shall be held inviolable, and neither the legislative, executive nor judicial powers of the United States shall have authority to alter, abrogate or infringe any part of the constitutions of the several States, which provide for the preservation of liberty in matters of religion.

2. That in controversies respecting property and in suits between man and man, trial by jury shall remain as heretofore, as well in the federal courts, as in those of the several States.

3. That in all capital and criminal prosecutions, a man has a right to demand the cause and nature of his accusation, as well in the federal courts, as in those of the several States; to be heard by himself or his counsel; to be confronted with the accusers and witnesses; to call for evidence in his favor, and a speedy trial, by an impartial jury of the vicinage, without whose unanimous consent he cannot be found guilty, nor can he be compelled to give evidence against himself; that no man be deprived of his liberty, except by the law of the land or the judgment of his peers.

4. That excessive bail ought not to be required, nor excessive fines imposed, nor cruel or unusual punishments inflicted.

5. That warrants unsupported by evidence, whereby any officer or messenger may be commanded or required to search suspected places, or to seize any person or persons, his or their property, not particularly described, are grievous and oppressive, and shall not be granted either by the magistrates of the federal government or others.

6. That the people have a right to the freedom of speech, of writing and of publishing their sentiments; therefore, the freedom of the press shall not be restrained by any law of the United States.

7. That the people have a right to bear arms for the defence of themselves and their own State, or the United States, or for the purpose of killing game; and no law shall be passed for disarming the people or any of them, unless for crimes committed, or real danger of public injury from individuals; and as standing armies in the time of peace are dangerous to liberty, they ought not to be kept up; and that the military shall be kept under strict subordination to and be governed by the civil power.

8. The inhabitants of the several States shall have liberty to fowl and hunt in seasonable times on the lands they hold, and on all other lands in the United States not inclosed, and in like manner to fish in all navigable waters, and others not private property, without being restrained therein by any laws to be passed by the legislature of the United States.

9. That no law shall be passed to restrain the legislatures of the several States from enacting laws for imposing taxes, except imposts and duties on goods exported and imported, and that no taxes, except imposts and duties upon goods imported and exported and postage on letters, shall be levied by the authority of Congress.

10. That elections shall remain free, that the house of representatives be properly increased in number, and that the several States shall have power to regulate the elections for senators and representatives, without being controlled either directly or indirectly by any interference on the part of Congress, and that elections of representatives be annual.

11. That the power of organizing, arming and disciplining the militia, (the manner of disciplining the militia to be prescribed by Congress) remain with the individual States, and that Congress shall not have authority to call or march any of the militia out of their own State, without the consent of such State, and for such length of time only as such State shall agree.

12. That the legislative, executive, and judicial powers be kept

separate, and to this end, that a constitutional council be appointed to advise and assist the President, who shall be responsible for the advice they give (hereby, the senators would be relieved from almost constant attendance); and also that the judges be made completely independent.

13. That no treaties which shall be directly opposed to the existing laws of the United States in Congress assembled, shall be valid until such laws shall be repealed or made conformable to such treaty, neither shall any treaties be valid which are contradictory to the constitution of the United States, or the constitutions of the individual States.

14. That the judiciary power of the United States shall be confined to cases affecting ambassadors, other public ministers and consuls, to cases of admiralty and maritime jurisdiction, to controversies to which the United States shall be a party, to controversies between two or more States—between a State and citizens of different States—between citizens claiming lands under grants of different States, and between a State or the citizens thereof and foreign States, and in criminal cases, to such only as are expressly enumerated in the constitution, and that the United States in Congress assembled, shall not have power to enact laws, which shall alter the laws of descents and distributions of the effects of deceased persons, the title of lands or goods, or the regulation of contracts in the individual States.

15. That the sovereignty, freedom and independency of the several States shall be retained, and every power, jurisdiction and right which is not by this constitution expressly delegated to the United States in Congress assembled.

Amendments Proposed by Massachusetts Convention
February 6, 1788

First, That it be explicitly declared that all Powers not expressly delegated by the aforesaid Constitution are reserved to the several States to be by them exercised.

Secondly, That there shall be one representative to every thirty thousand persons according to the Census mentioned in the Constitution until the whole number of the Representatives amounts to Two hundred.

Thirdly, That Congress do not exercise the powers vested in them by the fourth Section of the first article, but in cases when a State shall neglect or refuse to make the regulations therein mentioned or shall make regulations subversive of the rights of the People to a free & equal representation in Congress agreeably to the Constitution.

Fourthly, That Congress do not lay direct Taxes but when the Monies arising from the Impost & Excise are insufficient for the publick exigencies nor then until Congress shall have first made a requisition upon the States to assess levy & pay their respective proportions of such Requisition agreeably to the Census fixed in the said Constitution; in such way & manner as the Legislature of the States shall think best, & in such case if any State shall neglect or refuse to pay its proportion pursuant to such requisition then Congress may assess & levy such State's proportion together with interest thereon at the rate of Six per cent per annum from the time of payment prescribed in such requisition

Fifthly, That Congress erect no Company of Merchants with exclusive advantages of commerce.

Sixthly, That no person shall be tried for any Crime by which he may incur an infamous punishment or loss of life until he be first indicted by a Grand Jury, except in such cases as may arise in the Government & regulation of the Land & Naval forces.

Seventhly, The Supreme Judicial Federal Court shall have no jurisdiction of Causes between Citizens of different States unless the matter in dispute whether it concerns the realty or personalty be of the value of three thousand dollars at the least. nor shall the Federal Judicial Powers extend to any actions between Citizens of different States where the matter in dispute whether it concerns the Realty or personalty is not of the value of Fifteen hundred dollars at the least.

Eighthly, In civil actions between Citizens of different States every issue of fact arising in Actions at common law shall be tried by a Jury if the parties or either of them request it.

Ninthly, Congress shall at no time consent that any person holding an office of trust or profit under the United States shall accept of a title of Nobility or any other title or office from any King, prince or Foreign State.

1. That Congress shall exercise no power but what is expressly delegated by this Constitution.

2. That there shall be a trial by jury in all criminal cases, according to the course of proceeding in the state where the offence is committed; and that there be no appeal from matter of fact, or second trial after acquittal; but this provision shall not extend to such cases as may arise in the government of the land or naval forces.

3. That, in all actions on debts or contracts, and in all other controversies respecting property, of which the inferior federal courts have jurisdiction, the trial of facts shall be by jury, if required by either party; and that it be expressly declared that the state courts, in such cases, have a concurrent jurisdiction with the federal courts, with an appeal from either, only as to matter of law, to the Supreme Federal Court, if the matter in dispute be of the value of ——— dollars.

4. That the inferior federal courts shall not have jurisdiction of less than ——— dollars; and there may be an appeal, in all cases of revenue, as well to matter of fact as law; and Congress may give the state courts jurisdiction of revenue cases, for such forms, and in such manner, as they may think proper.

5. That, in all cases of trespasses done within the body of a county, and within the inferior federal jurisdiction, the party injured shall be entitled to trial by jury in the state where the injury shall be committed; and that it be expressly declared that the state courts, in such cases, shall have concurrent jurisdiction with the federal courts, and there shall be no appeal from either, except on matter of law; and that no person be exempt from such

jurisdiction and trial but ambassadors and ministers privileged by the law of nations.

6. That the federal courts shall not be entitled to jurisdiction by fictions or collusion.

7. That the federal judges do not hold any other office of profit, or receive the profits of any other office under Congress, during the time they hold their commission.

8. That all warrants without oath, or affirmation of a person conscientiously scrupulous of taking an oath, to search suspected places, or seize any person or his property, are grievous and oppressive; and all general warrants to search suspected places, or to apprehend any person suspected, without naming or describing the place or person in special, are dangerous, and ought not to be granted.

9. That no soldier be enlisted for a longer time than four years, except in time of war, and then only during the war.

10. That soldiers be not quartered, in time of peace, upon private houses, without the consent of the owners.

11. That no mutiny bill continue in force longer than two years.

12. That the freedom of the press be inviolably preserved.

13. That the militia shall not be subject to martial law, except in time of war, invasion, or rebellion.

ADDITIONAL PROPOSALS OF MINORITY

1. That the militia, unless selected by lot, or voluntarily enlisted, shall not be marched beyond the limits of an adjoining state, without the consent of their legislature or executive.

2. That the Congress shall have no power to alter or change the time, place, or manner of holding elections for senators or representatives, unless a state shall neglect to make regulations, or to execute its regulations, or shall be prevented by invasion or rebellion; in which cases only, Congress may interfere, until the cause be removed.

3. That, in every law of Congress imposing direct taxes, the

collection thereof shall be suspended for a certain reasonable time, therein limited; and on payment of the sum by any state, by the time appointed, such taxes shall not be collected.

4. That no standing army shall be kept up in time of peace, unless with the consent of two thirds of the members present of each branch of Congress.

5. That the President shall not command the army in person, without the consent of Congress.

6. That no treaty shall be effectual to repeal or abrogate the constitutions or bills of rights of the states, or any part of them.

7. That no regulation of commerce, or navigation act, shall be made, unless with the consent of two thirds of the members of each branch of Congress.

8. That no member of Congress shall be eligible to any office of profit under Congress, during the time for which he shall be appointed.

9. That Congress shall have no power to lay a poll tax.

10. That no person conscientiously scrupulous of bearing arms, in any case, shall be compelled personally to serve as a soldier.

11. That there be a responsible council to the President.

12. That there be no national religion established by law; but that all persons be equally entitled to protection in their religious liberty.

13. That all imposts and duties laid by Congress shall be placed to the credit of the state in which the same shall be collected, and be deducted out of such state's quota of the common or general expenses of government.

14. That every man hath a right to petition the legislature for the redress of grievances, in a peaceable and orderly manner.

15. That it be declared, that all persons intrusted [*sic*] with the legislative or executive powers of government are the trustees and servants of the people; and, as such, accountable for their conduct. Wherefore, whenever the ends of government are perverted, and public liberty manifestly endangered, and all other means of redress are ineffectual, the people may, and of right

ought to, reform the old, or establish a new government. The doctrine of non-resistance against arbitrary power and oppression is absurd, slavish, and destructive of the good and happiness of mankind.

Amendments Proposed by South Carolina Convention
May 23, 1788

And Whereas it is essential to the preservation of the rights reserved to the several states, and the freedom of the people under the operations of a General government that the right of prescribing the manner time and places of holding the Elections to the Federal Legislature, should be for ever inseperably [*sic*] annexed to the sovereignty of the several states. This convention doth declare that the same ought to remain to all posterity a perpetual and fundamental right in the local, exclusive of the interference of the General Government except in cases where the Legislatures of the States, shall refuse or neglect to perform and fulfil the same according to the tenor of the said Constitution.

This Convention doth also declare that no Section or paragraph of the said Constitution warrants a Construction that the states do not retain every power not expressly relinquished by them and vested in the General Government of the Union.

Resolved that the general Government of the United States ought never to impose direct taxes, *but* where the monies arising from the duties, imposts and excise are insufficient for the public exigencies *nor then until* Congress shall have made a requisition upon the states to Assess levy and pay their respective proportions of such requisitions And in case any state shall neglect or refuse to pay its proportion pursuant to such requisition then Congress may assess and levy such state's proportion together with Interest thereon at the rate of six per centum per annum from the time of payment prescribed by such requisition—

Resolved that the third section of the Sixth Article ought to be amended by inserting the word *"other"* between the words *"no"* and *"religious"*

First That it be Explicitly declared that all Powers not expressly & particularly Delegated by the aforesaid Constitution are reserved to the several States to be, by them Exercised.—

Secondly, That there shall be one Representative to every Thirty thousand Persons according to the Census mentioned in the Constitution, untill the whole number of Representatives amount to Two hundred.—

Thirdly That Congress do not Exercise the Powers vested in them, by the fourth Section of the first Article, but in Cases when a State shall neglect or refuse to make the Regulations therein mentioned, or shall make regulations Subversive of the rights of the People to a free and equal Representation in Congress. Nor shall Congress in any Case make regulations contrary to a free and equal Representation.—

Fourthly That Congress do not lay direct Taxes but when the money arising from Impost, Excise and their other resources are insufficient for the Publick Exigencies; nor then, untill Congress shall have first made a Requisition upon the States, to Assess, Levy, & pay their respective proportions, of such requisition agreeably to the Census fixed in the said Constitution in such way & manner as the Legislature of the State shall think best and in such Case if any State shall neglect, then Congress may Assess & Levy such States proportion together with the Interest thereon at the rate of six per Cent per Annum from the Time of payment prescribed in such requisition—

Fifthly That Congress shall erect no Company of Merchants with exclusive advantages of Commerce.—

Sixthly That no Person shall be Tryed for any Crime by which he may incur an Infamous Punishment, or loss of Life, untill he first be indicted by a Grand Jury except in such Cases as may arise in the Government and regulation of the Land & Naval Forces.—

Seventhly All Common Law Cases between Citizens of dif-

ferent States shall be commenced in the Common Law-Courts of the respective States & no appeal shall be allowed to the Federal Court in such Cases unless the sum or value of the thing in Controversy amount to three Thousand Dollars.—

Eighthly In Civil Actions between Citizens of different States every Issue of Fact arising in Actions at Common Law shall be Tryed by Jury, if the Parties, or either of them request it—

Ninthly—Congress shall at no Time consent that any Person holding an Office of Trust or profit under the United States shall accept any Title of Nobility or any other Title or Office from any King, Prince, or Foreign State.—

Tenth,

That no standing Army shall be Kept up in time of Peace unless with the consent of three fourths of the Members of each branch of Congress, nor shall Soldiers in Time of Peace be quartered upon private Houses without the consent of the Owners.—

Eleventh

Congress shall make no Laws touching Religion, or to infringe the rights of Conscience—

Twelfth

Congress shall never disarm any Citizen unless such as are or have been in Actual Rebellion.—

Amendments Proposed by Virginia Convention
June 27, 1788

That there be a Declaration or Bill of Rights asserting and securing from encroachment the essential and unalienable Rights of the People in some such manner as the following;

First, That there are certain natural rights of which men, when they form a social compact cannot deprive or divest their posterity, among which are the enjoyment of life and liberty, with the means of acquiring, possessing and protecting property, and pursuing and obtaining happiness and safety.

Second. That all power is naturally vested in and consequently derived from the people; that Magistrates, therefore, are their trustees and agents and at all times amenable to them.

Third, That Government ought to be instituted for the common benefit, protection and security of the People; and that the doctrine of non-resistance against arbitrary power and oppression is absurd slavish, and destructive of the good and happiness of mankind.

Fourth, That no man or set of Men are entitled to exclusive or seperate [sic] public emoluments or privileges from the community, but in Consideration of public services; which not being descendible, neither ought the offices of Magistrate, Legislator or Judge, or any other public office to be hereditary.

Fifth, That the legislative, executive, and judiciary powers of Government should be seperate [sic] and distinct, and that the members of the two first may be restrained from oppression by feeling and participating the public burthens, they should, at fixt periods be reduced to a private station, return into the mass of the people; and the vacancies be supplied by certain and regular elections; in which all or any part of the former members to be eligible or ineligible, as the rules of the Constitution of Government, and the laws shall direct.

Sixth, That elections of representatives in the legislature ought to be free and frequent, and all men having sufficient evidence of permanent common interest with and attachment to the Community ought to have the right of suffrage: and no aid, charge, tax or fee can be set, rated, or levied upon the people without their own consent, or that of their representatives so elected, nor can they be bound by any law to which they have not in like manner assented for the public good.

Seventh, That all power of suspending laws or the execution of laws by any authority, without the consent of the representatives of the people in the legislature is injurious to their rights, and ought not to be exercised.

Eighth, That in all capital and criminal prosecutions, a man hath a right to demand the cause and nature of his accusation, to be confronted with the accusers and witnesses, to call for evidence and be allowed counsel in his favor, and to a fair and speedy trial by an impartial Jury of his vicinage, without whose unanimous consent he cannot be found guilty, (except in the government of the land and naval forces) nor can he be compelled to give evidence against himself.

Ninth. That no freeman ought to be taken, imprisoned, or disseised of his freehold, liberties, privileges or franchises, or outlawed or exiled, or in any manner destroyed or deprived of his life, liberty or property but by the law of the land.

Tenth. That every freeman restrained of his liberty is entitled to a remedy to enquire into the lawfulness thereof, and to remove the same, if unlawful, and that such remedy ought not to be denied nor delayed.

Eleventh. That in controversies respecting property, and in suits between man and man, the ancient trial by Jury is one of the greatest Securities to the rights of the people, and ought to remain sacred and inviolable.

Twelfth. That every freeman ought to find a certain remedy by recourse to the laws for all injuries and wrongs he may receive in his person, property or character. He ought to obtain right and justice freely without sale, compleatly [*sic*] and without denial, promptly and without delay, and that all establishments or regulations contravening these rights, are oppressive and unjust.

Thirteenth, That excessive Bail ought not be required, nor excessive fines imposed, nor cruel and unusual punishments inflicted.

Fourteenth, That every freeman has a right to be secure from all unreasonable searches and siezures [*sic*] of his person, his papers and his property; all warrants, therefore, to search suspected places, or sieze [*sic*] any freeman, his papers or property, without information upon Oath (or affirmation of a person religiously scrupulous of taking an oath) of legal and sufficient cause, are grievous and oppressive; and all general Warrants to search suspected places, or to apprehend any suspected person, without specially naming or describing the place or person, are dangerous and ought not to be granted.

Fifteenth, That the people have a right peaceably to assemble together to consult for the common good, or to instruct their

Representatives; and that every freeman has a right to petition or apply to the legislature for redress of grievances.

Sixteenth, That the people have a right to freedom of speech, and of writing and publishing their Sentiments; but the freedom of the press is one of the greatest bulwarks of liberty and ought not to be violated.

Seventeenth, That the people have a right to keep and bear arms; that a well regulated Militia composed of the body of the people trained to arms is the proper, natural and safe defence of a free State. That standing armies in time of peace are dangerous to liberty, and therefore ought to be avoided, as far as the circumstances and protection of the Community will admit; and that in all cases the military should be under strict subordination to and governed by the Civil power.

Eighteenth, That no Soldier in time of peace ought to be quartered in any house without the consent of the owner, and in time of war in such manner only as the laws direct.

Nineteenth, That any person religiously scrupulous of bearing arms ought to be exempted upon payment of an equivalent to employ another to bear arms in his stead.

Twentieth, That religion or the duty which we owe to our Creator, and the manner of discharging it can be directed only by reason and conviction, not by force or violence, and therefore all men have an equal, natural and unalienable right to the free exercise of religion according to the dictates of conscience, and that no particular religious sect or society ought to be favored or established by Law in preference to others.

AMENDMENTS TO THE BODY OF THE CONSTITUTION

First, That each State in the Union shall respectively retain every power, jurisdiction and right which is not by this Constitution delegated to the Congress of the United States or to the departments of the Foederal [sic] Government.

Second, That there shall be one representative for every thirty thousand, according to the Enumeration or Census mentioned in the Constitution, until the whole number of representatives amounts to two hundred; after which that number shall be continued or encreased [*sic*] as the Congress shall direct, upon the principles fixed by the Constitution by apportioning the Representatives of each State to some greater number of people from time to time as population encreases [*sic*].

Third, When Congress shall lay direct taxes or excises, they shall immediately inform the Executive power of each State of the quota of such state according to the Census herein directed, which is proposed to be thereby raised; And if the Legislature of any State shall pass a law which shall be effectual for raising such quota at the time required by Congress, the taxes and excises laid by Congress shall not be collected, in such State.

Fourth, That the members of the Senate and House of Representatives shall be ineligible to, and incapable of holding, any civil office under the authority of the United States, during the time for which they shall respectively be elected.

Fifth, That the Journals of the proceedings of the Senate and House of Representatives shall be published at least once in every year, except such parts thereof relating to treaties, alliances or military operations, as in their judgment require secrecy.

Sixth, That a regular statement and account of the receipts and expenditures of all public money shall be published at least once in every year.

Seventh, That no commercial treaty shall be ratified without the concurrence of two thirds of the whole number of the members of the Senate; and no Treaty ceding, contracting, restraining or suspending the territorial rights or claims of the United States, or any of them or their, or any of their rights or claims to fishing in the American seas, or navigating the American rivers shall be [made] but in cases of the most urgent and extreme necessity, nor shall any such treaty be ratified without the concurrence of three fourths of the whole number of the members of both houses respectively.

Eighth, That no navigation law, or law regulating Commerce

shall be passed without the consent of two thirds of the Members present in both houses.

Ninth, That no standing army or regular troops shall be raised or kept up in time of peace, without the consent of two thirds of the members present in both houses.

Tenth, That no soldier shall be inlisted [*sic*] for any longer term than four years, except in time of war, and then for no longer term than the continuance of the war.

Eleventh, That each State respectively shall have the power to provide for organizing, arming and disciplining it's own Militia, whensoever Congress shall omit or neglect to provide for the same. That the Militia shall not be subject to Martial law, except when in actual service in time of war, invasion, or rebellion; and when not in the actual service of the United States, shall be subject only to such fines, penalties and punishments as shall be directed or inflicted by the laws of its own State.

Twelfth That the exclusive power of legislation given to Congress over the Foederal [*sic*] Town and its adjacent District and other places purchased or to be purchased by Congress of any of the States shall extend only to such regulations as respect the police and good government thereof.

Thirteenth, That no person shall be capable of being President of the United States for more than eight years in any term of sixteen years.

Fourteenth That the judicial power of the United States shall be vested in one supreme Court, and in such courts of Admiralty as Congress may from time to time ordain and establish in any of the different States: The Judicial power shall extend to all cases in Law and Equity arising under treaties made, or which shall be made under the authority of the United States; to all cases affecting ambassadors other foreign ministers and consuls; to all cases of Admiralty and maritime jurisdiction; to controversies to which the United States shall be a party; to controversies between two or [more] States, and between parties claiming lands under the grants of different States. In all cases affecting ambassadors, other foreign ministers and Consuls, and those in which a State shall be a party, the supreme court shall have original jurisdiction; in all other cases before mentioned the supreme Court shall have appellate jurisdiction as to matters of law only: except in cases of equity, and of admiralty and maritime jurisdiction, in which the Supreme Court shall have appellate jurisdiction both as to law and fact, with such exceptions and under such regulations as the Congress shall make. But the judicial power of the United States shall extend to no case where the cause of action shall have originated before the ratification of this Constitution; except in disputes between States about their Territory, disputes between persons claiming lands under the grants of different States, and suits for debts due to the United States.

Fifteenth, That in criminal prosecutions no man shall be restrained in the exercise of the usual and accustomed right of challenging or excepting to the Jury.

Sixteenth, That Congress shall not alter, modify or interfere in the times, places, or manner of holding elections for Senators and Representatives or either of them, except when the legislature of any State shall neglect, refuse or be disabled by invasion or rebellion to prescribe the same.

Seventeenth, That those clauses which declare that Congress shall not exercise certain powers be not interpreted in any manner whatsoever to extend the powers of Congress. But that they may be construed either as making exceptions to the specified powers where this shall be the case, or otherwise as inserted merely for greater caution.

Eighteenth, That the laws ascertaining the compensation to Senators and Representatives for their services be postponed in their operation, until after the election of Representatives immediately succeeding the passing thereof; that excepted, which shall first be passed on the Subject.

Nineteenth, That some Tribunal other than the Senate be provided for trying impeachments of Senators.

Twentieth, That the Salary of a Judge shall not be encreased [sic] or diminished during his continuance in Office, otherwise than by general regulations of Salary which may take place on a revision of the subject at stated periods of not less than seven years to commence from the time such Salaries shall be first ascertained by Congress.

Amendments Proposed by New York Convention
July 26, 1788

WE the Delegates of the People of the State of New York . . . Do declare and make known.

That all Power is originally vested in and consequently derived from the People, and that Government is instituted by them for their common Interest Protection and Security.

That the enjoyment of Life, Liberty and the pursuit of Happiness are essential rights which every Government ought to respect and preserve.

That the Powers of Government may be reassumed by the People, whensoever it shall become necessary to their Happiness; that every Power, Jurisdiction and right, which is not by the said Constitution clearly delegated to the Congress of the United States, or the departments of the Government thereof, remains to the People of the several States, or to their respective State Governments to whom they may have granted the same; And that those Clauses in the said Constitution, which declare, that Congress shall not have or exercise certain Powers, do not imply that Congress is entitled to any Powers not given by the said Constitution; but such Clauses are to be construed either as exceptions to certain specified Powers, or as inserted merely for greater Caution.

That the People have an equal, natural and unalienable right, freely and peaceably to Exercise their Religion according to the dictates of Conscience, and that no Religious Sect or Society ought to be favoured or established by Law in preference of others.

That the People have a right to keep and bear Arms; that a well regulated Militia, including the body of the People *capable of bearing Arms,* is the proper, natural and safe defence of a free State;

That the Militia should not be subject to Martial Law except in time of War, Rebellion or Insurrection.

That standing Armies in time of Peace are dangerous to Liberty, and ought not to be kept up, except in Cases of necessity; and that at all times, the Military should be under strict Subordination to the civil Power.

That in time of Peace no Soldier ought to be quartered in any House without the consent of the Owner, and in time of War only by the Civil Magistrate in such manner as the Laws may direct.

That no Person ought to be taken imprisoned or disseised of his freehold, or be exiled or deprived of his Privileges, Franchises, Life, Liberty or Property but by due process of Law.

That no Person ought to be put twice in Jeopardy of Life or Limb for one and the same Offence, nor, unless in case of impeachment, be punished more than once for the same Offence.

That every Person restrained of his Liberty is entitled to an enquiry into the lawfulness of such restraint, and to a removal thereof if unlawful, and that such enquiry and removal ought not to be denied or delayed, except when on account of Public Danger the Congress shall suspend the privilege of the Writ of Habeas Corpus.

That excessive Bail ought not to be required; nor excessive Fines imposed; nor Cruel or unusual Punishments inflicted.

That (except in the Government of the Land and Naval Forces, and of the Militia when in actual Service, and in cases of Impeachment) a Presentment or Indictment by a Grand Jury ought to be observed as a necessary preliminary to the trial of all Crimes cognizable by the Judiciary of the United States, and such Trial should be speedy, public, and by an impartial Jury of the County where the Crime was committed; and that no person can be found Guilty without the unanimous consent of such Jury. But in cases of Crimes not committed within any County of any of the United States, and in Cases of Crimes committed within any County in which a general Insurrection may prevail, or which may be in the possession of a foreign Enemy, the enquiry and trial may be in such County as the Congress shall by Law direct; which County in the two Cases last mentioned should be as near as conveniently may be to that County in which the Crime may have been committed. And that in all Criminal Prosecutions, the Accused ought to be informed of the cause and nature of his Accusation, to be confronted with his accusers and the Witnesses against him, to have the means of producing his Witnesses, and the assistance of Council [sic] for his defense, and should not be compelled to give Evidence against himself.

That the trial by Jury in the extent that it obtains by the Common Law of England is one of the greatest securities to the rights of a free People, and ought to remain inviolate.

That every Freeman has a right to be secure from all unreasonable searches and seizures of his person his papers or his property, and therefore, that all Warrants to search suspected places or seize any Freeman his papers or property, without information upon Oath or Affirmation of sufficient cause, are grievous and oppressive; and that all general Warrants (or such in which the place or person suspected are not particularly designated) are dangerous and ought not to be granted.

That the People have a right peaceably to assemble together to consult for their common good, or to instruct their Representatives; and that every person has a right to Petition or apply to the Legislature for redress of Grievances.—That the Freedom of the Press ought not to be violated or restrained.

That there should be once in four years an Election of the President and Vice President, so that no Officer who may be appointed by the Congress to act as President in case of the removal, death, resignation or inability of the President and Vice President can in any case continue to act beyond the termination of the period for which the last President and Vice President were elected.

That nothing contained in the said Constitution is to be construed to prevent the Legislature of any State from passing Laws at its discretion from time to time to divide such State into convenient Districts, and to apportion its Representatives to and amongst such Districts.

That the Prohibition contained in the said Constitution against *ex post facto* Laws, extends only to Laws concerning Crimes.

That all Appeals in Causes determineable [*sic*] according to the course of the common Law, ought to be by Writ of Error and not otherwise.

That the Judicial Power of the United States in cases in which a State may be a party, does not extend to criminal Prosecutions, or to authorize any Suit by any Person against a State.

That the Judicial Power of the United States as to Controversies between Citizens of the same State claiming Lands under Grants of different States is not to be construed to extend to any other Controversies between them except those which relate to such Lands, so claimed under Grants of different States.

That the Jurisdiction of the Supreme Court of the United States, or of any other Court to be instituted by the Congress, is not in any case to be encreased [*sic*] enlarged or extended by any Fiction Collusion or mere suggestion;—And That no Treaty is to be construed so to operate as to alter the Constitution of any State.

Under these impressions and declaring that the rights aforesaid cannot be abridged or violated, and that the Explanations aforesaid are consistent with the said Constitution, And in confidence that the Amendments which shall have been proposed to the said Constitution will receive an early and mature Consideration: We the said Delegates, in the Name and in the behalf of the People of the State of New York Do by these presents Assent to and Ratify the said Constitution. In full Confidence nevertheless that until a Convention shall be called and convened for proposing Amendments to the said Constitution, the Militia of this State will not be continued in Service out of this State for a longer term than six weeks without the Consent of the Legislature thereof;—that the Congress will not make or alter any Regulation in this State respecting the times places and manner of holding Elections for Senators or Representatives unless the Legislature of this State shall neglect or refuse to make Laws or regulations for the purpose, or from any circumstance be incapable of making the same, and that in those cases such power will only be exercised until the Legislature of this State shall make provision in the Premises;—that no Excise will be imposed on any Article of the Growth production or Manufacture of the United States, or any of them within this State, Ardent Spirits excepted; And that the Congress will not lay direct Taxes within this State, but when the Monies arising from the Impost and Excise shall be insufficient for the public Exigencies, nor then, until Congress shall first have made a Requisition upon this State to assess levy and pay the Amount of such Requisition made agreably [*sic*] to the Census fixed in the said Constitution in such way and manner as the Legislature of this State shall judge best, but that in such case, if the State shall neglect or refuse to pay its proportion pursuant to such Requisition, then the Congress may assess and levy this States [*sic*] proportion together with Interest at the Rate of six per Centum per Annum from the time at which the same was required to be paid. . . .

AND the Convention do in the Name and Behalf of the People of the State of New York enjoin it upon their Representatives in the Congress, to Exert all their Influence, and use all reasonable means to Obtain a Ratification of the following Amendments to the said Constitution in the manner prescribed therein; and in all Laws to be passed by the Congress in the meantime to conform to the spirit of the said Amendments as far as the Constitution will admit.

That there shall be one Representative for every thirty thousand Inhabitants, according to the enumeration or Census mentioned in the Constitution, until the whole number of Representatives amounts to two hundred; after which that number shall be continued or encreased [*sic*] but not diminished, as Congress shall direct, and according to such ratio as the Congress shall fix, in conformity to the rule prescribed for the Apportionment of Representatives and direct Taxes.

That the Congress do not impose any Excise on any Article (except Ardent Spirits) of the Growth Production or Manufacture of the United States, or any of them.

That Congress do not lay direct Taxes but when the Monies arising from the Impost and Excise shall be insufficient for the Public Exigencies, nor then until Congress shall first have made a Requisition upon the States to assess levy and pay their respective proportions of such Requisition, agreably [sic] to the Census fixed in the said Constitution, in such way and manner as the Legislatures of the respective States shall judge best; and in such Case, if any State shall neglect or refuse to pay its proportion pursuant to such Requisition, then Congress may assess and levy such States [sic] proportion, together with Interest at the rate of six per Centum per Annum, from the time of Payment prescribed in such Requisition.

That the Congress shall not make or alter any Regulation in any State respecting the times places and manner of holding Elections for Senators or Representatives, unless the Legislature of such State shall neglect or refuse to make Laws or Regulations for the purpose, or from any circumstance be incapable of making the same; and then only until the Legislature of such State shall make provision in the premises; provided that Congress may prescribe the time for the Election of Representatives.

That no Persons except natural born Citizens, or such as were Citizens on or before the fourth day of July one thousand seven hundred and seventy six, or such as held Commissions under the United States during the War, and have at any time since the fourth day of July one thousand seven hundred and seventy six become Citizens of one or other of the United States, and who shall be Freeholders, shall be eligible to the Places of President, Vice President, or Members of either House of the Congress of the United States.

That the Congress do not grant Monopolies or erect any Company with exclusive Advantages of Commerce.

That no standing Army or regular Troops shall be raised or kept up in time of peace, without the consent of two-thirds of the Senators and Representatives present, in each House.

That no Money be borrowed on the Credit of the United States without the Assent of two-thirds of the Senators and Representatives present in each House.

That the Congress shall not declare War without the concurrence of two-thirds of the Senators and Representatives present in each House.

That the Privilege of the *Habeas Corpus* shall not by any Law be suspended for a longer term than six Months, or until twenty days after the Meeting of the Congress next following the passing of the Act for such suspension.

That the Right of the Congress to exercise exclusive Legislation over such District, not exceeding ten Miles square, as may by cession of a particular State, and the acceptance of Congress, become the Seat of the Government of the United States, shall not be so exercised, as to exempt the Inhabitants of such District from paying the like Taxes Imposts Duties and Excises, as shall be imposed on the other Inhabitants of the State in which such District may be; and that no person shall be privileged within the said District from Arrest for Crimes committed, or Debts contracted out of the said District.

That the Right of exclusive Legislation with respect to such places as may be purchased for the Erection of Forts, Magazines, Arsenals, Dockyards and other needful Buildings, shall not authorize the Congress to make any Law to prevent the Laws of the States respectively in which they may be, from extending to such places in all civil and Criminal Matters except as to such Persons as shall be in the Service of the United States; nor to them with respect to Crimes committed without such Places.

That the Compensation for the Senators and Representatives be ascertained by standing Laws; and that no alteration of the existing rate of Compensation shall operate for the Benefit of the Representatives, until after a subsequent Election shall have been had.

That the Journals of the Congress shall be published at least once a year, with the exception of such parts relating to Treaties or Military operations, as in the Judgment of either House shall require Secrecy; and that both Houses of Congress shall always keep their Doors open during their Sessions, unless the Business may in their Opinion requires [*sic*] Secrecy. That the yeas & nays shall be entered on the Journals whenever two Members in either House may require it.

That no Capitation Tax shall ever be laid by the Congress.

That no Person be eligible as a Senator for more than six years in any term of twelve years; and that the Legislatures of the respective States may recal [*sic*] their Senators or either of them, and elect others in their stead, to serve the remainder of the time for which the Senators so recalled were appointed.

That no Senator or Representative shall during the time for which he was elected be appointed to any Office under the Authority of the United States.

That the Authority given to the Executives of the States to fill the vacancies of Senators be abolished, and that such vacancies be filled by the respective Legislatures.

That the Power of Congress to pass uniform Laws concerning Bankruptcy shall only extend to Merchants and other Traders; and that the States respectively may pass Laws for the relief of other Insolvent Debtors.

That no Person shall be eligible to the Office of President of the United States a third time.

That the Executive shall not grant Pardons for Treason, unless with the Consent of the Congress; but may at his discretion grant Reprieves to persons convicted of Treason, until their Cases, can be laid before the Congress.

That the President or person exercising his Powers for the time being, shall not command an Army in the Field in person, without the previous desire of the Congress.

That all Letters Patent, Commissions, Pardons, Writs and Process of the United States, shall run in the Name of *the People of the United States,* and be tested in the Name of the President of the United States, or the person exercising his powers for the time being, or the first Judge of the Court out of which the same shall issue, as the case may be.

That the Congress shall not constitute ordain or establish any Tribunals or Inferior Courts, with any other than Appellate Jurisdiction, except such as may be necessary for the Tryal [*sic*] of Causes of Admiralty and Maritime Jurisdiction, and for the Trial of Piracies and Felonies committed on the High Seas; and in all other Cases to which the Judicial Power of the United States extends, and in which the Supreme Court of the United States has not original Jurisdiction, the Causes shall be heard tried, and determined in some one of the State Courts, with the right of Appeal to the Supreme Court of the United States, or other proper Tribunal to be established for that purpose by the Congress, with such exceptions, and under such regulations as the Congress shall make.

That the Court for the Trial of Impeachments shall consist of the Senate, the Judges of the Supreme Court of the United States, and the first or Senior Judge for the time being, of the highest Court of general and ordinary common Law Jurisdiction in each State;—that the Congress shall by standing Laws designate the Courts in the respective States answering this Description, and in States having no Courts exactly answering this Description, shall designate some other Court, preferring such if any there be, whose Judge or Judges may hold their places during good Behaviour— Provided that no more than one Judge, other than Judges of the Supreme Court of the United States, shall come from one State— That the Congress be authorized to pass Laws for compensating the said Judges for such Services and for compelling their Attendance—and that a Majority at least of the said Judges shall be requisite to constitute the said Court—that no person impeached shall sit as a Member thereof. That each Member shall previous to the entering upon any Trial take an Oath or Affirmation, honestly and impartially to hear and determine the Cause—and that a Majority of the Members present shall be necessary to a Conviction.

That persons aggrieved by any Judgment, Sentence or Decree of the Supreme Court of the United States, in any Cause in which that Court has original Jurisdiction, with such exceptions and under such Regulations as the Congress shall make concerning the same, shall upon application, have a Commission to be issued by the President of the United States, to such Men learned in the

Law as he shall nominate, and by and with the Advice and consent of the Senate appoint, not less than seven, authorizing such Commissioners, or any seven or more of them, to correct the Errors in such Judgment or to review such Sentence and Decree, as the case may be, and to do Justice to the parties in the Premises.

That no Judge of the Supreme Court of the United States shall hold any other Office under the United States, or any of them.

That the Judicial Power of the United States shall extend to no Controversies respecting Land, unless it relate to Claims of Territory or Jurisdiction between States, or to Claims of Land between Individuals, or between States and Individuals under the Grants of different States.

That the Militia of any State shall not be compelled to serve without the limits of the State for a longer term than six weeks, without the Consent of the Legislature thereof.

That the words *without the Consent of the Congress* in the seventh Clause of the ninth Section of the first Article of the Constitution, be expunged.

That the Senators and Representatives and all Executive and Judicial Officers of the United States shall be bound by Oath or Affirmation not to infringe or violate the Constitutions or Rights of the respective States.

That the Legislatures of the respective States may make Provision by Law, that the Electors of the Election Districts to be by them appointed shall chuse [*sic*] a Citizen of the United States who shall have been an Inhabitant of such District for the Term of one year immediately preceeding [*sic*] the time of his Election, for one of the Representatives of such State.

Amendments Proposed by North Carolina Convention
August 1, 1788

DECLARATION OF RIGHTS.

1st That there are certain natural rights of which men, when they form a social compact, cannot deprive or divest their posterity, among which are the enjoyment of life, and liberty, with the means of acquiring, possessing and protecting property, and pursuing and obtaining happiness and safety.

2d. That all power is naturally vested in, and consequently derived from the people; that magistrates therefore are their trustees, and agents, and at all times amenable to them.

3d. That Government ought to be instituted for the common benefit, protection and security of the people; and that the doctrine of non-resistance against arbitrary power and oppression is absurd, slavish, and destructive to the good and happiness of mankind.

4th That no man or set of men are entitled to exclusive or separate public emoluments or privileges from the community, but in consideration of public services; which not being descendible, neither ought the offices of magistrate, legislator or judge, or any other public office to be hereditary.

5th. That the legislative, executive and judiciary powers of government should be separate and distinct, and that the members of the two first may be restrained from oppression by feeling and participating the public burthens, they should at fixed periods be reduced to a private station, return into the mass of the people; and the vacancies be supplied by certain and regular elections; in which all or any part of the former members to be eligible or ineligible, as the rules of the Constitution of Government, and the laws shall direct.

6th. That elections of Representatives in the legislature ought to be free and frequent, and all men having sufficient evidence of permanent common interest with, and attachment to the community, ought to have the right of suffrage: and no aid, charge, tax or fee can be set, rated, or levied upon the people without their own consent, or that of their representatives, so elected, nor can they be bound by any law, to which they have not in like manner assented for the public good.

7th. That all power of suspending laws, or the execution of laws by any authority without the consent of the representatives, of the people in the Legislature, is injurious to their rights, and ought not to be exercised.

8th. That in all capital and criminal prosecutions, a man hath a right to demand the cause and nature of his accusation, to be confronted with the accusers and witnesses, to call for evidence and be allowed counsel in his favor, and to a fair and speedy trial by an impartial jury of his vicinage, without whose unanimous consent he cannot be found guilty (except in the government of the land and naval forces) nor can he be compelled to give evidence against himself.

9th That no freeman ought to be taken, imprisoned, or disseized of his freehold, liberties, privileges or franchises, or outlawed or exiled, or in any manner destroyed or deprived of his life, liberty, or property but by the law of the land.

10th. That every freeman restrained of his liberty is entitled to a remedy to inquire into the lawfulness thereof, and to remove the same, if unlawful, and that such remedy ought not to be denied nor delayed.

11th. That in controversies respecting property, and in suits between man and man, the ancient trial by jury is one of the greatest securities to the rights of the people, and ought to remain sacred and inviolable.

12th. That every freeman ought to find a certain remedy by recourse to the laws for all injuries and wrongs he may receive in his person, property, or character. He ought to obtain right and justice freely without sale, completely and without denial, promptly and without delay, and that all establishments, or regulations contravening these rights, are oppressive and unjust.

13th. That excessive bail ought not to be required, nor excessive fines imposed, nor cruel and unusual punishments inflicted,

14. That every freeman has a right to be secure from all unreasonable searches, and seizures of his person, his papers, and property: all warrants therefore to search suspected places, or seize any freeman, his papers or property, without information upon oath (or affirmation of a person religiously scrupulous of taking an oath) of legal and sufficient cause, are grievous and oppressive, and all general warrants to search suspected places, or to appre-

hend any suspected person without specially naming or describing the place or person, are dangerous and ought not to be granted.

15th. That the people have a right peaceably to assemble together to consult for the common good, or to instruct their representatives; and that every freeman has a right to petition or apply to the Legislature for redress of grievances.

16th. That the people have a right to freedom of speech, and of writing and publishing their sentiments; that the freedom of the press is one of the greatest bulwarks of Liberty, and ought not to be violated.

17th. That the people have a right to keep and bear arms; that a well regulated militia composed of the body of the people, trained to arms, is the proper, natural and safe defence of a free state. That standing armies in time of peace are dangerous to Liberty, and therefore ought to be avoided, as far as the circumstances and protection of the community will admit; and that in all cases, the military should be under strict subordination to, and governed by the civil power.

18th. That no soldier in time of peace ought to be quartered in any house without the consent of the owner, and in time of war in such manner only as the Laws direct

19th. That any person religiously scrupulous of bearing arms ought to be exempted upon payment of an equivalent to employ another to bear arms in his stead.

10. [20th] That religion, or the duty which we owe to our Creator, and the manner of discharging it, can be directed only by reason and conviction, not by force or violence, and therefore all men have an equal, natural and unalienable right to the free exercise of religion according to the dictates of conscience, and that no particular religious sect or society ought to be favoured or established by law in preference to others.

AMENDMENTS TO THE CONSTITUTION.

I. THAT each state in the union shall, respectively, retain every power, jurisdiction and right, which is not by this constitution delegated to the Congress of the United States, or to the departments of the Federal Government.

II. That there shall be one representative for every 30,000, according to the enumeration or census, mentioned in the constitution, until the whole number of representatives amounts to two hundred; after which, that number shall be continued or increased, as Congress shall direct, upon the principles fixed in the constitution, by apportioning the representatives of each state to some greater number of people from time to time, as population encreases [sic].

III. When Congress shall lay direct taxes or excises, they shall immediately inform the executive power of each state, of the quota of such State, according to the census herein directed, which is proposed to be thereby raised: And if the legislature of any state shall pass a law, which shall be effectual for raising such quota at the time required by Congress, the taxes and excises laid by Congress shall not be collected in such state.

IV. That the members of the senate and house of representatives shall be ineligible to, and incapable of holding any civil office under the authority of the United States, during the time for which they shall, respectively, be elected.

V. That the journals of the proceedings of the senate and house of representatives shall be published at least once in every year, except such parts thereof relating to treaties, alliances, or military operations, as in their judgment require secrecy.

VI. That a regular statement and account of the receipts and expenditures of the public money shall be published at least once in every year.

VII. That no commercial treaty shall be ratified without the concurrence of two-thirds of the whole number of the members of the Senate: And no treaty, ceding, contracting, or restraining or suspending the territorial rights or claims of the United States, or any of them or their, or any of their rights or claims to fishing in the American seas, or navigating the American rivers shall be made, but in cases of the most urgent and extreme necessity; nor shall any such treaty be ratified without the concurrence of three-fourths of the whole number of the members of both houses respectively.

VIII. That no navigation law, or law regulating commerce shall be passed without the consent of two-thirds of the members present in both houses.

IX. That no standing army or regular troops shall be raised or kept up in time of peace, without the consent of two thirds of the members present in both houses.

X. That no soldier shall be enlisted for any longer term than four years, except in time of war, and then for no longer term than the continuance of the war

XI. That each state, respectively, shall have the power to provide for organizing, arming and disciplining its own militia whensoever Congress shall omit or neglect to provide for the same. That the militia shall not be subject to martial law, except when in actual service in time of war, invasion or rebellion: And when not in the actual service of the United States, shall be subject only to such fines, penalties, and punishments as shall be directed or inflicted by the laws of its own state.

XII. That Congress shall not declare any state to be in rebellion without the consent of at least two-thirds of all the members present of both houses.

XIII. That the exclusive power of Legislation given to Congress over the federal town and its adjacent district, and other places, purchased or to be purchased by Congress, of any of the states, shall extend only to such regulations as respect the police and good government thereof.

XIV. That no person shall be capable of being president of the United States for more than eight years in any term of sixteen years.

XV. That the judicial power of the United States shall be vested in one supreme court, and in such courts of admiralty as Congress may from time to time ordain and establish in any of the different states. The judicial power shall extend to all cases in law and equity, arising under treaties made, or which shall be made under the authority of the United States; to all cases affecting ambassadors, other foreign ministers and consuls; to all cases of admiralty, and maritime jurisdiction; to controversies to which the United States shall be a party; to controversies between two or more states, and between parties claiming lands under the grants of different states. In all cases affecting ambassadors, other foreign ministers and consuls, and those in which a state shall be a party; the supreme court shall have original jurisdiction, in all other cases before mentioned; the supreme court shall have appellate jurisdiction as to matters of law only, except in cases of equity, and of admiralty and maritime jurisdiction, in which the supreme court shall have appelate [*sic*] jurisdiction both as to law and fact, with such exceptions, and under such regulations as the Congress shall make. But the judicial power of the United States shall extend to no case where the cause of action shall have originated before the ratification of this constitution, except in disputes between states about their territory; disputes between persons claiming lands under the grants of different states, and suits for debts due to the united states [*sic*].

XVI That in criminal prosecutions, no man shall be restrained in the exercise of the usual and accustomed right of challenging or excepting to the jury.

XVII. That Congress shall not alter, modify, or interfere in the times, places, or manner of holding elections for senators and representatives, or either of them, except when the legislature of any state shall neglect, refuse or be disabled by invasion or rebellion, to prescribe the same.

XVIII. That those clauses which declare that Congress shall not exercise certain powers, be not interpreted in any manner whatsoever to extend the powers of Congress; but that they be construed either as making exceptions to the specified powers where this shall be the case, or otherwise, as inserted merely for greater caution.

XIX That the laws ascertaining the compensation of senators and representatives for their services be posponed [*sic*] in their operation, until after the election of representatives immediately succeeding the passing thereof, that excepted, which shall first be passed on the subject,

XX. That some tribunal, other than the senate, be provided for trying impeachments of senators.

XXI That the salary of a judge shall not be increased or diminished during his continuance in office, otherwise than by general regulations of salary which may take place, on a revision of the subject at stated periods of not less than seven years, to commence from the time such salaries shall be first ascertained by Congress.

XXII. That Congress erect no company of merchants with exclusive advantages of commerce.

XXIII. That no treaties which shall be directly opposed to the existing laws of the United States in Congress assembled, shall be valid until such laws shall be repealed, or made conformable to such treaty; nor shall any treaty be valid which is contradictory to the constitution of the United States.

XXIV. That the latter part of the fifth paragraph of the 9th section of the first article be altered to read thus,—Nor shall vessels bound to a particular state be obliged to enter or pay duties in any other; nor when bound from any one of the States be obliged to clear in another.

XXV. That Congress shall not directly or indirectly, either by themselves or thro' the judiciary, interfere with any one of the states in the redemption of paper money already emitted and now in circulation, or in liquidating and discharging the public securities of any one of the states: But each and every state shall have the exclusive right of making such laws and regulations for the above purposes as they shall think proper.

XXVI That Congress shall not introduce foreign troops into the United States without the consent of two-thirds of the members present of both houses.

5. AMENDMENTS OFFERED IN CONGRESS BY MADISON

June 8, 1789

First. That there be prefixed to the Constitution a declaration, that all power is originally vested in, and consequently derived from, the people.

That Government is instituted and ought to be exercised for the benefit of the people; which consists in the enjoyment of life and liberty, with the right of acquiring and using property, and generally of pursuing and obtaining happiness and safety.

That the people have an indubitable, unalienable, and indefeasible right to reform or change their Government, whenever it be found adverse or inadequate to the purposes of its institution.

Secondly. That in article 1st, section 2, clause 3, these words be struck out, to wit: "The number of Representatives shall not exceed one for every thirty thousand, but each State shall have at least one Representative, and until such enumeration shall be made;" and that in place thereof be inserted these words, to wit: "After the first actual enumeration, there shall be one Representative for every thirty thousand, until the number amounts to ———, after which the proportion shall be so regulated by Congress, that the number shall never be less than ———, nor more than ———, but each State shall, after the first enumeration, have at least two Representatives; and prior thereto."

Thirdly. That in article 1st, section 6, clause 1, there be added to the end of the first sentence, these words, to wit: "But no law varying the compensation last ascertained shall operate before the next ensuing election of Representatives."

Fourthly. That in article 1st, section 9, between clauses 3 and 4, be inserted these clauses, to wit: The civil rights of none shall be abridged on account of religious belief or worship, nor shall any national religion be established, nor shall the full and equal rights of conscience be in any manner, or on any pretext, infringed.

The people shall not be deprived or abridged of their right to speak, to write, or to publish their sentiments; and the freedom of the press, as one of the great bulwarks of liberty, shall be inviolable.

The people shall not be restrained from peaceably assembling and consulting for their common good; nor from applying to the Legislature by petitions, or remonstrances, for redress of their grievances.

The right of the people to keep and bear arms shall not be infringed; a well armed and well regulated militia being the best security of a free country: but no person religiously scrupulous of bearing arms shall be compelled to render military service in person.

No soldiers shall in time of peace be quartered in any house without the consent of the owner; nor at any time, but in a manner warranted by law.

No person shall be subject, except in cases of impeachment, to more than one punishment or one trial for the same offence; nor shall be compelled to be a witness against himself; nor be deprived of life, liberty, or property, without due process of law; nor be obliged to relinquish his property, where it may be necessary for public use, without a just compensation.

Excessive bail shall not be required, nor excessive fines imposed, nor cruel and unusual punishments inflicted.

The rights of the people to be secured in their persons, their houses, their papers, and their other property, from all unreasonable searches and seizures, shall not be violated by warrants issued without probable cause, supported by oath or affirmation, or not particularly describing the places to be searched, or the persons or things to be seized.

In all criminal prosecutions, the accused shall enjoy the right to a speedy and public trial, to be informed of the cause and nature of the accusation, to be confronted with his accusers, and the witnesses against him; to have a compulsory process for obtaining witnesses in his favor; and to have the assistance of counsel for his defence.

The exceptions here or elsewhere in the Constitution, made in favor of particular rights, shall not be so construed as to diminish the just importance of other rights retained by the people, or as to enlarge the powers delegated by the Constitution; but either as actual limitations of such powers, or as inserted merely for greater caution.

Fifthly. That in article 1st, section 10, between clauses 1 and 2, be inserted this clause, to wit:

No State shall violate the equal rights of conscience, or the freedom of the press, or the trial by jury in criminal cases.

Sixthly. That, in article 3d, section 2, be annexed to the end of clause 2d, these words, to wit:

But no appeal to such court shall be allowed where the value in controversy shall not amount to ——— dollars: nor shall any fact triable by jury, according to the course of common law, be otherwise re-examinable than may consist with the principles of common law.

Seventhly. That in article 3d, section 2, the third clause be struck out, and in its place be inserted the clauses following, to wit:

The trial of all crimes (except in cases of impeachments, and cases arising in the land or naval forces, or the militia when on actual service, in time of war or public danger) shall be by an impartial jury of freeholders of the vicinage, with the requisite of unanimity for conviction, of the right of challenge, and other accustomed requisites; and in all crimes punishable with loss of life or member, presentment or indictment by a grand jury shall be an essential preliminary, provided that in cases of crimes committed within any county which may be in possession of an enemy, or in which a general insurrection may prevail, the trial may by law be authorized in some other county of the same State, as near as may be to the seat of the offence.

In cases of crimes committed not within any county, the trial may by law be in such county as the laws shall have prescribed. In suits at common law, between man and man, the trial by jury, as one of the best securities to the rights of the people, ought to remain inviolate.

Eighthly. That immediately after article 6th, be inserted, as article 7th, the clauses following, to wit:

The powers delegated by this Constitution are appropriated to the departments to which they are respectively distributed: so that the Legislative Department shall never exercise the powers vested in the Executive or Judicial, nor the Executive exercise the powers vested in the Legislative or Judicial, nor the Judicial exercise the powers vested in the Legislative or Executive Departments.

The powers not delegated by this Constitution, nor prohibited by it to the States, are reserved to the States respectively.

Ninthly. That article 7th be numbered as article 8th.

6. AMENDMENTS REPORTED
BY THE SELECT COMMITTEE
July 28, 1789

In the introductory paragraph before the words, "*We the people*," add, "Government being intended for the benefit of the people, and the rightful establishment thereof being derived from their authority alone."

Art. 1, Sec. 2, Par. 3—Strike out all between the words, "*direct*" and "*and until such*," and instead thereof insert, "After the first enumeration there shall be one representative for every thirty thousand until the number shall amount to one hundred; after which the proportion shall be so regulated by Congress that the number of Representatives shall never be less than one hundred, nor more than one hundred and seventy-five, but each State shall always have at least one Representative."

Art. 1, Sec. 6—Between the words "*United States*," and "*shall in all cases*," strike out "*they*," and insert, "But no law varying the compensation shall take effect until an election of Representatives shall have intervened. The members."

Art. 1, Sec. 9—Between Par. 2 and 3 insert, "No religion shall be established by law, nor shall the equal rights of conscience be infringed."

"The freedom of speech, and of the press, and the right of the people peaceably to assemble and consult for their common good, and to apply to the government for redress of grievances, shall not be infringed."

"A well regulated militia, composed of the body of the people, being the best security of a free State, the right of the people to keep and bear arms shall not be infringed, but no person religiously scrupulous shall be compelled to bear arms."

"No soldier shall in time of peace be quartered in any house without the consent of the owner, nor in time of war but in a manner to be prescribed by law."

"No person shall be subject, except in case of impeachment, to more than one trial or one punishment for the same offence, nor shall be compelled to be a witness against himself, nor be deprived of life, liberty, or property without due process of law; nor shall private property be taken for public use without just compensation."

"Excessive bail shall not be required, nor excessive fines imposed, nor cruel and unusual punishments inflicted."

"The right of the people to be secure in their person, houses, papers and effects, shall not be violated by warrants issuing, without probable cause supported by oath or affirmation, and not particularly describing the places to be searched, and the persons or things to be seized."

"The enumeration in this Constitution of certain rights shall not be construed to deny or disparage others retained by the people."

ART. 1, SEC. 10, between the 1st and 2d PAR. insert, "No State shall infringe the equal rights of conscience, nor the freedom of speech, or of the press, nor of the right of trial by jury in criminal cases."

ART. 3, SEC. 2, add to the 2d PAR. "But no appeal to such court shall be allowed, where the value in controversy shall not amount to one thousand dollars; nor shall any fact, triable by a Jury according to the course of the common law, be otherwise re-examinable than according to the rules of common law."

ART. 3, SEC. 2—Strike out the whole of the 3d paragraph, and insert—"In all criminal prosecutions the accused shall enjoy the right to a speedy and public trial, to be informed of the nature and cause of the accusation, to be confronted with the witnesses against him, to have compulsory process for obtaining witnesses in his favor, and to have the assistance of counsel for his defence."

"The trial of all crimes (except in cases of impeachment, and in cases arising in the land or naval forces, or in the militia, when in actual service in time of war or public danger) shall be by an impartial jury of freeholders of the vicinage, with the requisite of unanimity for conviction, the right of challenge and other accustomed requisites; and no person shall be held to answer for a capital, or otherwise infamous crime, unless on a presentment or indictment by a Grand Jury; but if a crime be committed in a place in the possession of an enemy, or in which an insurrection may prevail, the indictment and trial may by law be authorized in some other place within the same State; and if it be committed in a place not within a State, the indictment and trial may be at such place or places as the law may have directed."

"In suits at common law the right of trial by jury shall be preserved."

"Immediately after ART. 6, the following to be inserted as ART. 7."

"The powers delegated by this Constitution to the government of the United States, shall be exercised as therein appropriated, so that the Legislative shall never exercise the powers vested in the Executive or the Judicial; nor the Executive the powers vested in the Legislative or Judicial; nor the Judicial the powers vested in the Legislative or Executive."

"The powers not delegated by this Constitution, nor prohibited by it to the States, are reserved to the States respectively."

ART. 7 to be made ART. 8.

ARTICLE THE TENTH.

The trial of all crimes (except in cases of impeachment, and in cases arising in the land or naval forces, or in the militia when in actual service in time of War or public danger) shall be by an Impartial Jury of the Vicinage, with the requisite of unanimity for conviction, the right of challenge, and other accostomed [*sic*] requisites; and no person shall be held to answer for a capital, or otherways [*sic*] infamous crime, unless on a presentment or indictment by a Grand Jury; but if a crime be committed in a place in the possession of an enemy, or in which an insurrection may prevail, the indictment and trial may by law be authorised in some other place within the same State.

ARTICLE THE ELEVENTH.

No appeal to the Supreme Court of the United States, shall be allowed, where the value in controversy shall not amount to one thousand dollars, nor shall any fact, triable by a Jury according to the course of the common law, be otherwise re-examinable, than according to the rules of common law.

ARTICLE THE TWELFTH.

In suits at common law, the right of trial by Jury shall be preserved.

ARTICLE THE THIRTEENTH.

Excessive bail shall not be required, nor excessive fines imposed, nor cruel and unusual punishments inflicted.

ARTICLE THE FOURTEENTH.

No State shall infringe the right of trial by Jury in criminal cases, nor the rights of conscience, nor the freedom of speech, or of the press.

ARTICLE THE FIFTEENTH.

The enumeration in the Constitution of certain rights, shall not be construed to deny or disparage others retained by the people.

ARTICLE THE SIXTEENTH.

The powers delegated by the Constitution to the government of the United States, shall be exercised as therein appropriated, so that the Legislative shall never exercise the powers vested in the Executive or Judicial; nor the Executive the powers vested in the Legislative or Judicial; nor the Judicial the powers vested in the Legislative or Executive.

ARTICLE THE SEVENTEENTH.

The powers not delegated by the Constitution, nor prohibited by it, to the States, are reserved to the States respectively.

8. AMENDMENTS PASSED
BY THE SENATE
September 9, 1789

ARTICLE THE FIRST.

After the first enumeration, required by the first article of the Constitution, there shall be one Representative for every thirty thousand, until the number shall amount to one hundred; to which number one Representative shall be added for every subsequent increase of forty thousand, until the Representatives shall amount to two hundred, to which number one Representative shall be added for every subsequent increase of sixty thousand persons.

ARTICLE THE SECOND.

No law, varying the compensation for the services of the Senators and Representatives, shall take effect, until an election of Representatives shall have intervened.

ARTICLE THE THIRD.

Congress shall make no law establishing articles of faith, or a mode of worship, or prohibiting the free exercise of religion, or abridging the freedom of speech, or of the press, or the right of the people peaceably to assemble, and to petition to the government for a redress of grievances.

ARTICLE THE FOURTH.

A well regulated militia, being necessary to the security of a free State, the right of the people to keep and bear arms, shall not be infringed.

ARTICLE THE FIFTH.

No soldier shall, in time of peace, be quartered in any house, without the consent of the owner, nor in time of war, but in a manner to be prescribed by law.

ARTICLE THE SIXTH.

The right of the people to be secure in their persons, houses, papers, and effects, against unreasonable searches and seizures, shall not be violated, and no warrants shall issue, but upon probable cause, supported by oath or affirmation, and particularly describing the place to be searched, and the persons or things to be seized.

ARTICLE THE SEVENTH.

No person shall be held to answer for a capital, or otherwise infamous crime, unless on a presentment or indictment of a Grand Jury, except in cases arising in the land or naval forces, or in the militia, when in actual service in time of war or public danger; nor shall any person be subject for the same offence to be twice put in jeopardy of life or limb; nor shall be compelled in any criminal case, to be a witness against himself, nor be deprived of life, liberty or property, without due process of law; nor shall private property be taken for public use without just compensation.

ARTICLE THE EIGHTH.

In all criminal prosecutions, the accused shall enjoy the right to a speedy and public trial, to be informed of the nature and cause of the accusation, to be confronted with the witnesses against him, to have compulsory process for obtaining witnesses in his favour, and to have the assistance of counsel for his defence.

ARTICLE THE NINTH.

In suits at common law, where the value in controversy shall exceed twenty dollars, the right of trial by Jury shall be preserved, and no fact, tried by a Jury, shall be otherwise re-examined in any court of the United States, than according to the rules of the common law.

ARTICLE THE TENTH.

Excessive bail shall not be required, nor excessive fines imposed, nor cruel and unusual punishments inflicted.

ARTICLE THE ELEVENTH.

The enumeration in the Constitution, of certain rights, shall not be construed to deny or disparage others retained by the people.

ARTICLE[2] THE TWELFTH.

The powers not delegated to the United States by the Constitution, nor prohibited by it to the States, are reserved to the States respectively, or to the people.

[2] This word in the printed document reads ACTICLE.

9.

AMENDMENTS AGREED TO AFTER

CONFERENCE AND PROPOSED

BY CONGRESS TO THE STATES

September 25, 1789

Article the first . . . After the first enumeration required by the first Article of the Constitution, there shall be one Representative for every thirty thousand, until the number shall amount to one hundred, after which, the proportion shall be so regulated by Congress, that there shall be not less than one hundred Representatives, nor less than one Representative for every forty thousand persons, until the number of Representatives shall amount to two hundred, after which the proportion shall be so regulated by Congress, that there shall not be less than two hundred Representatives, nor more than one Representative for every fifty thousand persons.

Article the second . . . No law, varying the compensation for the services of the Senators and Representatives, shall take effect, until an election of Representatives shall have intervened.

Article the third . . . Congress shall make no law respecting an establishment of religion, or prohibiting the free exercise thereof; or abridging the freedom of speech, or of the press, or the right of the people peaceably to assemble, and to petition the Government for a redress of grievances.

Article the fourth . . . A well regulated Militia, being necessary to the security of a free State, the right of the people to keep and bear Arms, shall not be infringed.

Article the fifth . . . No Soldier shall, in time of peace be quartered in any house, without the consent of the Owner, nor in time of war, but in a manner to be prescribed by law.

Article the sixth . . . The right of the people to be secure in their persons, houses, papers, and effects, against unreasonable searches and seizures, shall not be violated, and no Warrants shall issue, but upon probable cause, supported by Oath or affirmation, and particularly describing the place to be searched, and the persons or things to be seized.

Article the seventh . . . No person shall be held to answer for a capital, or otherwise infamous crime, unless on a presentment or indictment of a Grand Jury, except in cases arising in the land or naval forces, or in the Militia, when in actual service in time of War or public danger; nor shall any person be subject for the same offence to be twice put in jeopardy of life or limb, nor shall be compelled in any criminal case to be a witness against himself, nor be deprived of life, liberty, or property, without due process of law; nor shall private property be taken for public use without just compensation.

Article the eighth . . . In all criminal prosecutions, the accused shall enjoy the right to a speedy and public trial, by an impartial jury of the State and district wherein the crime shall have been committed, which district shall have been previously ascertained by law, and to be informed of the nature and cause of the accusation; to be confronted with the witnesses against him; to have compulsory process for obtaining witnesses in his favor, and to have the Assistance of Counsel for his defence.

Article the ninth . . . In suits at common law, where the value in controversy shall exceed twenty dollars, the right of trial by jury shall be preserved, and no fact tried by a jury shall be otherwise re-examined in any Court of the United States, than according to the rules of the common law.

Article the tenth . . . Excessive bail shall not be required, nor excessive fines imposed, nor cruel and unusual punishments inflicted.

Article the eleventh . . . The enumeration in the Constitution,

221

of certain rights, shall not be construed to deny or disparage others
retained by the people.

Article the twelfth . . . The powers not delegated to the United
States by the Constitution, nor prohibited by it to the States, are
reserved to the States respectively, or to the people.

BIBLIOGRAPHY

MANUSCRIPT SOURCES

Library of Congress, Washington, D. C. Manuscripts Division.
Thomas Jefferson Papers.
James Madison Papers.
George Mason Papers.
National Archives, Washington, D. C.

JUDICIAL DECISIONS AND STATUTES
English Reports:

Coke, Sir Edward. *The Reports.* 4th edition. 13 vols. London, 1738.
(cited Rep.) The acknowledged pre-eminence of Lord Coke as an
oracle of the law and doughty champion of constitutional rights is
such that when a lawyer cites simply "the Reports" (or, more briefly,
"Rep.") the reference is to Coke's *Reports.* When any other reports
are cited, the name of the reporter, or of the jurisdiction referred to,
must be given. The first part of Coke's reports was published in 1600.
Ten more were issued during the author's lifetime, the last in 1615.
A second edition appeared before Coke's death on September 3,
1634. Parts Twelve and Thirteen were published posthumously,
in 1656 and 1659 respectively, after most of Coke's papers (seized
by the Crown as seditious while he lay on his deathbed) had been
returned to his heir in 1641.
Croke, Sir George. . . . *Reports . . . of Such Select Cases, As Were
Adjudged . . . [during the Reign] of the Late Queen Elizabeth . . .
Revised and Published in English, By Sir Harbottle Grimston . . .*
London, 1669. (cited Cro. Eliz.)
Leonard, William. *Reports and Cases of Law Argued and Adjudged
in the Courts at Westminster in the Times of the late Queen Eliza-
beth and King James.* 2nd edition. 4 vols. London, 1687.
Moore, Sir Francis. *Cases . . .* London, 1675.

Federal:

Federal Reporter (second series) and Federal Supplement.
Reports of the Supreme Court of the United States.
Statutes at Large of the United States.
United States Code Annotated.

State Reports:

Massachusetts Reports.
New York Reports.
New York Supplement.
North Carolina Reports.

NEWSPAPERS

New York Daily Advertiser, June 12, 1789.

PRINTED PUBLIC RECORDS AND DOCUMENTS

*Annals of Congress (The Debates and Proceedings in the Congress of
the United States; . . . Compiled from Authentic Materials,* by
Joseph Gales, Senior, Vol. I). Washington, 1834.

Bouton, Nathaniel (ed.). *Miscellaneous Documents and Records Relating to New Hampshire at Different Periods.* Vol. X. Concord,
N. H., 1877. (Contains the proceedings of the New Hampshire
ratifying convention.)

Charters of Freedom. (National Archives Publication No. 53–14.)
Washington, 1952.

*Conventions and Constitutions of Pennsylvania (The Proceedings
Relative to Calling the Conventions of 1776 and 1790. The Min-
utes of the Convention that Formed the Present Constitution of
Pennsylvania, together with the Charter to William Penn, the
Constitutions of 1776 and 1790, and a View of the Proceedings of
the Convention of 1776, and the Council of Censors).* Harrisburg,
Pa., 1825.

*Debates and Other Proceedings of the Convention of Virginia, Con-
vened at Richmond, on Monday the 2d Day of June, 1788, for
the Purpose of Deliberating on the Constitution Recommended by
the Grand Federal Convention.* 3 vols. Petersburg, Va., 1788–89.

*The Debates and Proceedings of the Convention of the State of New-
York, Assembled at Poughkeepsie, on the 17th June, 1788. . . .*
New York, 1788.

224

Debates Which Arose in the House of Representatives of South Carolina, on the Constitution Framed for the United States, by the Convention of Delegates, Assembled at Philadelphia. Charleston, S. C., 1788.

Documentary History of the Constitution of the United States. Vol. II. Washington, 1894.

Documents Illustrative of the Formation of the Union of the American States. (69th Congress, 1st Session, House Document No. 398.) Washington, 1927.

Elliot, Jonathan. *The Debates . . . on the Adoption of the Federal Constitution.* 5 vols. Washington, 1827–45. 2nd ed. Philadelphia, 1881.

Farrand, Max. *The Records of the Federal Convention of 1787.* 4 vols. New Haven, 1911–37.

The Formation of the Union: An Exhibit. (National Archives Publication No. 53–15.) Washington, 1952.

History of Congress; Exhibiting a Classification of the Proceedings of the Senate, and the House of Representatives, from March 4, 1789, to March 3, 1793; Embracing the First Term of the Administration of General Washington. Philadelphia, 1843. (First published 1834.)

Journal of the Convention of South Carolina Which Ratified the Constitution of the United States May 23, 1788. Atlanta, Georgia, 1928.

Journal of the House of Representatives. New York, 1789. (Reprinted, Washington, 1826.)

Journal of the First Session of the Senate. New York, 1789. (Reprinted, Washington, 1820.)

Lloyd, Thomas. *The Congressional Register; or, History of the Proceedings and Debates of the First House of Representatives of the United States of America.* 4 vols. New York, 1789–90.

———. *Debates . . . on the Constitution Proposed for the Government of the United States.* 2 vols. Philadelphia, 1788.

McMaster, John B., and Frederick D. Stone. *Pennsylvania and the Federal Constitution 1787–1788.* Philadelphia, 1888.

A National Program for the Publication of Historical Documents. Washington, 1954.

Peirce, Bradford K. and Charles Hale. *Debates and Proceedings in the Convention of the Commonwealth of Massachusetts, Held in* the Year *1788, and Which Finally Ratified the Constitution of the United States*. Boston, 1856.

Poore, Ben: Perley. *The Federal and State Constitutions, Colonial Charters, and Other Organic Laws of the United States*. 2nd ed. 2 vols. Washington, 1878.

Proceedings and Debates of the Convention of North-Carolina, Convened at Hillsborough on Monday the 21st day of July, 1788. . . . Edenton, N. C., 1789.

The Ratifications of the New Foederal Constitution, together with the Amendments, Proposed by the Several States. Richmond, 1788. (Mrs. Mina R. Bryan has identified this as the pamphlet enclosed by Madison to Jefferson on October 17, 1788.)

A Reprint of the Twelve Proposed Amendments to the Federal Constitution as Submitted to the States for Ratification in 1789. San Marino, Calif., 1943.

Strayer, Joseph R. *The Delegate from New York or Proceedings of the Federal Convention of 1787 from the Notes of John Lansing, Jr.* Princeton, 1939.

Thorpe, Francis N. *The Federal and State Constitutions, Colonial Charters, and Other Organic Laws of the States, Territories, and Colonies Now or Heretofore Forming the United States of America*. 5 vols. Washington, 1909.

WRITINGS OF CONTEMPORARY STATESMEN

Adams, John. *The Works of John Adams*. Edited by Charles Francis Adams. 10 vols. Boston, 1850–56.

Jay, John. *Correspondence and Public Papers of John Jay*. Edited by Henry P. Johnston. 4 vols. New York, 1890–93.

Jefferson, Thomas. *The Papers of Thomas Jefferson*. Edited by Julian P. Boyd. 12 vols. to date. Princeton, 1950–.

———. *The Works of Thomas Jefferson*. Edited by Paul Leicester Ford. 12 vols. New York, 1904.

———. *The Writings of Thomas Jefferson*. Edited by Andrew A. Lipscomb and Albert E. Bergh. Memorial Edition. 20 vols. Washington, 1903–1904.

Lee, Richard Henry. *The Letters of Richard Henry Lee*. Edited by James C. Ballagh. 2 vols. New York, 1911–14.

Lodge, Henry Cabot, ed. *The Federalist*. New York, 1888.

Madison, James. *The Writings of James Madison.* Edited by Gaillard Hunt. 9 vols. New York, 1910.

Washington, George. *The Writings of George Washington.* Edited by John C. Fitzpatrick. 39 vols. Washington, 1931–44.

BOOKS

Adams, Henry. *The Life of Albert Gallatin.* Philadelphia, 1879.

Ames, Herman V. *The Proposed Amendments to the Constitution of the United States During the First Century of Its History.* Washington, 1897. (Annual Report of the American Historical Association for 1896, Vol. II; 54 Cong., 2 sess., H. Doc. No. 353, pt. 2.)

Anthologia Grotiana. The Hague, 1955.

Bancroft, George. *History of the Formation of the Constitution of the United States.* 2 vols. New York, 1882.

Beaney, William M. *The Right to Counsel in American Courts.* Ann Arbor, Mich., 1955.

Biographical Directory of the American Congress, 1774–1949. (81 Cong., 2 sess., H. Doc. No. 607.) Washington, 1950.

Blackstone, William. *Commentaries on the Laws of England.* 4 vols. Oxford, 1765–69.

Brant, Irving. *James Madison.* 4 vols. to date. Indianapolis, 1941–.

Chafee, Zechariah, Jr. *The Blessings of Liberty.* Philadelphia, 1956.

———. *Free Speech in the United States.* Cambridge, Mass., 1941.

———. *Freedom of Speech.* New York, 1920.

———. *How Human Rights Got into the Constitution.* Boston, 1952.

Cobb, Sanford H. *The Rise of Religious Liberty in America.* New York, 1902.

Cohen, Felix S. *Ethical Systems and Legal Ideals.* New York, 1933.

Conway, Moncure D. *Omitted Chapters of History Disclosed in the Life and Papers of Edmund Randolph.* New York, 1888.

Corwin, Edward S. *The Commerce Power versus States Rights.* Princeton, 1936.

———. *The Constitution and What It Means Today.* 10th ed. Princeton, 1948.

———. *A Constitution of Powers in a Secular State.* Charlottesville, Va., 1951.

———. *The Constitution of the United States of America: Analysis and Interpretation. Annotations of Cases Decided by the Supreme*

Court of the United States to June 30, 1952. 82 Cong., 2 sess., Sen. Doc. No. 170. Washington, 1953.
————. *Constitutional Revolution, Ltd.* Claremont, Calif., 1941.
————. *Court over Constitution.* Princeton, 1938.
Crowl, Philip A. *Maryland during and after the Revolution.* Baltimore, 1943.
Cushing, Harry A. *History of the Transition from Provincial to Commonwealth Government in Massachusetts.* New York, 1896.
Davis, Elmer. *But We Were Born Free.* Garden City, N. Y., 1954.
Davis, John W. *The Constitution—A Thing of Life.* Rochester, N. Y., 1925.
Dickinson, John. *Administrative Justice and the Supremacy of Law in the United States.* Cambridge, Mass., 1927.
Dumbauld, Edward. *The Declaration of Independence and What It Means Today.* Norman, Okla., 1950.
————. *The Political Writings of Thomas Jefferson.* New York, 1955.
Eckenrode, Hamilton J. *Separation of Church and State In Virginia.* Richmond, 1910.
Ehler, Sidney Z. and John B. Morrall. *Church and State through the Centuries.* London, 1954.
Eisenman, Nathaniel J. *The Ratification of the Federal Constitution by the State of New Hampshire.* (mimeographed.) Washington, 1938.
Ferguson, Russell J. *Early Western Pennsylvania Politics.* Pittsburgh, 1938.
Ford, Paul Leicester (ed.). *Essays on the Constitution of the United States, Published during Its Discussion by the People 1787–1788.* Brooklyn, N. Y., 1892.
————. *The Origin, Purpose and Result of the Harrisburg Convention of 1788.* Brooklyn, N. Y., 1890.
————. *Pamphlets on the Constitution.* Brooklyn, N. Y., 1888.
Ford, Worthington C. *The Federal Constitution in Virginia. 1787–1788.* Cambridge, Mass., 1903. (Reprint from *Proceedings* of Massachusetts Historical Society, 2nd series, Vol. XVII, 450–510.)
Frankfurter, Felix (ed.). *Mr. Justice Holmes.* New York, 1931.
Freeman, Douglas. *George Washington.* 6 vols. New York, 1948–54.
Grigsby, Hugh Blair. *The History of the Virginia Federal Convention of 1788, with Some Account of the Eminent Virginians of That*

228

Era Who Were Members of the Body. 2 vols. Richmond, 1890–91.

————. *The Virginia Convention of 1776.* Richmond, 1855.

Griswold, Erwin N. *The Fifth Amendment Today.* Cambridge, Mass., 1955.

Haines, Charles G. *The Revival of Natural Law Concepts.* Cambridge, Mass., 1930.

————. *The Role of the Supreme Court in American Government and Politics 1789–1835.* Berkeley, Calif., 1944.

Harding, Samuel B. *The Contest over the Ratification of the Federal Constitution in the State of Massachusetts.* New York, 1896.

Harris, George W. (ed.). *Sketches of Debate in the First Senate of the United States, in 1789–90–91.* Harrisburg, Pa., 1880.

Heller, Francis H. *The Sixth Amendment to the Constitution of the United States.* Lawrence, Kan., 1951.

Hening, William Waller. *The Statutes at Large.* 13 vols. Richmond and Philadelphia, 1809–1823.

Henry, William W. *Patrick Henry: Life, Correspondence and Speeches.* 3 vols. New York, 1891.

Hicks, Frederick C. *Men and Books Famous in the Law.* Rochester, N. Y., 1921.

Holdsworth, William S. *A History of English Law.* 9 vols. London, 1922–1926.

Howell, T. B. *A Complete Collection of State Trials and Proceedings for High Treason and Other Crimes and Misdemeanors from the Earliest Times to the Year 1783.* 21 vols. London, 1816.

Hughes, Charles E. *Addresses and Papers of Charles Evans Hughes Governor of New York 1906–1908.* New York, 1908.

Hunt, Gaillard. *The Life of James Madison.* New York, 1902.

Jackson, Robert H. *The Struggle for Judicial Supremacy.* New York, 1941.

————. *The Supreme Court in the American System of Government.* Cambridge, Mass., 1955.

James, Charles F. *Documentary History of the Struggle for Religious Liberty in Virginia.* Lynchburg, Va., 1900.

Koch, Adrienne. *Jefferson and Madison.* New York, 1950.

Lasson, Nelson B. *The History and Development of the Fourth Amendment to the United States Constitution.* Baltimore, 1937.

Leake, Isaac Q. *Memoir of the Life and Times of General John Lamb.* Albany, 1850.

Libby, Orin Grant. *The Geographical Distribution of the Vote of the Thirteen States on the Federal Constitution, 1787–8.* Madison, Wis., 1894.

Lincoln, Charles H. *The Revolutionary Movement in Pennsylvania.* Philadelphia, 1901.

Lingley, Charles R. *The Transition in Virginia from Colony to Commonwealth.* New York, 1910.

Lippmann, Walter. *Public Opinion.* New York, 1922.

McLaughlin, Andrew C. *A Constitutional History of the United States.* New York, 1935.

Maclay, Edgar S. (ed.). *Journal of William Maclay, United States Senator from Pennsylvania, 1789–1791.* New York, 1890.

Maitland, Frederick W. *The Constitutional History of England.* Cambridge, 1908.

Malone, Dumas. *Jefferson and His Time.* 2 vols. to date. Boston, 1948–.

Mays, David J. *Edmund Pendleton, 1720–1803.* 2 vols. Cambridge, Mass., 1952.

Meigs, William M. *The Growth of the Constitution in the Federal Convention of 1787.* Philadelphia, 1900.

Meyer, Jacob C. *Church and State in Massachusetts From 1740 to 1833.* Cleveland, 1930.

Mill, John Stuart. *On Liberty.* (First published 1859.) Everyman's Library Edition. London, 1910.

Milton, John. *The Works of John Milton.* Edited by Frank A. Patterson. Vol. IV. New York, 1931.

Miner, Clarence E. *The Ratification of the Federal Constitution by the State of New York.* New York, 1921.

Monaghan, Frank. *Heritage of Freedom.* Princeton, 1948.

Mott, Rodney D. *Due Process of Law.* Indianapolis, 1926.

Murphy, John S. (ed.). *Interesting Documents. Containing: . . . A Sketch of the proceedings of the convention of the State of New-York, which adopted the Constitution. . . .* New York, 1819.

Myers, Denys P. *Massachusetts and the First Ten Amendments to the Constitution.* (74 Cong., 2 sess., S. Doc. No. 181.) Washington, 1936.

———. *The Process of Constitutional Amendment.* (76 Cong., 3 sess., S. Doc. No. 314.) Washington, 1940.

230

Patterson, Bennett B. *The Forgotten Ninth Amendment.* Indianapolis, 1955.
Patterson, Caleb P. *The Constitutional Principles of Thomas Jefferson.* Austin, Texas, 1953.
Pfeffer, Leo. *Church, State, and Freedom.* Boston, 1953.
Plato. *The Apology.* In *The Trial and Death of Socrates.* Translated by F. J. Church. London, 1886.
Proceedings . . . In Memory of Robert Houghwout Jackson. Washington, 1955.
Roberts, Owen J. *The Court and the Constitution.* Cambridge, Mass., 1951.
Robertson, David. *Reports of the Trials of Colonel Aaron Burr.* 2 vols. Philadelphia, 1808.
Roosevelt, Franklin D. *The Public Papers and Addresses of Franklin D. Roosevelt.* Vol. IV. New York, 1938.
Rowland, Kate Mason. *The Life of George Mason.* 2 vols. New York, 1892.
Rutland, Robert A. *The Birth of the Bill of Rights 1776–1791.* Chapel Hill, N. C., 1955.
Schaff, Philip. *Church and State in the United States.* Washington, 1888.
Selsam, John P. *The Pennsylvania Constitution of 1776.* Philadelphia, 1936.
Shriver, Harry C. *Justice Oliver Wendell Holmes: His Book Notices and Uncollected Letters and Papers.* Washington, 1936.
Siebert, Fredrick S. *Freedom of the Press in England, 1476–1776.* Urbana, Ill., 1952.
Stephen, Sir James Fitzjames. *A History of the Criminal Law of England.* 3 vols. London, 1883.
Stokes, Anson P. *Church and State in the United States.* 3 vols. New York, 1950.
Stryker, Lloyd P. *For the Defense: Thomas Erskine, the Most Enlightened Liberal of His Times 1750–1823.* Garden City, N. Y., 1947.
Thomas, Earl Bruce. *Political Tendencies in Pennsylvania, 1783–1794.* Philadelphia, 1938.
Thorpe, Francis N. *The Constitutional History of the United States.* 3 vols. Chicago, 1901.

Torpey, William G. *Judicial Doctrines of Religious Rights in America.* Chapel Hill, 1948.
Trenholme, Louise I. *The Ratification of the Federal Constitution in North Carolina.* New York, 1932.
United States Code Annotated. Constitution, Amendments 1 to 13. St. Paul, Minn., 1944. With 1955 Cumulative Annual Pocket Part For Use During 1956. St. Paul, Minn., 1955.
Warren, Charles. *Congress, the Constitution, and the Supreme Court.* Boston, 1925. 2nd ed. Boston, 1935.
———. *The Making of the Constitution.* Boston, 1928.
———. *The Supreme Court in United States History.* 3 vols. Boston, 1922.
White, Thomas Raeburn. *Commentaries on the Constitution of Pennsylvania.* Philadelphia, 1907.

ARTICLES

Brant, Irving. "Madison: On the Separation of Church and State," *William and Mary Quarterly,* third series, Vol. VIII, No. 1 (January, 1951), 3–24.
Braucher, Robert. "Requisition at a Ceiling Price," *Harvard Law Review,* Vol. LXIV, No. 7 (May, 1951), 1103–1124.
Butterfield, Lyman H. "Elder John Leland, Jeffersonian Itinerant," American Antiquarian Society *Proceedings,* LXII, part 2 (October, 1952), 155–242.
Chafee, Zechariah, Jr. "Federal and State Powers Under the UN Covenant on Human Rights," *Wisconsin Law Review* (May, 1951), 389–473.
Clapp, Alfred C. "Privilege against Self-Incrimination," *Rutgers Law Review,* Vol. X, No. 3 (Spring, 1956), 541–573.
Corwin, Edward S. "The 'Higher Law' Background of American Constitutional Law," *Harvard Law Review,* Vol. XLII, No. 2 (December, 1928), 149–185; No. 3 (January, 1929), 365–409.
———. "The Supreme Court's Construction of the Self-Incrimination Clause," *Michigan Law Review,* Vol. XXIX, No. 1 (November, 1930), 1–27; No. 2 (December, 1930), 191–207.
Crowl, Philip A. "Anti-Federalism in Maryland, 1787–1788," *William and Mary Quarterly,* 3rd series, Vol. IV, No. 4 (October, 1947), 449–469.
Dumbauld, Edward. "John Marshall and the Law of Nations," *Uni-*

versity of Pennsylvania Law Review, Vol. CIV, No. 1 (August, 1955), 38–56.

————. "John Marshall and Treaty Law," *American Journal of International Law,* Vol. L, No. 1 (January, 1956), 69–80.

————. "Judicial Review and Popular Sovereignty," *University of Pennsylvania Law Review,* Vol. XCIX, No. 2 (November, 1950), 197–210.

————. "Thomas Jefferson and American Constitutional Law," *Journal of Public Law,* Vol. II, No. 2 (Fall, 1953), 370–389.

Eaton, Vincent L. "Bill of Rights," *New Colophon,* Vol. II, part 2 (September, 1949), 279–282.

Fairman, Charles. "Does the Fourteenth Amendment Incorporate the Bill of Rights?" *Stanford Law Review,* Vol. II, No. 1 (December, 1949), 5–139.

————. "Robert H. Jackson: 1892–1954; Associate Justice of the Supreme Court," *Columbia Law Review,* Vol. LV, No. 4 (April, 1955), 445–487.

Farrand, Max. "The Delaware Bill of Rights of 1776," *American Historical Review,* Vol. III, No. 4 (July, 1898), 641–649.

Ford, Worthington C. "The Federal Constitution in Virginia, 1787–1788," *Proceedings of the Massachusetts Historical Society,* 2nd Series, Vol. XVII (1903), 450–510.

Fraenkel, Osmond K. "Concerning Searches and Seizures," *Harvard Law Review,* Vol. XXXIV, No. 4 (February, 1921), 361–387.

Frankfurter, Felix and Thomas G. Corcoran, "Petty Federal Offenses and the Constitutional Guaranty of Trial by Jury," *Harvard Law Review,* Vol. XXXIX, No. 8 (June, 1926), 917–1019.

Freund, Paul A. "The Supreme Court and Civil Liberties," *Vanderbilt Law Review,* Vol. IV, No. 3 (April, 1951), 533–554.

Friendly, Henry. "The Historic Basis of Diversity Jurisdiction," *Harvard Law Review,* Vol. XLI, No. 4 (February, 1928), 483–510.

Gerhart, Eugene C. "A Decade of Mr. Justice Jackson," *New York University Law Review,* Vol. XXVIII, No. 5 (May, 1953), 927–974.

Grant, J. A. C. "The Higher Law Background of Eminent Domain," *Wisconsin Law Review,* Vol. VI, No. 2 (February, 1931), 67–85.

————. "Immunity from Compulsory Self-Incrimination in a Federal System of Government," *Temple Law Quarterly,* Vol. IX, No. 1 (November, 1934), 57–70; No. 2 (February, 1935), 194–212.

————. "The Natural Law Background of Due Process," *Columbia Law Review*, Vol. XXXI, No. 1 (January, 1931), 56–81.

————. "Self-Incrimination in the Modern American Law," *Temple Law Quarterly*, Vol. V, No. 3 (April, 1931), 368–403.

Harris, Whitney R. "Jury Trial in Civil Cases," *Southwestern Law Journal*, Vol. VII, No. 1 (Winter, 1953), 1–20.

Hazeltine, Harold D. "The Influence of Magna Carta on American Constitutional Development," *Columbia Law Review*, Vol. XVII, No. 1 (January, 1917), 1–33.

Jackson, Robert H. "Tribute to Country Lawyers: a Review," *American Bar Association Journal*, Vol. XXX, No. 3 (March, 1944), 136–39.

Jarrett, James M. and Vernon A. Mund. "The Right of Assembly," *New York University Law Quarterly Review*, Vol. IX, No. 1 (September, 1931), 1–38.

Knox, John C. "Self Incrimination," *University of Pennsylvania Law Review*, Vol. LXXIV, No. 2 (December, 1925), 139–154.

Lowell, A. Lawrence. "The Judicial Use of Torture," *Harvard Law Review*, Vol. XI, No. 4 (November, 1897), 220–233; No. 5 (December, 1897), 290–300.

McIlwain, Charles H. "Due Process of Law in Magna Carta," *Columbia Law Review*, Vol. XIV, No. 1 (January, 1914), 26–51.

Mason, Alpheus T. "The Core of Free Government, 1938–40: Mr. Justice Stone and 'Preferred Freedoms,'" *Yale Law Journal*, Vol. LXV, No. 5 (April, 1956), 597–628.

Meltzer, Bernard D. "Required Records, the McCarran Act, and the Privilege against Self-Incrimination," *University of Chicago Law Review*, Vol. XVIII, No. 4 (Summer, 1951), 687–728.

Meyer, Alfred W. "The Blaine Amendment and the Bill of Rights," *Harvard Law Review*, Vol. LXIV, No. 6 (April, 1951), 939–945.

Morgan, Edmund M. "The Privilege against Self-Incrimination," *Minnesota Law Review*, Vol. XXXIV, No. 1 (December, 1949), 1–45.

Murphy, Jay. "Free Speech and the Interest in Local Law and Order," *Journal of Public Law*, Vol. I, No. 1 (Spring, 1952), 40–70.

Pittman, R. Carter. "The Colonial and Constitutional History of the Privilege against Self-Incrimination in America," *Virginia Law Review*, Vol. XXI, No. 7 (May, 1935), 763–789.

————. "The Fifth Amendment: Yesterday, Today and Tomorrow," *American Bar Association Journal,* Vol. XLII, No. 6 (June, 1956), 509–512, 588–94.

Rackow, Felix. "The Right to Counsel: English and American Precedents," *William and Mary Quarterly,* third series, Vol. XI, No. 1 (January, 1954), 3–27.

Radin, Max. "The Right to a Public Trial," *Temple Law Quarterly,* Vol. VI, No. 3 (April, 1932), 381–398.

Smith, Edward P. "The Movement towards a Second Constitutional Convention in 1788," in J. Franklin Jameson, ed., *Essays on the Constitutional History of the United States in the Formative Period, 1775–1789* (Boston, 1889), 46–115.

Waite, Edward F. "The Debt of Constitutional Law to Jehovah's Witnesses," *Minnesota Law Review,* Vol. XXVIII, No. 4 (March, 1944), 209–246.

Warren, Charles. "The New 'Liberty' under the Fourteenth Amendment," *Harvard Law Review,* Vol. XXXIX, No. 4 (February, 1926), 431–463.

———. "New Light on the History of the Federal Judiciary Act of 1789," *Harvard Law Review,* Vol. XXXVII, No. 1 (November, 1923), 49–132.

———. "Political Practice and the Constitution," *University of Pennsylvania Law Review,* Vol. LXXXIX, No. 8 (June, 1941), 1003–1025.

Wigmore, John H. "The Privilege against Self-Incrimination; Its History," *Harvard Law Review,* Vol. XV, No. 8 (April, 1902), 617–637.

Willcox, Alanson W. "Invasions of the First Amendment through Conditioned Spending," *Cornell Law Quarterly,* Vol. XLI, No. 1 (Fall, 1955), 12–56.

INDEX

Blackstone, William: 53n., 123
Borrowing power: 28
Boudinot, Elias: 36n., 42
Bradshaw, John: 82
Brandeis, Justice Louis D.: 97, 115ff.,
  119, 149–50, 151n., 152n.
Burke, Aedanus: 36n., 40, 43, 76n.
Burton, Henry: 81
Butler, Justice Pierce: 130

Cardozo, Justice Benjamin N.: 135n.
Carroll, Daniel: 42n.
Ceiling price: 101
Chafee, Zechariah, Jr.: x, 115, 133,
  150, 151n.
Christians, early: 151
Civil power, supremacy of over mili-
  tary: 5, 13, 23, 46, 63
Clear and present danger: 113, 114n.,
  115–26, 129
Clinton, George: 27
Clymer, George: 36n.
Coke, Sir Edward: 78–79, 223
Commerce power: 65, 105
Communism: 70n., 82, 85n., 91n., 94,
  96, 119–22, 125, 144
Company town: 130
Compensation, just: 37, 40, 46, 52,
  77, 98–103, 134–35
Compensation of members of Congress:
  26, 28, 36, 39, 45
Congress, Continental: 9
Conscience, rights of: see religion,
  freedom of
Conscientious scruples: 19, 23, 40,
  111, 113
Conscription: 18, 25, 94n.
Constitution, U. S.: vii, viii, 3, 6, 8n.,
  14, 27, 38, 39, 140f., 159; Amendments to, adopted by Congress, x,
  48; Amendment I, 21n., 50, 59f.,
  64, 95n., 103–33, 136, 150; Amendment II, 21n., 51, 59f., 62, 134;
  Amendment III, 21n., 52, 59f., 62,
  134; Amendment IV, 52, 59f., 71f.,
  134; Amendment V, 22, 46, 52, 59f.,
  62n., 69n., 72, 76–103, 133, 143f.,

153; Amendment VI, 53, 59f., 67ff.,
  137; Amendment VII, 46, 54, 59,
  66f., 138; Amendment VIII, 46,
  55, 59, 68, 70f., 138; Amendment
  IX, 24n., 55, 59, 63–65, 105, 138;
  Amendment X, 15n., 24n., 55, 59,
  64, 65–66, 138, 143; Amendment
  XIV, 22, 67n., 69, 71n., 74n., 77n.,
  93n., 104n., 133, 136, 138, 144;
  provisions of, quoted, 15n., 16n., 20,
  31n.; ratifications of, 10, 14, 17, 20,
  21n., 27, 30f.; rejected by North
  Carolina, 30
Constitutional Convention of 1787: 9;
  rejects bill of rights, 4–6, 26
Constitutionality, presumption of:
  128f.
Constitutions, written: 8n.
Contract, freedom of: 133
Convention, second, proposal for:
  15n., 27n., 30
Cook, John: 82
Coplon, Judith: 73n.
Council, executive: 13, 19
Counsel, right to: 22, 37, 54, 69, 138
Court of High Commission: 78
Court of Star Chamber: 78f., 81f.

Declaration of Independence: viii,
  5n., 6n., 31n., 51n., 54, 61n., 67n.,
  111, 141, 159
Discovery: 144
Dissenters, prosecution of: 78
Diversity of citizenship jurisdiction:
  13, 16, 25, 42n., 46n.
Double jeopardy: 18, 37, 40, 46, 52f.,
  76, 134
Douglas, Justice William O.: 66n.,
  75n., 88n., 122n., 127n., 135
Due process of law: 12, 22, 33, 37, 40,
  46, 77, 90–98, 134; procedural due
  process: 91–92, 144, 153; substantive due process, 77n., 89, 90–91,
  93–98, 144

Eaton, Vincent: ix, 159
Eisenhower, Dwight D.: xi

238

67; not applicable against states, 137f.; re-examination of facts found by jury, 37, 54

Kent, James: 53n.

Land, value of: 100
Lattimore, Owen: 68
Laurence, John: 40
Lee, Richard Henry: *ix*, 9, 11n., 17n., 22n., 45
Libel: 115, 126–27, 136
Lilburne, John: 79–82
Livermore, Samuel: 39, 41, 71n.
Lobbying: 95
Long Parliament: 78n., 81
Loyalty oath laws: 96

MacArthur, Douglas: 63
McCollum, Mrs. Vashti: 109
Maclay, William: 44n.
McReynolds, Justice James C.: 130n.
Madison, James: *viii, ix,* 7f., 12, 15n., 21, 23, 25n., 27n., 36n., 44, 57, 63, 108, 132, 133n., 139, 146; avoids doubtful proposals, 24, 26, 34, 40, 43; honor-bound to propose amendments, 24n., 33; proposals in Congress, *x,* 24, 36–38, 206–29; on conference committee, 48
Magna Charta: 22, 53n., 70n., 82, 90, 141
Marshall, Chief Justice John: *x,* 99n., 127n., 132, 154
Martin, Luther: 6
Maryland committee, proposals of: 17–20, 177–80
Mason, George: *ix,* 3n., 4f., 11n., 13n., 16n., 22n.
Massachusetts, proposals of: 14–16, 175–77
Massachusetts Bill of Rights: 3
Military, subordination of to civil power: *see* civil power
Military affairs: 62
Military tribunal: 67f., 92
Militia, control of: 13, 19, 25, 29, 33

Mill, John Stuart: 115, 148
Milton, John: 115, 147
Mindszenty, Cardinal: 153
Monopolies: 8, 16, 28, 33, 44, 48
Moving pictures: 123–24
Murphy, Justice Frank: 110n.
Mutiny bill: 18

Natural law: 64n., 90n., 135, 136, 138n., 145
Navigation act: 19, 25, 26
New Hampshire, proposals of: 20–21, 39, 181–82
New York, proposals of: 26–30, 189–98
North Carolina, proposals of: 30–31, 198–205

Ordered liberty theory: 127n., 135–38
Otis, James: 52, 71n.

Paper money: 31
Pardoning power: 29
Parks: 131
Pennsylvania Declaration of Rights: 3, 11n., 51
Pennsylvania minority, proposals of: *viii,* 10–14, 15, 173–75
Pennsylvania ratifying convention: 7
Pepper, George Wharton: *xi*
Petition, right of: 19, 22, 33, 37, 61n.; protected against states, 134
Picketing: 130
Pinckney, Charles: 5f.
Pinckney, Charles Cotesworth: 7
Political creed: 8n., 57n., 146f.
Polygamy: 111n.
Power, undelegated, retention of: 14f., 18, 24, 33, 38, 41–42, 47, 55
Preferred position: 114n., 117n., 127–32
Press, freedom of the: 5f., 8, 10n., 19, 23, 33, 37, 40, 50, 145; protected against states, 134
Prior restraint: 123f.
Process: 29

240

Property: 98; power of Congress over, 14
Prynn, William: 81
Publication of proceedings and accounts: 24, 28–29
Public records: 85
Public use: 99
Punishment, prerequisites to infliction of: 68
Punishments, cruel and unusual: 71; see also bail
Pupil benefit theory: 106f., 142n.

Quartering soldiers: 6, 18, 21, 23, 33, 37, 40, 46, 52

Racial test: 93, 96n.
Radio: 124
Randolph, Edmund: 5
Rate regulation: 96
Rational basis test: 114, 127n., 128n., 129
Rebellion: 31
Reed, Justice Stanley: 109n., 127n.
Rejected proposals: in House, 42n.; in Senate, 47n.
Released time: 108–10, 132, 142n.
Religion, establishment of: 104–106, 136n.; in New England, 104, 133
Religion, freedom of: 8, 10n., 12, 19, 21, 23, 33, 37, 39, 43, 45, 49f., 103–15, 145, 152; twofold aspect of, 110–11, 136n.; unconventional forms protected, 112; protected against states, 134
Religious test: 6n., 20, 42n., 44, 48
Renegotiation of contracts: 94
Rent control: 97
Representative legislature: 145
Representatives, number of: 13, 15, 24, 28, 33, 36, 39, 45; qualifications of, 30
Requisitions: 16, 19, 24, 26n., 28, 42n., 43, 48
Rhode Island, belated proposals of: 11n., 31–32

Rights, pre-constitutional: 61, 64n., 138n.
Rights of accused: 12, 22, 37, 41, 46, 54
Riot, incitement to: 118, 124–26
Roberts, Justice Owen J.: 130
Rogge, O. John: 125
Roosevelt, Mrs. Eleanor: 126
Roosevelt, Franklin D.: 58n.
Rutledge, Justice Wiley: 108, 110n.

Searches and seizures: 10n., 18, 22, 33, 37, 40, 46, 52, 72–75, 134; without warrant, 73–74; stomach pump case, 74n., 75n.
Sedgwick, Theodore: 41, 44
Segregation: 93, 154
Select Committee: appointed, 36; reports, 39; report of, ix, 35n., 41, 210–12
Self-incrimination: 22, 37, 40, 46, 53, 76, 77–89, 134, 143, 153; see also Fifth Amendment
Senate, U. S.: Journal of, ix, 34–35n.; debate in, 44–48; twelve articles passed by, ix, 217–19; amends article on religious freedom, 45; rejects restrictions on states, 46; rewrites two articles, 46; rejects separation of powers, 47; accepts conference report, 48
Separation of powers: 13, 38, 41, 46–47, 145
Sherman, Rogers: 6n., 36n., 38n., 39, 42n., 44, 48
Smilie, John: 4
Smith, Gerald L. K.: 126
Smith, William Loughton: 71n.
Snake-handling: 111n.
Social compact philosophy: 64n., 145
Socrates: 151
Sound equipment: 113n., 123, 128n.
South Carolina, proposals of: 20, 180
Spain, lack of religious freedom in: 152
Speech, freedom of: 13, 23, 33, 37, 40,

51; protected against states, 134; value of, 147-51